IBM® GRAPHICS
FROM THE GROUND UP
DAVID E. SIMON

HAYDEN BOOK COMPANY
a division of Hayden Publishing Company, Inc.
Hasbrouck Heights, New Jersey

To my family, and especially to my brother Charles,
who started it all.

EQUIPMENT NEEDED

To use the programs in this book, you will need the following equipment:
- An IBM PC or XT with 64K of memory
- A Color/Graphics Monitor Adapter (or equivalent)
- An IBM Personal Computer Color Display (or equivalent)
- A Diskette Drive
- The IBM DOS Diskette

Optional equipment used in some of the examples:
- A Monochrome Display and Printer Adapter
- A Monochrome Display
- An IBM Personal Computer Printer (or equivalent)
- A Game Adapter
- A Joystick

Acquisitions Editor: M. C. VARLEY

Production Editor: MAUREEN CONNELLY

Developmental Editor: JOHN BRAGG III

Original artwork: JOHN McAUSLAND

Cover illustration: ANDY ZITO

Production service: GANIS AND HARRIS, INC.

Printed and bound by: THE MAPLE-VAIL BOOK MANUFACTURING GROUP

Library of Congress Cataloging in Publication Data

Simon, David E.
    IBM graphics from the ground up.

    Includes index.
    1. Computer graphics. 2. IBM Personal computer—Programming. 3. IBM
Personal computer XT—Programming. 4. Basic (Computer program language)
I. Title. II. Title: I.B.M. graphics from the ground up.
T385.S54 1984   001.64'43   84-9063
ISBN 0-8104-6375-X

IBM is a registered trademark of International Business Machines Corp., which is
not affiliated with Hayden Book Company.

1	2	3	4	5	6	7	8	9 PRINTING
84	85	86	87	88	89	90	91	92 YEAR

Preface

This book is intended to help you use BASIC to program your IBM Personal Computer or IBM Personal Computer XT to do graphics. It assumes that you know about the LET statement, FOR-NEXT loops, the GOSUB statement, and a few other elementary BASIC statements, but it assumes that you know nothing about computer graphics. You need not be an expert with BASIC: we expect that you do not know about all of the little crannies in BASIC, and we assume that you may have had only a little practice with BASIC, although a lot of practice will be helpful, of course.

This book uses very little mathematics. If you have solved simple problems using BASIC, you have enough mathematical background for this book. However, since the most straightforward way to do computer graphics sometimes depends on trigonometry or linear algebra, avoiding mathematics means sometimes presenting formulas without explaining their derivations and sometimes using roundabout solutions to the problems at hand. In these cases, subsequent sections for the mathematically inclined explain simpler ways to solve the problems based on more advanced mathematical concepts. We have avoided examples that use trigonometry or linear algebra; readers familiar with these fields of mathematics will be able to apply their mathematical skills after they have become familiar with the general principles of computer graphics.

Books about computer programming, this one included, make unexciting bedtime reading, so you should periodically put down this book, turn on your computer, and try out some of the applications you are reading about. You have no doubt purchased this book to learn to write programs that solve the problems you want your computer to solve; you might try writing some of these programs. Some of the program examples in this book are intended for you to type in, run, modify, and generally fool with. Others are too long for this; learn from them without typing them into your computer. Just how long is too long, however, depends on how fast you type and how patient you are, so we haven't labeled the examples one way or the other. You can try the IBM sample programs on the DOS diskette, discussed further below, without typing anything. You can modify and generally fool with the sample programs, also, but it isn't easy, as they are complex.

We have made every effort to make the examples in this book as clear as possible. We have used extra-long, descriptive variable names; we have used lots of comments; we have used straightforward algorithms and not patchworks of bailing wire and chewing gum. The examples range from the very shortest, which you can type in just to see how something works, to the more complicated, which will give you some idea how graphics can be used in the context of larger programs.

IBM provides a number of sample programs along with the DOS diskette. Figuring out how they work is quite frustrating, since they were obviously not written with the idea that someone else might want to figure them out, although they do work well enough. This book contains rewritten versions of these IBM sample programs:

ART
CIRCLE
BALL
MUSIC
COLORBAR
SPACE
DONKEY
PIECHART

Without changing what they do or how they work, we have massaged the programs into more human-readable form, and we have explained the resulting programs in detail in the text. You can run the programs provided by IBM to see what they do and read the programs in the text to figure out how they do it.

Chapters 1 and 2 contain a general introduction to computer graphics. Chapters 3 and 4 discuss all of the nitty-gritty details of using BASIC for graphics on the IBM Personal Computer. You must read at least a good chunk of Chapters 3 and 4 before going on to the following chapters. Chapters 5, 6, and 8 are relatively independent of one another. Each uses the material from Chapters 3 and 4 for a particular graphics application: games, business, and three-dimensional graphics. Chapter 7 discusses using a printer for graphics.

Section 4.6 assumes that you understand musical notation and terminology.

The manuscript for this book was prepared on an IBM Personal Computer with the help of the WordStar word processing software package. We tried out all of the programs in the figures on that computer. When we had made them work, they were printed by that computer, and the printout was photo-reproduced into this book. Many of the figures depicting the display from a program were also printed out by the computer and photo-reproduced into this book. This was done to ensure that program examples and figures are accurate.

Hardware Requirements

To try out the program examples in this book, you need:

An IBM PC or XT with 64K of memory
A Color/Graphics Monitor Adapter (or equivalent)
An IBM Personal Computer Color Display (or equivalent)
A Diskette Drive
The IBM DOS Diskette

Optional equipment used in some of the examples is:

A Monochrome Display and Printer Adapter
A Monochrome Display
An IBM Personal Computer Printer (or equivalent)
A Game Control Adapter
A Joystick

Various outfits sell products more or less equivalent to the IBM Color/Graphics Monitor Adapter. The acid test to find out if a given product is "equivalent" enough is to run the IBM sample programs provided on the DOS diskette. If these programs work on the look-alike product, then the programs in this book will work, also. Instead of the IBM Personal Computer Color Display, you can purchase a color monitor from any outfit that sells one intended for use with the IBM Personal Computer. You can also use a standard television set and purchase a Sup-R-Mod or other inexpensive gadget from a computer store to hook your computer and television set together. In fact, the author did this until it became apparent that writing a book about graphics involves staring at a graphics display for long stretches, at which point he decided that the better-quality picture on the IBM Personal Computer Color Display was worth the extra expense.

This book is mostly about drawing pictures on the display screen. One section discusses drawing pictures on a printer; the programs in that section work with the IBM Personal Computer Printer and the Epson MX series printer, which is the same printer with a different label on it. One section discusses the use of joysticks for input. The hardware requirements for the use of a joystick are discussed in that section.

Contents

1 Introduction to Graphics

A picture is worth a thousand words.

Since the advent of computer-drawn pictures, previously unimagined uses for computers have been found in management, entertainment, and engineering. Although most computers continue to compute with thousands of words or numbers, many computer tasks are now done more gracefully with a few pictures instead.

Computer graphics can present data processing results as graphs and charts instead of as tables of numbers. Most people find it easier to spot trends and to extract important facts from among masses of irrelevant data by looking at a graph or chart rather than at a printout: human eyes are very good at perceiving overall patterns in a picture and ignoring extraneous, unimportant detail. No such intuition applies to printed tables composed of numbers, however, and the recipient of the computer-printed listing must pore over the data to ascertain its meaning.

Computer graphics has brought us the now almost ubiquitous video game, an amusement in which a box containing a small, specialized computer presents a picture on a screen, and the player jockeys his or her man around the screen by manipulating the game's controls. Pac-Man, Frogger, and many similar entries from the likes of Atari, Activision, and other companies demonstrate the possibilities. Computer graphics stirs the player's imagination and allows him to use his well-developed hand-eye coordination. No one could or would play the game if Pac-Man printed descriptions of the player's and monsters' locations and expected the player to type in the direction in which he or she wished to move. The game would be difficult and boring.

Computer-aided design has sprung to life with the advent of computer graphics. Drawings are an accepted and effective medium of communication among engineers, designers, and manufacturing and repair departments

1

and are hence here to stay; printed listings will not replace drawings, computer revolution or no. With graphics, however, drawings can be created on a computer rather than with pencil and paper. Computer drawings offer significant advantages over those done with pencil and paper: erasing mistakes from a computer screen is easier than from a piece of paper; the computer can be harnessed to check that an object shown in the drawings will do its job; it can determine that several drawings are consistent with one another; it can add dimensions and notes to drawings; it can figure the best way to manufacture a product; it can estimate manufacturing costs; the computer can even produce control tapes for the machines that manufacture the object. Computers draw with very steady mechanical hands and can therefore produce high-quality drawings, whether the engineer's handwriting is good or not.

Unfortunately, a picture is worth a thousand words in large part because it takes a thousand words to describe one, even in a computer. Therefore, handling a picture requires a computer that can compute quickly with a lot of data. Furthermore, specialized equipment is required to produce pictures; it is a more complex process than just producing the twenty-six letters of the alphabet and the ten digits.

A variety of computer graphics equipment has been developed. This book is mostly about the *graphics display and controller,* a device capable of drawing pictures on a screen under computer control. The screen itself is not novel, being basically just a (usually high-quality) television tube; but controllers, the electronics necessary to tie computer and display together, have become reasonably effective at affordable prices only recently.

Computers can draw pictures with equipment other than screen displays. One such piece of equipment is a *plotter* or *pen plotter,* which holds a pen in a mechanical arm whose motion the computer directs. Pen plotters are available in various sizes, speeds, and qualities; their prices vary from under a thousand to tens of thousands of dollars. Pictures can also be drawn with printers. *Character printers* or *line printers* can print only letters, numbers, some punctuation marks, and perhaps some special symbols; hence, any picture drawn with such a printer consists of clever patterns of letters, numbers, and so on. The so-called *dot matrix printers,* however, of which the IBM Personal Computer Printer is an example, form letters, numbers, and other symbols by printing patterns of dots that look like them. In addition to printing letters and numbers, most of these printers can create pictures on the paper by printing dots in any pattern the programmer chooses.

Various ways of getting graphics information into computers have been developed recently. One way is to use a *mouse,* a device that the computer user rolls around the desk next to the computer. The computer can detect the motion of the mouse and can be programmed to respond accordingly. Mice (or is the plural "mouses"?) allow the user to "point" at something on the screen by controlling the motion of some kind of marker on the screen. If the user moves the mouse to the left, for example, the marker on the screen moves to the left, and so on. In addition to pointing at a feature of a picture, mice allow users to point at, for example, a word to delete from text being edited by a word processing program, or a number to change on a spread-sheet.

A less costly device that performs much the same function as a mouse is the *joystick*. A joystick is a box with a lever that the user can press in different directions. The computer determines the direction the user is pushing the lever and, like a mouse, moves a screen marker accordingly. Joysticks usually are harder to learn to use than mice are.

Other available input devices include a *tablet* or *digitizing tablet* and a *light pen*. The tablet is a tablelike piece of equipment whose embedded electronics determine where on its surface the user is pointing. A user most often tapes a drawing to the tablet and then traces the drawing. The computer detects where the user's stylus moves during the tracing process and hence knows what the drawing looks like. Tablets are large and expensive, but if your work involves tracing drawings into the computer, tablets are indispensable. The light pen is a hand-held gadget the size and shape of a largish ball-point pen (hence the name). When the user points the pen at a location on the screen, the light pen's electronics can tell the computer where that location is.

Programs to draw pictures on various pieces of computer equipment work by dividing the pictures into *primitives* that the equipment knows how to draw. One primitive understood by display screens is "Change the color of one small dot." Programs that draw pictures on graphics displays work by changing the colors of the dots on the screen. Most display screen systems also let the programmer use lines, circles, and filled-in areas as primitives, often by having internal software that converts these other primitives into dots. With a pen plotter, the most basic primitive is often a line. Some pen plotters, in fact, can draw only lines, and every drawing must be divided up into lines. Many of today's plotters, however, can also draw circles, dashed lines, letters, and so forth.

In this book, we shall consider how to program an IBM Personal Computer equipped with a graphics display and controller. We shall also discuss the use of a joystick for input and a printer for output, since these items are relatively standard. Because IBM sells a Color/Graphics Monitor Adapter (the controller for a graphics screen), a Game Controller for connect-ing joysticks, and a dot matrix printer capable of producing graphics, IBM's competitors have designed equipment that, for the most part, is programmed the same way as the IBM counterpart.

If you purchase equipment such as pen plotters, light pens, and tablets, you will have to spend some time studying the equipment manual—and scratching your head—before you get your computer and these items communicating properly. This book will teach you the basic principles on which all graphics programming is based, but each plotter and each tablet has its own idiosyncrasies that you will have to learn about.

2 | Introduction to Graphics Programming

This chapter discusses basic principles of graphics programming. Its purposes are to help you understand what happens inside the computer when you are doing graphics on a screen display, to provide conceptual hooks on which to hang some of the information in the next chapter, and to present general background information relevant to all aspects of graphics programming. Since BASIC includes statements and functions to help you to draw pictures on a graphics display using the IBM Color/Graphics Monitor Adapter, and since this book is primarily about that display, most of our discussion concerns the workings of a display and that adapter.

The Screen

Any screen you might connect to the Color/Graphics Monitor Adapter on your IBM Personal Computer—be it the official IBM Personal Computer Color Display, a color *monitor* from another manufacturer, or even a household television set—works in basically the same way. The screen face is the front of a large vacuum tube, and its inner surface is coated with a chemical material that glows whenever electrons hit it. At the back of the tube, an electron gun projects a tightly controlled beam of electrons to the screen. If you turn the gun on and point it at a particular place on the screen, that place on the screen will glow. Everywhere else on the screen will remain dark. Whenever you move the gun from one location to another on the screen, the first location quickly fades to dark.

Since any location on the screen fades out whenever the electron gun is not pointing at it, and since the electron gun can point at only one location at a time, it must spend a little time pointing at every spot on the screen that should be light rather than dark. It does this by continuously scanning

5

Fig. 2-1   Raster Lines on a Video Screen

A television screen divides the picture into horizontal stripes. The electron gun scans the stripes one at a time, turning the electron beam on and off as it does so. The resulting bright and dim spots on the screen form the picture.

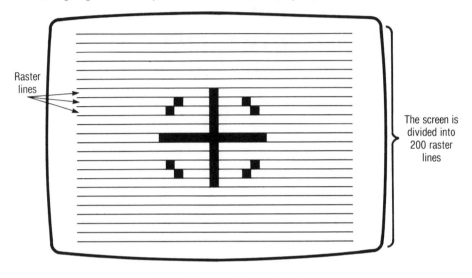

Raster lines

The screen is divided into 200 raster lines

horizontally across the screen. The screen is divided into 200 horizontal stripes, one above another, called *raster lines* or *rasters,* and the electron gun scans all 200 in a thirtieth of a second. As it scans, the electron gun modifies the intensity of its electron beam to create a series of bright and dark places on the screen. See Fig. 2-1. As soon as it is done, it repeats the process. Even if the picture never changes—as, for instance, when a television station broadcasts a test pattern—the electron gun must continue to scan the screen over and over again, for if it stopped, the screen would immediately fade to darkness.

A color display is about the same as a black and white display except that it has tiny dots of various chemical materials that glow in several different colors; and it has a lot of complicated electronics that allow the electron gun to pick out individual dots in order to select the color that a particular location on the screen should be.

A standard television set uses the signal from the television station to control the intensity of the electron gun as it scans across the lines on the screen. It has some fancy electronics to capture a signal from an antenna and some more fancy electronics to separate the signal of the station you are

Fig. 2-2   Workings of a Television Set

The signal from the antenna is filtered to get the signal from the one channel you want to watch. Then that signal is converted to electrical impulses that control the electron gun in the television tube.

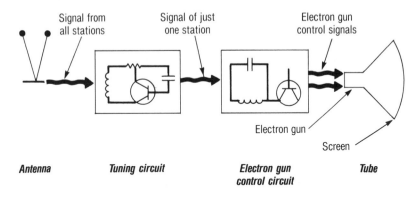

watching from the signals of all of the other stations on the air and yet some more fancy electronics to turn the signal into impulses to send to its electron gun. The signal from the broadcasting station varies to indicate the various shades of grey (for black and white) or the various shades of different colors; and as the signal varies, the television set changes what it does with its electron gun. See Fig. 2-2.

A computer monitor such as the IBM Personal Computer Color Display uses a signal from the computer to decide what to do with its electron gun. It is the same as a television set with all of the front-end electronics replaced by a cable running directly from the computer to the monitor. See Fig. 2-3.

Fig. 2-3   IBM Personal Computer with Color Monitor Attached

The IBM Personal Computer sends a signal directly to the electron gun in the color tube either through the nine-pin connector of the Color/Graphics Monitor Adapter board or through the composite video output.

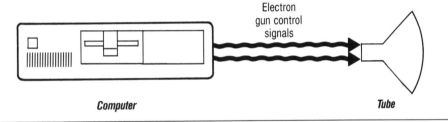

Fig. 2-4   IBM Personal Computer with Television Set Attached

The signal from the IBM Personal Computer is put on channel 33 and then fed into the television set's regular circuitry. The television thinks that the computer is a station broadcasting on channel 33.

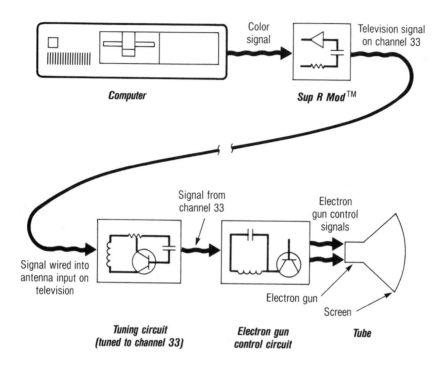

When a television set is used as a computer monitor, the computer "broadcasts" its signal along the cable on channel 33, and the resultant signal goes through the tuning circuitry on the television set. See Fig. 2-4.

The computer divides each raster line into a series of adjacent dots. The IBM Personal Computer works in two graphics modes. In *high resolution* graphics, each raster line contains 640 dots, and the picture is black and white. In *medium resolution* graphics, each line has 320 dots, and the picture is in color. In either mode, each dot is referred to as a *pixel*, or *point*. See Fig. 2-5. In black and white graphics, each pixel can be either black (the electron gun is off as it scans by) or white (the electron gun is on). There is no

Fig. 2-5   Pixels on a Computer Display

Each raster line is divided into a series of dots called *pixels*. In medium resolution graphics, each pixel can be one of four colors. In high resolution graphics, each line has twice as many pixels, but each can be only one of two colors: black or white.

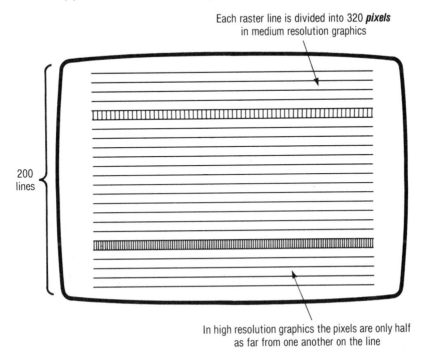

Each raster line is divided into 320 *pixels* in medium resolution graphics

200 lines

In high resolution graphics the pixels are only half as far from one another on the line

grey, as there is on black and white television. In color graphics, each pixel can be one of sixteen colors, represented by a combination of colored phosphors being lit.

The Color/Graphics Monitor Adapter

To put a picture on the screen, the computer must send a signal to control the electron gun, and it has to send it fast, since the electron gun runs across all 200 lines on the screen in a thirtieth of a second. If the computer itself did this, it would spend most of its time just producing a signal and would have little if any time left over to make changes in the picture or to perform general computing. Therefore, responsibility for sending this signal is turned over to the Color/Graphics Monitor Adapter, which is why you must have this adapter or a similar board from another manufacturer (see the discussion in the Preface concerning non-IBM equipment) if you wish to do graphics on your IBM Personal Computer.

The Color/Graphics Monitor Adapter is a chunk of electronics that does four things necessary for graphics:

1. It stores the data representing the picture you want displayed—that is, it stores the color of each pixel on the screen. It uses this data to produce the signal to the screen.

2. It keeps track of the colors that are being displayed on the screen. On the IBM Personal Computer you can use up to sixteen colors, but you cannot use more than four at once. The Color/Graphics Monitor Adapter keeps track of which four you are using.

3. It sends the signal that keeps the picture on the screen to the electron gun in the monitor.

4. It communicates graphics data to and from the main part of the computer. The IBM Personal Computer and the BASIC program running in it can direct the Color/Graphics Monitor Adapter to make changes in the picture on the screen and can ask it certain questions about the picture that is already there.

The Color/Graphics Monitor Adapter is able to cope with its first task because it contains a *display buffer*. This is nothing more than a large chunk of memory organized in such a way as to store graphics data conveniently. To keep track of what colors are being used, the adapter has several special memory spaces. The task of sending a signal to the screen is accomplished by a block of electronics that reads repeatedly through the memory that makes up the display buffer and sends what it finds to the screen. The fourth task is done by electronics that receive signals from the main part of the IBM Personal Computer, decide what changes to the picture are intended, and modify the display buffer appropriately. This is done by a *CRT controller*, which is also responsible for coordinating all of the other operations on the board. The data flow involved in this process is shown in Fig. 2-6.

The Display Buffer

The display buffer memory is like any other computer memory in some ways. You can write data into it and subsequently read it back, for example, and it forgets its data when you turn the power off. In two ways, however, the display buffer is unlike other computer memory. First, two electronic processes take place continuously in the display buffer: the picture is being

Fig. 2-6   Data Flow in Color/Graphics Monitor Adapter

Instructions from the computer are received by the *CRT controller* on the Color/
Graphics Monitor Adapter. The picture is stored in the *display buffer,* which can be
changed by the CRT controller when a program running in the computer requests it,
and which is read continuously by the *display generator.* The color registers control the
colors currently in use. This information is set by the CRT controller and used by the
display generator.

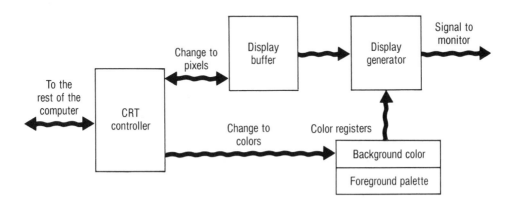

modified by the computer in response to the BASIC program drawing the
picture, and the screen signal is constantly being read out of it by the display
generator. Second, whereas other computer memory is organized so as to
store numbers or strings, the display buffer is organized so as to store a
graphics picture. (Actually, this is mostly a function of how the other
electronics in the computer interpret the data in the memory rather than a
difference in the memory itself.)

In high resolution (black and white) graphics, the display buffer must
store one fact for each pixel on the screen: whether it is black or white. It
does this by assigning one *bit* in the memory to each pixel on the screen and
then storing in each bit either a 1 to indicate that the corresponding pixel
should be white or a 0 to indicate that the corresponding pixel should be
black. Since there are 200 raster lines, each with 640 pixels, the computer
needs 128,000 bits (or 16,000 *bytes* with eight bits each) to store the picture.
The Color/Graphics Monitor Adapter has 16,000 bytes of memory on it.

In medium resolution graphics, each pixel on the screen can be any one
of four colors. The colors are numbered 0, 1, 2, and 3. The computer assigns
two bits in the display buffer for each pixel on the screen, since two bits can
represent four values.

If the two bits in the display buffer are:		then the pixel on the screen has color:
Bit 1	*Bit 2*	*Color*
0	0	0
0	1	1
1	0	2
1	1	3

(Readers familiar with binary arithmetic will notice that the two bits in the display buffer represent the color number in base 2.) If both bits are 0, this pixel is colored with the *background color,* color 0. If one bit or the other is 1 or if both bits are 1, then one of three *foreground colors*—colors 1, 2, and 3—is displayed at this pixel. In medium resolution graphics, there are 200 raster lines, each with 320 pixels, for a total of 64,000 pixels. Since the computer uses two bits to represent the color of each pixel, it needs 128,000 bits to store the picture. The difference, therefore, between high resolution graphics and medium resolution graphics is just a matter of how the computer interprets the display buffer.

The computer can put text on a graphics monitor in one of two ways. If you are doing graphics, the computer can display text by forming each letter from a suitable collection of pixels. To display the letter I, for example, the computer changes the colors of pixels in a vertical row on the screen. Alternatively, if you are doing only text and not graphics, the Color/Graphics Monitor Adapter can reinterpret its display buffer in yet another way that stores only text. It does this by dividing the display buffer into sixteen-bit pieces, each of which corresponds to a letter location on the screen. It then uses eight of those bits to remember what letter is at that screen location and the other eight bits to remember what color the letter is, what color the background for the letter is, and whether or not it is flashing. With 128,000 bits of memory, the computer can store 8,000 letters, or eight screenfuls. This capability is not discussed in this book, but is discussed in the IBM BASIC manual.

The Color Registers

In color graphics, each pixel is represented by two bits, so each pixel can be one of four colors, represented by the four possible patterns in which two bits can be 1 or 0. The display, however, can handle many more than four colors. In order to allow the computer to make use of more than four colors,

the Color/Graphics Monitor Adapter does not decide what colors are represented by the four bit patterns until the display generator is sending the signal
to the display. At that point, the adapter looks at two *color registers* located
in the adapter to find out what colors to use. If both bits corresponding to a
pixel are 0, indicating that the background color, color 0, should be
displayed, then the adapter displays whichever of the sixteen possible colors
is stored in the *background color register.* If one or both of the bits are 1, the
system looks at the *palette register,* which indicates which of two *color
palettes* is being used. Each color palette is a set of three foreground colors.
When the adapter has discovered which palette is in use, it then knows what
color to use for the pixels in colors 1, 2, and 3.

Cartesian Coordinates

Readers familiar with Cartesian coordinates can skip this section after
noting one fact: the coordinate system used on the IBM Personal Computer is
"upside down," that is, larger y coordinates are lower on the screen rather
than higher, as they would be in the normal Cartesian coordinate system,
and the origin is therefore at the upper left-hand corner of the screen rather
than at the lower left, where you might have expected to find it.

Readers to whom Cartesian coordinates are a new concept may find this
discussion brief. It has intentionally been kept short in order to get on with
programming. If you get to the end of the discussion of Cartesian coordinates
and find that you are not yet an expert, read on as far as the end of Section
3.4. After you have read the discussion here plus the program examples in
Section 3.4, it will become clear.

To draw pictures on the computer display, you must change the colors of
one or more pixels on the display. To do this, you must store new data in the
display buffer, and to do this, you must tell the computer where in the buffer
you want data stored. You do this by using a convention called *Cartesian
coordinates,* named after the seventeenth-century French mathematician
René Descartes. Using Cartesian coordinates, you refer to each pixel (and its
corresponding bits in the display buffer) by a pair of numbers. The first
number, or *coordinate,* in the pair indicates the pixel's horizontal position on
the raster line. The pixel at the left-hand edge of the screen on each raster
line is pixel number 0. The next one to the right is pixel number 1, then pixel
number 2, and so on to the right-hand edge of the screen. In medium
resolution graphics, the pixel at the right-hand edge of the screen is pixel
number 319. In high resolution, the pixel at the right-hand edge of the screen

is number 639. The second coordinate denotes the pixel's vertical position by indicating on which raster line the pixel is located. The raster line at the top of the screen is number 0; the next one down is number 1; and so on to the line at the bottom of the screen, which is number 199 in both high resolution and medium resolution graphics.

A pixel's coordinates are commonly written enclosed in parentheses and separated by a comma. For example,

(5,29)

represents the fifth pixel from the left-hand edge of the screen on the twenty-ninth line from the top of the screen.

The first coordinate in a pair is usually called the x *coordinate,* and the second coordinate is called the y *coordinate.*

Let us consider a few examples. The pixel whose coordinates are

(0,0)

is the left-most pixel on the top line of the screen—that is, it is the point at the upper left-hand corner of the screen. The pixel whose coordinates are (0,0) is often called the *origin.* The pixel at

(0,199)

is the pixel at the left-hand end of the lowest line on the screen. In medium resolution graphics, the pixels

(319,0) and (319,199)

are at the top right and bottom right corners of the screen, respectively, and

(160,100)

is almost exactly in the center of the screen. See Fig. 2-7.

All of the pixels on the same horizontal line have the same second coordinate. Here is an example of a series of pixels that make up a short horizontal line:

(149,117)
(150,117)
(151,117)
(152,117)
(153,117)
(154,117)
(155,117)

Fig. 2-7   Cartesian Coordinates

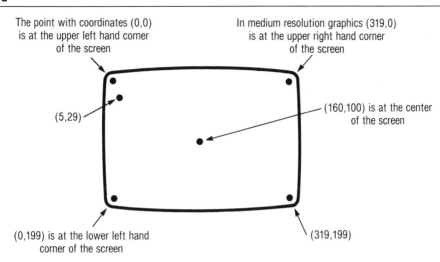

The point with coordinates (0,0) is at the upper left hand corner of the screen

In medium resolution graphics (319,0) is at the upper right hand corner of the screen

(5,29)

(160,100) is at the center of the screen

(0,199) is at the lower left hand corner of the screen

(319,199)

A row of pixels with the same second coordinate forms a horizontal line.

(149,117)   (150,117)   (151,117)   (155,117)

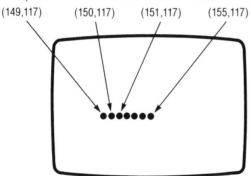

Pixels with the same first coordinate lie on a vertical line.

(93,49)   (93,57)   (93,113)   (93,126)

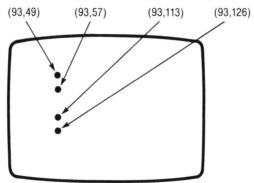

continued on p. 16

continued from p. 15

The coordinates (123,14) are to the right of (100,14) because 123 is greater than 100, and (15,107) is below (15,15) because 107 is greater than 15.

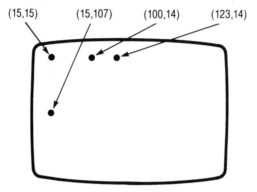

The distance between (15,27) and (33,27) is 33 minus 15, or 18.

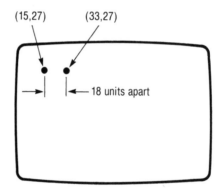

Similarly, the first coordinates of the pixels on a vertical line are all the same. These pixels all lie directly above one another, although there is blank space among them:

(93,49)
(93,57)
(93,113)
(93,126)

The horizontal line through the pixel at (0,0) (on which all pixels have a y coordinate of 0) is called the x *axis*. The vertical line through the origin (on which all pixels have an x coordinate of 0) is called the y *axis*.

A pixel with a larger first coordinate is to the right of one with a smaller first coordinate:

(123,14) is to the right of (100,14)

A pixel with a larger second coordinate is below one with a smaller second coordinate:

(15,107) is below (15,15)

You can find the distance between two pixels on a horizontal line by subtracting the first coordinate of one from the first coordinate of the other:

(15,27) is 18 from (33,27)

Similarly, you can find the distance between two pixels on a vertical line by finding the difference between their second coordinates. To find the distance between two points not above each other, use this formula:

$$\sqrt{(X1 - X2)^2 + (Y1 - Y2)^2}$$

Readers with some geometry can see that this formula is a consequence of the Pythagorean theorem:

$$X^2 + Y^2 = Z^2$$

BASIC makes extensive use of Cartesian coordinates, as we shall see.

Shape of the Screen

One problem that arises in computer graphics is that the distance between the raster lines on the screen is most likely different from the distance between the pixels on the raster lines. For example, 320 pixels on each of 200 raster lines may fill a screen 10 inches wide by 7 inches high, which makes the pixels 0.0325 inches apart and the raster lines 0.0350 inches apart. In this case, a "square" whose corners are

(0,0)   (100,0)

(0,100)   (100,100)

appears to be a rectangle 3.25 inches wide by 3.50 inches high. Similarly, circles appear to be ellipses, and every other figure on the screen appears a little taller and thinner than it should.

The ratio between the horizontal spacing among the pixels and the vertical spacing among the raster lines is called the *aspect ratio* of the screen. Every screen model has a slightly different aspect ratio; the best way to find out about yours is to draw squares on it (as we shall in Section 3.5) and see if they appear square. If they do, then the aspect ratio of your screen is 1:1, and you are in the fortunate position of not having to worry about it. In the more likely event that they do not look square, you will have to correct for this situation whenever you write a program in which the exact shape of what appears on the screen is critical. In the example above, to get a true square 3.5 inches on a side, you would have to program the computer to draw a "square" whose coordinates are

(0,0)   (108,0)

(0,100)   (108,100)

where the additional pixels in the horizontal direction make up for the fact that the pixels are closer to one another than are the raster lines. You could also correct the number of raster lines and program a 3.25-inch square, whose corners would be:

(0,0)   (100,0)

(0,93)   (100,93)

Graphics devices other than screens also have aspect ratios, and you must deal with them similarly. Pen plotters most often have an aspect ratio of 1:1; you therefore do not have to make aspect corrections for pen plotters. If you use a printer as a graphics output device, however, you must deal with the fact that the distance from letter to letter on the line is usually 1/10 inch while the distance from line to line is 1/6 inch. On dot matrix printers such as the IBM Personal Computer Printer, dots are typically 72 to the inch horizontally and 60 to the inch vertically. You must correct for these ratios in programs that use these devices.

The figures in this book were made with an Epson MX-80, a dot matrix printer that is basically identical to the IBM Personal Computer Printer. No correction was applied in the program. The square

(0,0)   (100,0)

(0,100)   (100,100)

was printed as a rectangle about 1.39 inches wide by 1.66 inches high.

BASIC

BASIC allows you to draw pictures on the screen without having to work directly with the CRT controller on the Color/Graphics Monitor Adapter. Your BASIC programs tell the computer to change the colors of given pixels or sets of pixels, and BASIC takes over the task of telling the adapter what to do.

The BASIC statements and their uses are summarized here:

SCREEN tells the system to switch to low or high resolution graphics mode.
CLS clears the screen.
PSET and PRESET change the color of just one pixel.
LINE draws a line on the screen by changing the colors of all the pixels in a row. This statement can also draw rectangle outlines and solid rectangles.
CIRCLE draws a circle. This statement can also draw ellipses and arcs.
PAINT fills in an area on the screen with a given color.
COLOR tells the system what colors to use.
GET and PUT copy a part of a picture to another part of the screen.
POINT finds out the color of a location on the screen.

3 BASIC Primitives for Constructing Pictures on the Screen

3.1 USING THE SCREENS

The various sections in this chapter discuss the different BASIC statements that allow you to use the Color/Graphics Monitor Adapter to draw pictures on the display. We assume that you have some familiarity with BASIC, and we will not discuss the standard constructions available in the language: LET, FOR-NEXT, GOTO, GOSUB, IF, arrays, strings, and so on.

This section explains how to tell the computer that you want to do graphics, how to tell it that you want to use your color monitor rather than your monochrome display (if you have both), how to choose high resolution or medium resolution graphics, and how to perform other mundane chores of this nature. These concerns are in the category of things-to-program-once-and-then-save-the-program-quick-so-that-you-can-do-it-whenever-you-need-to. They are not the reason you are reading a book about computer graphics. Unfortunately, until you get past these concerns, you can't do anything else.

Getting Started If You Have Only the Monochrome Adapter

Two sorts of adapters are available to connect displays to the Personal Computer: the Monochrome Display and Parallel Printer Adapter and the Color/Graphics Monitor Adapter. If your computer contains only the Monochrome Display Adapter or an equivalent adapter, then you can't do graphics on your computer, because these adapters can't do graphics. If you want graphics, you should put down this book and buy a Color/Graphics

Monitor Adapter for your computer. (Or you can read on and decide later if you want to pay for one.) If you have only the Color/Graphics Monitor Adapter in your Personal Computer, then go on to the next section, which tells you how to get started on graphics. If you have one of each type of adapter, then skip the next section and read the following one, which addresses problems peculiar to that situation.

Getting Started If You Have Only the Color/Graphics Adapter

If your Personal Computer has just the Color/Graphics Monitor Adapter, then whenever you turn the computer on and start up either BASIC or DOS, the computer wakes up automatically putting its output on whatever screen you have attached to your Color/Graphics Monitor Adapter. It hasn't any choice in the matter: that is the only screen there is. The computer also wakes up thinking that you want to use the screen for text, not for graphics. Before you can use graphics, therefore, you must warn the computer about it. You do this with the SCREEN command:

SCREEN 1,0

This command tells the computer that you wish to use the screen for medium resolution (color) graphics. If you want to switch to high resolution (black and white) graphics, then you use this command:

SCREEN 2,0

After you have given one of these commands—and *only* after you have given one of these commands—the computer will let you use the various BASIC graphics statements discussed in the rest of this chapter.

When you use the screen in one of these *graphics modes,* the computer can still display text on the screen in the usual way—when you edit your programs, for example—but the text draws and scrolls very slowly, and it is harder to read than the text that is printed in the *text mode* that the computer woke up using. Although it is convenient to make minor changes in a program without switching back to text mode, you will nonetheless want to switch back if you have to make a lot of changes. You do this with the command:

SCREEN 0

You can use any of the above commands as a statement just by preceding it with a line number.

Whenever you use any of these commands (or whenever one of them is executed as a statement in one of your programs), the computer clears the screen.

Getting Started If You Have Both Adapters

If you have both the Monochrome Display Adapter and the Color/Graphics Monitor Adapter, then whenever you turn the computer on and start up either BASIC or DOS, the computer wakes up automatically putting its output on whatever screen you have attached to your Monochrome Display Adapter. Since the computer can't do graphics without using the Color/Graphics Monitor Adapter, you must first tell the computer to use that adapter instead of the monochrome. Since the computer uses a particular memory location in its regular memory to keep track of which adapter is in use, you must change the contents of that memory location. Here is a two-statement program that directs future output to the Color/Graphics Monitor Adapter:

```
10 DEF SEG = 0
20 POKE &H410, (PEEK(&H410) OR &H30)
```

Here is a two-statement program to change back:

```
10 DEF SEG = 0
20 POKE &H410, (PEEK(&H410) AND &HCF) OR &H10
```

In addition to telling the computer which adapter it should send output to, you must also tell it the characteristics of the screen that it is now using. The steps that do this are: (1) use the SCREEN statement, which tells the computer that you wish to work in medium resolution graphics mode, in high resolution graphics mode, or in text mode; (2) give your computer the WIDTH statement to tell it whether your screen is 40 characters wide (as it is if it is attached to the Color/Graphics Monitor Adapter) or 80 characters wide (as it is if it is attached to the Monochrome Display Adapter); and (3) use the LOCATE statement, which tells the computer what kind of flashing cursor will look good on this screen. Here are two short programs that will allow you to do all these things at once.

The program that switches you from the monochrome display to the color display is as follows:

```
21000 DEF SEG = 0
21010 POKE &H410, (PEEK(&H410) AND &HCF) OR &H10
21020 SCREEN 1,0,0,0
21025 SCREEN 0
21030 WIDTH 40
21035 LOCATE ,,1,6,7
21040 STOP
```

We recommend that you type this program into your computer verbatim and save it for use whenever you want to do graphics. The choice of line numbers is entirely up to you. However, choosing very large line numbers such as these allows you to use this program later as a subroutine if you want a larger program to change screens automatically. This program leaves the computer expecting to do text. Before you can use graphics, therefore, you must warn the computer about it. You do this with the SCREEN command:

SCREEN 1,0

This command tells the computer that you wish to use the screen for medium resolution (color) graphics. If you want to switch to high resolution (black and white) graphics, then you use this command:

SCREEN 2,0

After you have given one of these commands—and *only* after you have given one of these commands—the computer will let you use the various BASIC graphics statements discussed in the rest of this chapter.

When you use the screen in one of these *graphics modes,* the computer can still display text on the screen in the usual way—when you edit your programs, for example—but the text draws and scrolls very slowly, and it is harder to read than the text that is printed in the *text mode* that the computer woke up using. Although it is convenient to make minor changes in a program without switching back to text mode, you will nonetheless want to switch back if you have to make a lot of changes. You do this with the command:

SCREEN 0

You can use any of the above commands as a statement just by preceding it with a line number.

Whenever you use any of these commands (or whenever one of them is executed as a statement in one of your programs), the computer clears the screen.

The program that switches you back from the color display to the monochrome display is as follows:

```
22000 DEF SEG = 0
22010 POKE &H410, (PEEK(&H410) OR &H30)
22020 SCREEN 0
22030 WIDTH 40
22040 WIDTH 80
22050 LOCATE ,,1,12,13
22060 STOP
```

We recommend that you type this program into your system and save it, also. Since the Monochrome Adapter can do only text, the SCREEN statements do not apply after you have shifted back to that adapter.

If you plan to use the two little programs above as subroutines for larger programs, then you should save them in ASCII files. You do this with the special "A" option on the BASIC SAVE command. This SAVE command will save a subroutine in an ASCII file called MONO2CLR:

SAVE "MONO2CLR",A

If you save these routines in ASCII files, as opposed to the usual way, then you can use the MERGE command later to add them to programs that you have already written and insert GOSUB statements to call these routines, and your programs will switch screens automatically.

In the rest of this book, the program examples usually assume that you have already switched to the Color/Graphics Monitor Adapter with the first of the routines above.

3.2 CLEARING THE SCREEN—THE CLS STATEMENT

Whenever you want to clear the screen you are using, you can do so with this command:

CLS

You can also use this as a statement within a program.

3.3 CARTESIAN COORDINATES IN BASIC

In Chapter 2, we discussed the Cartesian coordinate system used to designate pixels on the screen. In this section we shall discuss how coordinate pairs are used in BASIC programs.

BASIC allows you to specify a coordinate pair by writing two numbers in parentheses with a comma between them, just as we did in Chapter 2. For example, the following are perfectly good BASIC coordinates:

(15,23)
(47,188)

In addition, you can use variables within your coordinates. If HERE and NOW are variables in your program, then the following are legal coordinates:

(11,HERE)
(NOW,22)

If you wish, you can include arithmetic calculations within coordinates. If HEARNO, SEENO, and SPEAKNO are variables in one of your BASIC programs, then you can use

(HEARNO + SEENO, SPEAKNO*16)

although you may not want to use it, since a BASIC statement with coordinates like this would be hard to type, hard to read, and hard to understand.

BASIC allows you to put fractional numbers into coordinates. You can, for example, use

(14.96,11.23)

BASIC rounds the numbers to the nearest integer before doing any graphics with them. The above coordinate pair behaves just as though you had given

(15,11)

You can even use floating point, double precision floating point, hexadecimal, or octal constants within coordinates, although they are not very useful.

In medium resolution graphics the screen is 320 pixels wide by 200 pixels high. Therefore, a coordinate pair whose first coordinate is not between 0 and 319 or whose second coordinate is not between 0 and 199 does not refer to a pixel on the screen. BASIC, however, deals properly with larger coordinates as long as they stay between − 32,768 and 32,767. (Later on, we will explain why you might want to refer to points that are not on the screen.) If you give a coordinate pair, one of whose numbers is not between − 32,768 and 32,767, you will get this error:

```
Overflow in line 497
```

(or in whatever line in your program the outsized coordinate appeared). If you see this error, it is probably because a variable used in a coordinate pair has grown too large.

Absolute Form and Relative Form Coordinates

Readers eager to get on with programming should skip on to Section 3.4 and read the following material at a later time. Readers who like learning things systematically should continue on.

BASIC allows you to specify coordinates either in *absolute form* or in *relative form*. In absolute form, the form we discussed in Chapter 2, the coordinates you give tell where the point is in relation to the point in the upper left-hand corner of the screen: a big first coordinate would mean, for example, that the point in question is far to the right of the upper left-hand corner of the screen, and a small second coordinate would mean that it is not very far down from the top of the screen. In relative form, the coordinate pair you give represents the location of the point not in relation to the point at the upper left-hand corner of the screen but in relation to a point to which you previously referred. For example, if you just referred to the point

(5,10)

(perhaps by turning that point green or by drawing a line from somewhere else to that point), and if you now want to talk about the point

(11,23)

you can do it in two ways. The first way is to tell the computer

"(11,23)"

The second is to tell the computer where (11,23) is in relation to (5,10). The point (11,23) is six pixels to the right of (5,10) and thirteen raster lines below it. You warn the computer that you are using relative form coordinates with the word STEP and then give these distances as your coordinates. Therefore, the relative form coordinate pair you could use would be

STEP (6,13)

Obviously, you can't use relative form coordinates until you have used at least one point with absolute form coordinates, since until you do so, the computer has no "last referred point" from which to figure out where the new point really is. Subsequently, you and the computer must agree about which point is the "last referred point" if you are using relative form coordinates. See Fig. 3-1.

When using relative form coordinates, it makes sense to use negative numbers as coordinates, since the second point you refer to might be above or to the left of the point you referred to before. If you had just referred to

(26,43)

Fig. 3-1   Where Is the Point Last Referred To?

In order to use relative coordinates, you and the computer must agree on what point was last referred to. In some instances, this is evident: when you tell the computer to change the color of a certain pixel, then that pixel is the one last referred to. When you tell the computer to draw a line from one point to another, then the point last referred to is the second endpoint of the line. In other cases, the point last referred to may not be so obvious. The table below summarizes what point is the one last referred to when you use the BASIC graphics statements. This figure will make more sense to you after we discuss the BASIC statements to which it refers. It is presented here so that this information will be all in one place for reference.

PSET (X,Y). (X,Y)—The point whose color changed is the last mentioned point.

LINE (X1,Y1)–(X2,Y2).—The second endpoint of the line (X2,Y2) is the last mentioned point.

CIRCLE (X,Y),R—The center of the circle is the last mentioned point. (The center of the circle may well *not* be the last drawn point.)

PAINT (X,Y).—The point (X,Y) is the last mentioned point (although it is obviously not the most recently drawn).

---

and now wanted to use

(11,100)

the relative form coordinates would be

STEP (−15,57)

The flexibility of and limitations on relative form coordinates are about the same as on absolute form coordinates: you may use variables and arithmetic within the coordinates; fractions are rounded to the nearest whole number; if the point you refer to is off the screen, that's okay; if you mention coordinates larger than 32,767 or smaller than −32,768, you can expect an error message. There is one new wrinkle: if you use relative form coordinates to refer to a point whose absolute form coordinates would be out of the range from −32,768 to 32,767, the computer loses track of where it is, and your program won't work right.

Fig. 3-2 Relative Form Coordinates

The three squares shown below can all be described with the same sequence of relative form coordinates once the upper left-hand corner has been specified.

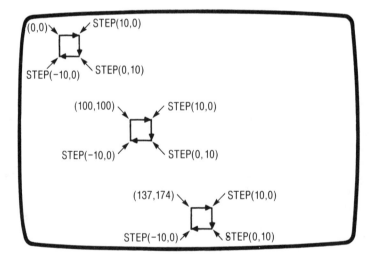

USING RELATIVE FORM COORDINATES

The application for absolute form coordinates is fairly obvious. When you decide where you want something drawn on the screen, you just tell the computer where that location is, using absolute form coordinates. The application for relative form coordinates is less obvious.

Suppose that you are writing a program to draw a square ten pixels high by ten pixels wide, but you don't know in advance where the box will be. The corners of the box might turn out to be:

   (0,0)   (10,0)

   (0,10)   (10,10)

or they might turn out to be

   (100,100)   (110,100)

   (100,110)   (110,110)

or they might even be

   (137,174)   (147,174)

   (137,184)   (147,184)

When your program finds out where to put the upper left-hand corner of the box, it could then do a lot of arithmetic to find absolute form coordinates for the other three corners. Alternatively, you could notice that once you have told the computer about the upper left-hand corner, the upper right-hand corner will be

   STEP (10,0)

in relative form. Having referred to this point, the lower right-hand corner is always

    STEP (0,10)

and after that, the lower left-hand corner is always

    STEP (–10,0)

3.4 CHANGING A PIXEL'S COLOR—
PSET AND PRESET

    So far, we have discussed theory. This and the next several sections consider practice: the BASIC statements that allow you to draw and change pictures on the graphics screen.

    The simplest operation you can perform is to change the color of a single pixel on the screen. The PSET and PRESET statements do this by telling the computer first, the coordinates of the pixel whose color is to change and, second, a number that represents the new color the pixel is to have. For example:

    179 PSET (160,100) , 2

This statement changes the pixel at location (160,100) from whatever color it was to color number 2. (Color number 2 is magenta until you get to Section 4.1, which discusses choosing what colors are used.) The 179 is just the statement number. The PRESET statement is identical in form:

    100 PRESET (160,100) , 2

and its function is only slightly different, as we shall discuss in a moment.

    The legal color numbers for the PSET and PRESET statements are 0, 1, 2, and 3, which correspond to colors as follows:

Number	Color
0	Black
1	Cyan (light blue)
2	Magenta
3	White

In Section 4.1, we shall discuss how to make the numbers correspond to different colors.

You may omit the color number from the PSET and PRESET statements. If you do, the PSET statement changes the pixel to color number 3. These two statements therefore have identical effect:

```
179 PSET (10,14) , 3
179 PSET (10,14)
```

If you omit the color number from a PRESET statement, on the other hand, the computer changes the pixel to color number 0. These statements have identical effect:

```
179 PRESET (10,14)
179 PRESET (10,14),0
```

They both set the pixel to color number 0. Since this is the only difference between the PSET and PRESET statements, we will use only the PSET statement in this book.

The program shown in Fig. 3-3 changes the screen to medium resolution graphics mode (statement 40), clears it (statement 50), and then colors the pixels at the four corners of the screen with color number 3 (statements 60 to 90). Color number 3 is white.

If your hardware includes both a Monochrome Adapter and a Color/ Graphics Monitor Adapter, remember to use the subroutine discussed in Chapter 2 to change to the Color/Graphics Monitor Adapter before you try out this program.

Fig. 3-3   Drawing a Dot in Each Corner of the Screen

```
10      ' --- PROGRAM TO DRAW A DOT IN EACH CORNER OF THE SCREEN
20      '
30      '
40          SCREEN 1,0
50          CLS
60          PSET (0,0)        ' THE UPPER LEFT HAND CORNER
70          PSET (0,199)      ' THE LOWER LEFT HAND CORNER
80          PSET (319,199)    ' THE LOWER RIGHT HAND CORNER
90          PSET (319,0)      ' THE UPPER RIGHT HAND CORNER
100     '
110         END
```

Note several things about the program. First, it draws the four pixels so fast that you will not notice that it does them one at a time. Second, the

Ok

which BASIC prints whenever a program ends, covers up the pixel at the upper left-hand corner of the screen. Third, this program leaves the screen in medium resolution graphics mode. If you now give the

LIST

command, the program will print differently than it did in text mode before you ran the program. Fourth, since the screen is still in graphics mode, you can eliminate statement 40, and the program will still work as long as you don't change the screen back to text mode with the SCREEN 0 command.

The first time this program runs, the CLS statement at line 50 is superfluous, since the SCREEN 1,0 statement at line 40 clears the screen and changes the system from text mode to medium resolution graphics mode. However, the second and subsequent times that the program runs, the screen will already be in medium resolution graphics mode. Therefore, statement 40 has no effect, and statement 50 is necessary to clear the screen. It is good practice to begin graphics programs with both a SCREEN 1,0 statement and a CLS statement. If the screen is in text mode when the program starts, then the SCREEN 1,0 statement changes it to graphics mode and clears it; the CLS statement has no effect. If the screen is already in graphics mode, then the SCREEN 1,0 statement does nothing and the CLS statement clears the screen. In either case, your programs will work well.

The program in Fig. 3-4 draws a magenta (color number 2) horizontal line from (100,100) to (200,100) by coloring the entire row of pixels that lie between these two points. The FOR-NEXT loop from line 50 to line 70 increments variable X from 100 to 200, and the PSET statement at line 60 therefore changes the color of each of these pixels in turn:

(100,100)
(101,100)
(102,100)
(103,100)
. . .

. . .
(199,100)
(200,100)

Fig. 3-4   Drawing a Line

```
10      ’ --- PROGRAM TO DRAW A HORIZONTAL LINE
20      ’
30      ’
35          SCREEN 1,0
40          CLS
50          FOR X = 100 TO 200
60              PSET (X,100),2
70          NEXT X
80      ’
90      ’
100         END
```

If you try out this program, you will see that the result on the screen looks like a line and not like a series of dots.

This program runs slowly enough so that you can see the line forming on the screen; in Section 3.5, we shall discuss a shorter and better way to draw lines that (1) is easier to program, and (2) runs faster.

The program in Fig. 3-5 draws a series of vertical blue (cyan) lines. The FOR-NEXT loop from line 60 to line 120 increments X from 10 to 310, and at each value for X, statements 75 to 110 draw a vertical line. Statements 75 and 80 calculate how tall a line to draw at each location, and statements 90 to 110 draw the line as did statements 40 to 60 in Fig. 3-4.

Fig. 3-5   More Lines

```
10      ’ --- PROGRAM TO DRAW VERTICAL LINES
20      ’
30      ’
35          SCREEN 1,0
50      ’
60          FOR X = 10 TO 310 STEP 10
70      ’       --- DRAW ONE LINE
75          LET TEMPX = 320 - X
80          LINE.HEIGHT = 199 - TEMPX * TEMPX / 500
90          FOR Y = 199 TO LINE.HEIGHT STEP -1
100             PSET (X,Y) , 1
110         NEXT Y
120         NEXT X
130     ’
140         END
```

Figure 3-6 shows a program that draws a red box and then fills it in with blue. The first four FOR-NEXT loops draw the four sides of the box. The nested FOR-NEXT loops in lines 290 to 330 change the color of every pixel inside the box. As with the pictures drawn by the programs in Fig. 3-4 and Fig. 3-5, the picture drawn by this program looks like a solid block of blue with a red boundary and does not look like a group of dots. We shall discuss shorter ways to draw this same picture with the LINE statement in Section 3.5 and with the PAINT statement in Section 3.7.

Fig. 3-6   Filling an Area

```
10      ' --- PROGRAM TO FILL A BOX
20      '
30      '
40          SCREEN 1,0
50      '
60      ' --- DRAW THE BOX
70      '
80      ' --- DRAW THE TOP
90          FOR X = 100 TO 125
100             PSET (X,30) , 2
110         NEXT X
120     '
130     ' --- DRAW THE BOTTEM
140         FOR X = 100 TO 125
150             PSET (X,150) , 2
160         NEXT X
170     '
180     ' --- DRAW THE LEFT HAND EDGE
190         FOR Y = 30 TO 150
200             PSET (100,Y) , 2
210         NEXT Y
220     '
230     ' --- DRAW THE RIGHT HAND EDGE
240         FOR Y = 30 TO 150
250             PSET (125,Y) , 2
260         NEXT Y
270     '
280     ' --- FILL THE BOX
290         FOR X = 101 TO 124
300             FOR Y = 31 TO 149
310                 PSET (X,Y) , 1
320             NEXT Y
330         NEXT X
340     '
350         END
```

Fig. 3-7   Circles

```
10      ' --- PROGRAM TO DRAW A CIRCLE
20      '
30      '
40          SCREEN 1,0
50          FOR THETA = 0 TO 6.28318 STEP .025
60              X = 160 + 25 * COS(THETA)
70              Y = 100 - 25 * SIN(THETA)
80              PSET (X,Y) , 2
90          NEXT THETA
100     '
110         END
```

Readers with mathematical skills can examine Fig. 3-7, which draws a circle. (Where is the center and what is the radius?) Readers who wish to have their computers draw circles but wish to skip the mathematical gymnastics should wait until Section 3.6, in which the easy way is presented.

NOTES

1. If the coordinates that you give to a PSET or PRESET statement are off the screen, then the statement has no effect (unless your coordinates are so big that you get the "Overflow" error discussed in the last section).

2. If a PSET statement tells the computer to change a pixel to a color when the pixel is already that color, then the statement has no effect.

3.5 DRAWING LINES—THE LINE STATEMENT

Several sample programs in Section 3.4 drew lines by changing the color of a row or column of pixels one pixel at a time. We promised to reveal an easier way.

The LINE statement tells the computer the coordinates of the two endpoints of a line and a color number for the line. For example:

246 LINE (100,100) – (200,100) , 2

draws a magenta (color number 2) line from (100,100) to (200,100) just as did the sample program in Fig. 3-4. The differences between the LINE statement and that program are that the LINE statement is easier to use and draws faster.

The starburst program shown in Fig. 3-8 and in Color Plate 1 uses the LINE statement. After the user of the program inputs a set of coordinates for the starburst's center point, the program draws fifty lines from that center point to randomly selected points. Statements 160 to 180 use the RND function to pick random second endpoints and colors for the lines, and statement 190 draws them. Figure 3-8 shows the appearance of the resulting screen if you input the point (101,100) as your center.

In Fig. 3-8, some of the lines look smooth while others appear quite jagged. The jagged lines occur because the system draws diagonal lines by coloring a series of pixels that approximate a line. For example, a line that is almost horizontal is approximated by a series of pixels on a particular raster line followed by a series of pixels on the next raster line up or down. Where the system jumps from one raster line to the next, the line appears jagged. Horizontal or vertical lines, such as those drawn in the sample programs in Section 3.4, can always be drawn smoothly, but diagonal lines must always be approximated in this way and always appear jagged to some extent.

Fig. 3-8   Starburst Program

This program draws fifty lines from a point the user picks to fifty random points.

```
10      ' --- PROGRAM TO DRAW A STARBURST
20      '
30      '
40      ' --- GET CENTER OF STARBURST FROM USER
50           PRINT "TYPE IN TWO NUMBERS"
60           PRINT "THE 1ST ONE MUST BE BETWEEN 0 AND 319"
70           PRINT "THE 2ND ONE MUST BE BETWEEN 0 AND 199"
80           PRINT "SEPARATE YOUR TWO NUMBERS WITH A COMMA."
90           INPUT "WHAT ARE YOUR NUMBERS?" , CENTER.X , CENTER.Y
100     '
110     ' --- DRAW THE STARBURST
120          SCREEN 1,0
130          CLS
140          RANDOMIZE(CENTER.X)
150          FOR I = 1 TO 50
160             LET X2 = 320 * RND
170             LET Y2 = 200 * RND
180             LET HUE = INT(3 * RND) + 1
190             LINE (X2,Y2) - (CENTER.X,CENTER.Y) , HUE
200          NEXT I
210     '
220          END
```

Output from the Starburst Program

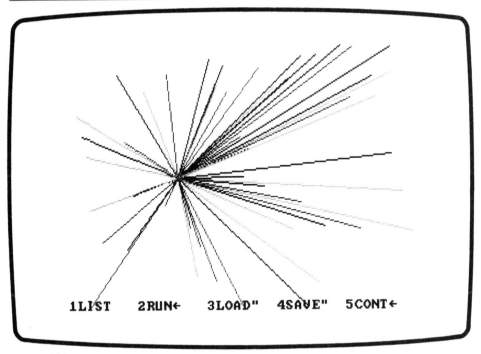

Jagged Lines

Diagonal lines appear jagged on the screen. The almost-horizontal line shown here is drawn by coloring several pixels on one raster line and then jumping to the raster line above. Where the jump is made, the line appears jagged.

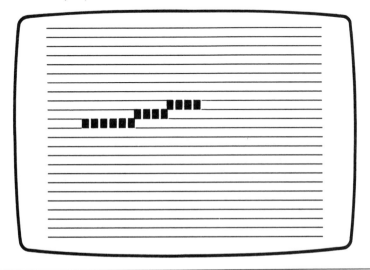

Omitting the First Endpoint and the Color

Suppose that you want a program to fill the screen with octagons as shown in Fig. 3-9. Since there are more lines in that figure than you will want to type LINE statements into a BASIC program, the program to draw that picture should be written with a subroutine to draw one octagon and a FOR-NEXT loop to call the subroutine repeatedly. Since you will call the subroutine many times to draw octagons at different locations on the screen, it must use relative form coordinates. (If you skipped Section 3.3 on relative form coordinates, this might be a good time to go back and read it.) Absolute form coordinates are difficult to use in this situation, because the subroutine doesn't know in advance where the lines it will be drawing on the screen will be.

Examine the program in Fig. 3-9, which draws the octagons in the figure.

Fig. 3-9   Using the STEP Option with Lines

```
10      ' --- PROGRAM TO DRAW A SET OF OCTAGONS
20      '
30      '
35          SCREEN 1,0
36          CLS
40          FOR X = 20 TO 260 STEP 24
50              FOR Y = 20 TO 140 STEP 24
60                  PSET (X,Y) , 0
70                  GOSUB 120
80              NEXT Y
90          NEXT X
95          END
100     '
110     '
120     ' --- SUBROUTINE TO DRAW ONE OCTAGON
130         LINE  - STEP (7,-7)
140         LINE  - STEP (10,0)
150         LINE  - STEP (7,7)
160         LINE  - STEP (0,10)
170         LINE  - STEP (-7,7)
180         LINE  - STEP (-10,0)
190         LINE  - STEP (-7,-7)
200         LINE  - STEP (0,-10)
210         RETURN
```

Octagons

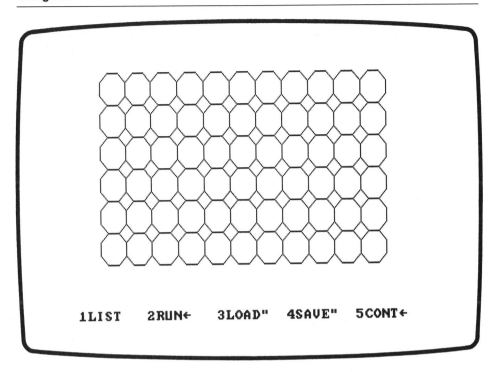

1LIST   2RUN←   3LOAD"   4SAVE"   5CONT←

The subroutine to draw one octagon starts at line 120. Each time through the nested FOR-NEXT loops, the PSET statement at line 60 colors the point that is to be the first point of the octagon and thereby establishes a base location for the relative form coordinates used in the subroutine. After using this PSET statement, the subroutine is called and its relative form coordinates will draw an octagon based on the location given in the PSET statement. The subroutine draws the eight lines that make up an octagon, starting from the point given in the PSET statement.

Since each line in the octagon starts where the previous line left off, you can omit the first endpoint in each of the LINE statements in the subroutine. Whenever you omit the first endpoint from a LINE statement, the computer draws a line to the given second endpoint from whatever point it drew just before executing the LINE statement. This is extremely convenient when you want to draw a series of lines, each of which starts where the previous one ended. This subroutine is a good example of this.

Note that since the LINE statements in the subroutine contain no color number, the computer will draw the octagons with color number 3 (white).

The Box and Box Fill Options

The program in Fig. 3-10 illustrates the "box" option with the LINE statement. If you add a comma and the letter B at the end of a LINE statement, the computer will draw a rectangle whose two opposite corners are the points that you give. For example, the statement

    445 LINE (50,60) – (70,100) , 2 , B

draws these four lines:

    (50,60) – (50,100)
    (50,100) – (70,100)
    (70,100) – (70,60)
    (70,60) – (50,60)

They form the rectangle whose corners are:

    (50,60)   (70,60)

    (50,100)   (70,100)

You can give the LINE statement the coordinates for either pair of opposite corners of the rectangle, and you can give them in either order. The following statements all have the same effect as the one above:

    445 LINE (50,100) – (70,60) , 2 , B
    445 LINE (70,100) – (50,60) , 2 , B
    445 LINE (70,60) – (50,100) , 2 , B

If you omit the color number when you are using the box option with the LINE statement, you must still put in both commas to indicate the space where the color number would be:

    445 LINE (50,100) – (70,60) , , B

Fig. 3-10   The Box Option on the LINE Statement

```
10      ' --- PROGRAM TO DRAW A SERIES OF BOXES
20      '
30      '
40          SCREEN 1,0
50          CLS
60          FOR I = 1 TO 25
70             X = 8 * I
80             Y = 6 * I
90             HUE = (I MOD 3)  + 1
100              LINE (X,Y) - STEP(12,9) , HUE , B
110         NEXT I
120     '
130         END
```

Boxes

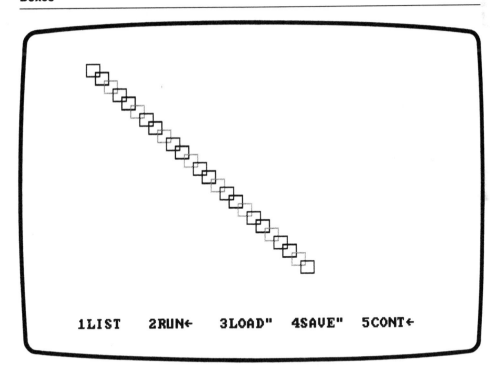

The computer just counts commas in a LINE statement to know whether the next item is a color number or the box option.

By adding a comma and the letters BF ("box fill") at the end of a LINE statement, you cause the computer to draw a box (as with the B option) and then to fill it solid with the given color. For example, the statement

443 LINE (50,50) – (100,100) , 1 , BF

changes to color number 1 all the pixels—more than 2,500 of them—in the box whose corners are:

(50,50)   (100,50)

(50,100)   (100,100)

IBM Sample Program "Art"

The program in Fig. 3-11 is a rewritten version of the sample program from IBM dubiously entitled "Art." It is the first of a number of IBM sample programs that have been rewritten and included in this book. Copies of these programs reside on the DOS diskette sold by IBM. You can try them out without bothering to type them into your computer by following these directions:

1. Insert your DOS diskette.
2. Start BASICA.
3. Give the LOAD command to load whatever program it is you wish to run. For example:

LOAD "ART"

4. Give the command

RUN

Although the versions of these programs printed in this book function almost identically to their IBM-written counterparts, they all differ in the following ways:

1. The programs in this book are much easier to read and understand than the IBM versions.

2. The programs in this book assume that you are using the graphics screen, whereas the IBM programs check to make sure that you are.

3. The programs in this book will not chain back to the master IBM program "Samples," whereas the IBM programs will.

Fig. 3-11   The IBM Sample Program "Art" (Simplified)

```
10     ' --- THE IBM 'ART' PROGRAM REVISITED
20     '
30     '
40         SCREEN 1,0
50         CLS
60     '
70     ' --- DRAW THE FRAME OF THE CITY
80         LINE (1,1)-(320,200),2,BF
90         LINE (30,30)-(290,170),0,BF
100        LINE (30,30)-(1,1),1
110        LINE (290,30)-(320,1),1
120        LINE (30,170)-(1,200),1
130        LINE (290,170)-(320,200),1
140        LINE (100,179)-(216,193),0,BF
150    '
160    '
170    ' --- DRAW 100 BUILDINGS
180        FOR BUILDING = 1 TO 100
190            LET SIDE1 = RND*250 + 35
200            LET SIDE2 = RND*250 + 35
210            LET SIDE2 = (SIDE1-SIDE2)/3 + SIDE2
220            LET TOP = RND*110 + 55
230            LET BOTTEM = 165
240    '
250    '        --- DRAW BUILDING AS A FILLED RECTANGLE
260            LINE (SIDE1,TOP)-(SIDE2,BOTTEM),RND*2+1,BF
270    '
280    '        --- ADD BLACK OUTLINE TO BUILDING
290            LINE (SIDE1,TOP)-(SIDE2,BOTTEM),0,B
300    '
310    '        --- ADD DARKER BLACK OUTLINE TO BUILDING
320            LINE (SIDE1+1,TOP+1)-(SIDE2-1,BOTTEM-1),0,B
330    '
340        NEXT BUILDING
350    '
360        END
```

Fig. 3-11, continued from p. 43

How a "Building" Is Drawn

1. Statement 260 draws a filled box

2. Statement 290 draws a black outline

3. Statement 320 draws a second outline

4. The programs in this book don't display the title page that the original programs display.

5. In general, the programs in this book stop after some fixed event, whereas the IBM counterparts usually run forever unless you press the "escape" key.

The rewritten versions have been tried out to see that they work.

The program in Fig. 3-11, the rewritten version of "Art," illustrates the "box fill" option of the LINE statement. In the program, each "building" is represented by a colored block (statement 260), a black outline (statement 290), and a second outline (statement 320). The two outlines merge into a double-thick row of black around the outside of the "building." In addition to the differences common to all the sample programs listed above, the rewritten version of "Art" differs from the IBM version in these ways:

1. The title "The City" does not appear at the bottom of the screen in this program.

2. The colors in the sample program "Art" are different from those in the program shown here. In Section 4.1 we shall discuss how to change the colors that are used in graphics.

3. This program makes no sounds. We'll discuss how to do this with the IBM Personal Computer in Sections 4.5 and 4.6.

Aspect Ratio Test Program

The program in Fig. 3-12 is the one we promised in Chapter 2 to help you determine the aspect ratio of your screen. The aspect ratio, as you may remember, is the ratio of the distance between two adjacent horizontal dots to the distance between two adjacent vertical dots. You should run the program several times, giving it various aspect ratios until the boxes it draws appear square. (If some of the boxes appear square while others do not, your screen may be out of adjustment.) On the author's IBM Personal Computer Color Display, an aspect ratio of 0.8 makes the boxes appear approximately square. They are then 24 pixels wide by 19 pixels high. If your monitor is a different brand, you can expect this number to be different, but it will probably be between 0.7 and 1.2.

Fig. 3-12 Aspect Ratio

```
10      ' --- PROGRAM TO TEST ASPECT RATIO OF SCREEN
20      '
30      '
40              SCREEN 1,0
45              INPUT "WHAT IS THE ASPECT RATIO?" , ARATIO
50              CLS
60              LINE (0,0) -(24,24*ARATIO) ,, B
70              LINE (319,0) - (295,24*ARATIO) ,, B
80              LINE (0,199) - (24,199 - 24*ARATIO) ,, B
90              LINE (319,199) - (295,199 - 24*ARATIO) ,, B
100             LINE (148,100 - 12*ARATIO) - (172,100 + 12*ARATIO) ,,B
110     '
120             END
```

3.6 CIRCLES AND ELLIPSES—THE CIRCLE STATEMENT

Circles are useful for making pie charts and bouncing balls and for playing Pac-Man, among other applications. Drawing a circle pixel by pixel is relatively complicated mathematically and a nuisance to write in BASIC. The CIRCLE statement, however, makes drawing circles quite simple.

Drawing Entire Circles

Just to draw a circle, you can use the simplest form of the CIRCLE statement, which tells the computer the center point of the circle and the *radius*. The radius, as you may remember from geometry class, is the distance from the center of the circle to the edge. (If you don't remember, Fig. 3-13 discusses various terms used in conjunction with circles.) As with the PSET and LINE statements, you can, if you wish, specify a color number.

Fig. 3-13 Terminology Associated with Circles

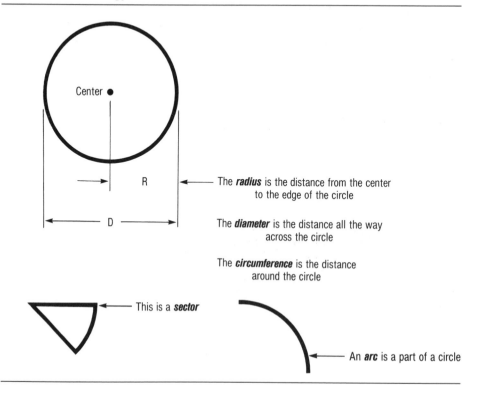

Center ●

R — The *radius* is the distance from the center to the edge of the circle

D — The *diameter* is the distance all the way across the circle

The *circumference* is the distance around the circle

This is a *sector*

An *arc* is a part of a circle

If you do, then the computer draws your circle with that color; if you give no color number, the computer uses color number 3. This CIRCLE statement:

273 CIRCLE (221,106) , 14 , 2

draws a circle with color number 2 centered at the point (221,106) with a radius of 14. Figure 3-14 contains a diagram of this circle.

The programs shown in Fig. 3-15 and Fig. 3-16 use the CIRCLE statement to produce geometric patterns on the screen. The first draws a series of circles at the center of the screen, all but one of which are white. As the computer executes the FOR-NEXT loop from statement 60 to statement 80, RADIUS gets smaller, and the computer draws smaller and smaller circles. The second program draws a series of white circles in an arc across the screen. Statements 70 and 80 compute a formula for the centers of the circles. Some of the circles drawn by these programs have a bad case of the jaggies just as did some of the lines drawn by programs in Section 3.5. As with diagonal lines, the computer has no way to draw perfectly smooth circles.

Fig. 3-14   Circle Drawn by Statement 273

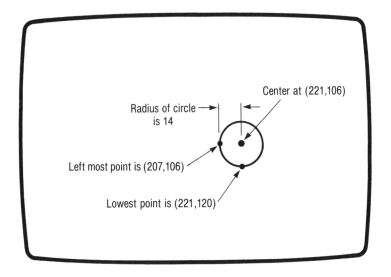

Fig. 3-15   Concentric Circles

This program draws a series of circles of various sizes, all with centers at the middle of the screen.

```
10      ' --- TARGET
20      '
30      '
40          SCREEN 1,0
50          CLS
60          FOR RADIUS = 95 TO 10 STEP -5
70              CIRCLE (160,100),RADIUS
80          NEXT RADIUS
90          CIRCLE (160,100) , 5 , 2
100     '
110     '
120         END
```

Concentric Circles Program Display

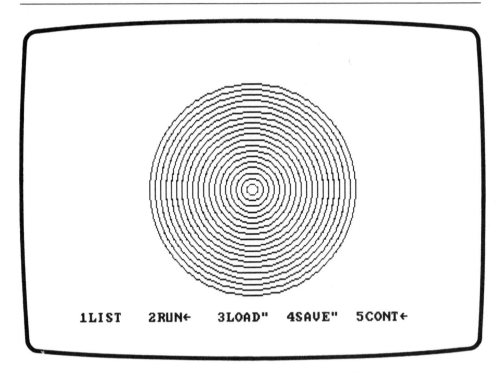

Fig. 3-16 More Circles

```
10      ' --- PROGRAM TO DRAW CIRCLES
20      '
30      '
40          SCREEN 1,0
50          CLS
60          FOR I = 0 TO 26
70              CENTER.X = 8*I + 50
80              CENTER.Y = 70 + .5 * (I-13)^2
90              RADIUS = 50 - (.2*(I-13)^2)
100             CIRCLE (CENTER.X,CENTER.Y),RADIUS
110         NEXT I
120     '
130         END
```

Display of Above Program

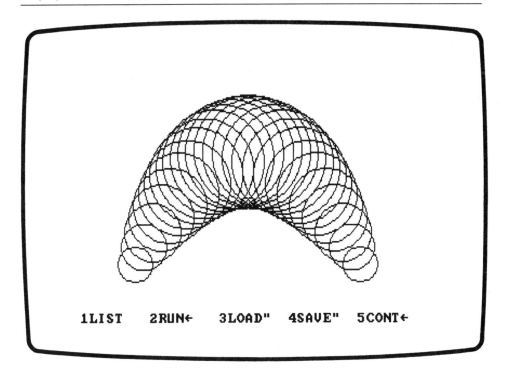

1LIST   2RUN←   3LOAD"   4SAVE"   5CONT←

Note that the center of the circle may be off the screen and that the radius may be too large for the entire circle to fit on the screen. When this happens, the computer figures out what parts of the circle, if any, appear on the screen and draws them, simply leaving off the parts of the circle that fall outside the screen boundaries.

Specifying Points on a Circle

The CIRCLE statement can draw parts of circles, called *arcs*, and pie-slice-shaped objects, called *sectors*. To tell the computer which part of a circle you want drawn, you tell it at what *angle* on the circle to start drawing and at what angle to stop. Angles are expressed in *radians* and are measured from a line starting at the center of the circle and extending to the right as shown in Fig. 3-17 and as described in the next paragraph. If your mathematics training included the study of figures like the one in Fig. 3-17, you may want to skip ahead to the section on drawing arcs and sectors.

To describe a point on the circle in terms of an angle—point X in Fig. 3-17, for example—first draw a horizontal line extending to the right from the center of the circle. Then draw a line from the center of the circle to point X. Finally, measure the angle between the two lines. That is the angle that represents point X. The angle to measure is always the one that runs counterclockwise starting at the horizontal line and ending at the line to the point you wish to describe. See, for example, points Y and Z in Fig. 3-17.

Fig. 3-17   Describing a Point on a Circle in Terms of an Angle

To describe point X in terms of an angle: (1) draw a horizontal line from the center of the circle to the circumference at the right; (2) draw a line from the center of the circle to point X; and (3) measure the angle between the two lines.

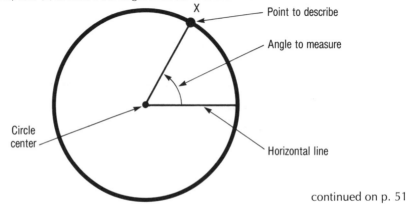

continued on p. 51

continued from p. 50

Find points Y and Z in the same manner.

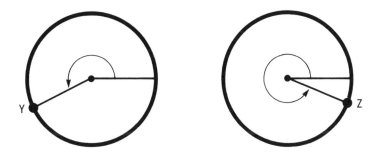

Some examples of angles that represent certain points.

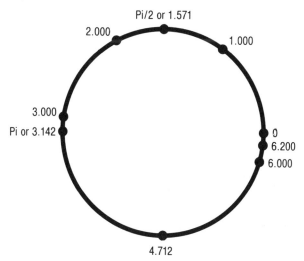

The point directly to the right of the center of the circle is represented by an angle of 0, and the points around the circle are represented by larger and larger angles as you proceed counterclockwise around the circle.

This method can describe points in terms of the number of degrees of angle measure around a circle. Points would then be described in terms of numbers from 0 to 360. The IBM Personal Computer, however, measures angles in terms of *radians*. Radians are an alternative unit of measurement of angles. The measures of angles around a circle range from 0 to approximately 6.283 radians. Why 6.283? Because if you draw a circle with a 1-inch radius, the distance around that circle will be approximately 6.283 inches. This is 2 times *pi*, the ratio of the circumference of a circle to its diameter. Pi is a never-ending, never-repeating decimal approximately equal to

3.1415926535897932384 . . .

Since the number of radians all the way around the circle is 2 times pi, the point that is halfway around the circle, which is the point directly to the left of the center of the circle, is represented by an angle whose size is pi radians. The point directly above the center of the circle is halfway between the right-hand point of the circle (angle 0) and the point at the left (angle pi), so its angle is pi divided by 2, or about

1.571

The point at the bottom of the circle is three times as far around the circle as is the point at the top, so its angle is three times as big:

4.712

Points in between these are at angles in between these values.

Drawing Arcs

The computer always draws circles in a counterclockwise direction. Actually, the pixels that make up circles and arcs do not always change color in counterclockwise order, but the computer does its thinking and deciding as though they did. In order to draw an arc, you must tell the computer at what point on the circle to start drawing and at what point to stop. For example, to draw the upper half of a circle, the computer should start drawing at the point with angle 0, which is directly to the right of the center of the circle, from whence it will draw counterclockwise, and stop at the point with angle 3.14, which is directly to the left of the center. A CIRCLE statement that draws the upper half of a circle is

401 CIRCLE (100,100) , 20 , 2 , 0 , 3.14

where 20 and 2 are the radius and the color of the arc, respectively, and 0 and 3.14 are the angles at which to start and stop drawing. See Fig. 3-18. To

Fig. 3-18   Arcs and Sectors

The arc drawn by 401 CIRCLE (100,100), 20, 2, 0, 3.14

The arc drawn by 402 CIRCLE (100,100), 20, 2, 3.14, 0

The sector drawn by 403 CIRCLE (100,100), 20, 2, -PI/2, -PI

draw the lower half of a circle, the computer must start at the point to the left of the center and stop at the point to the right:

402 CIRCLE (100,100) , 20 , 2 , 3.14 , 0

Note that the stopping angle can be smaller than the starting angle. The computer doesn't check. It just draws from wherever you tell it to start to wherever you tell it to stop.

NOTES

The computer does not allow angles outside the range from 0 to 2 times pi (6.283). If you use one, you will get the error

```
Illegal function call
```

and no arc.

If you omit the color number, you must nonetheless put in the commas that would be there if you put it in. The computer figures out which numbers are radii, which are colors, and which are angles by counting commas. It expects three commas before it finds a starting angle. If it finds fewer than three, it will treat your start angle as though it were a radius or a color number.

Since pi is such an important number when you are dealing with arcs, we recommend that you name a variable PI and set it to 3.14159 early in any program that uses arcs:

    10 LET PI = 3.14159

This allows you to use the value without having to remember it all the time.

Drawing Sectors

A pie-slice-shaped object called a *sector* is an arc with lines drawn from each end to the center of the circle. To draw a sector, you use the CIRCLE statement with a start angle and a stop angle as for an arc, but you give negative angles. When a negative angle appears as a start or stop angle in a CIRCLE statement, it indicates to the computer that a line should be drawn from that end of the arc to the center of the circle. The computer just ignores the fact that the angle is negative when it figures out where to stop or start the arc. If you give −1.3 as an angle, for example, the computer figures out where on the circle it would be if you had given the angle as 1.3, and starts there. To draw a sector that is the upper left quarter of a circle, you could use this statement:

    403 CIRCLE (100,100) , 20 , 2 , −PI/2 , −PI

where PI is a variable that was set to 3.14159 earlier in the program.

If you give one positive angle and one negative angle, then one end of your arc will be connected to the center of the circle, and the other end won't be. This does not affect the way that the arc is drawn. Figure 3-19 contains a program that draws a series of these half-sectors. Try it out to see what it does.

Note that you cannot give the computer a −0 and have it draw a sector starting at angle 0. Instead, you must give it −6.283, that is, negative 2 times pi.

Fig. 3-19   Sectors

```
10    ' --- SECTORS
20    '
30    '
40        SCREEN 1,0
50        CLS
55        LET PI = 3.14159
60        FOR RADIUS = 95 TO 10 STEP -5
61            ANGLE = -RADIUS/33
62            ANGLE2 = -ANGLE + PI
70            CIRCLE (160,100),RADIUS,,ANGLE,ANGLE2
80        NEXT RADIUS
90        CIRCLE (160,100),5,1
100   '
110   '
120       END
```

Display from Above Program

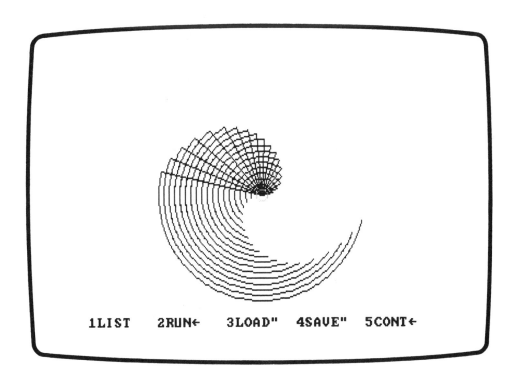

Fig. 3-20 Ellipses with Various Aspect Ratios

The ellipses shown here all have radius 5.

An ellipse with aspect ratio 2:

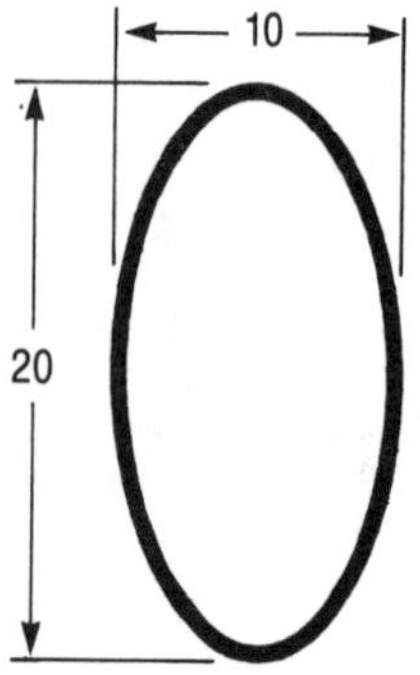

An ellipse with aspect ratio 1.5:

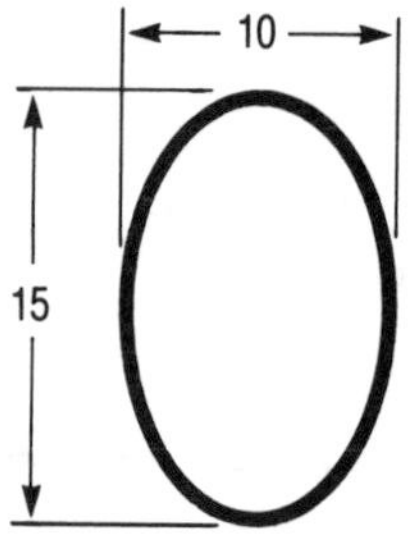

An ellipse with aspect ratio 1 (a circle):

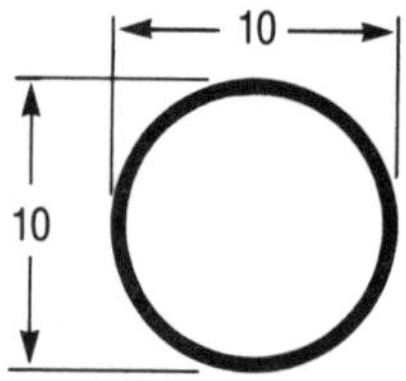

An ellipse with aspect ratio 0.5:

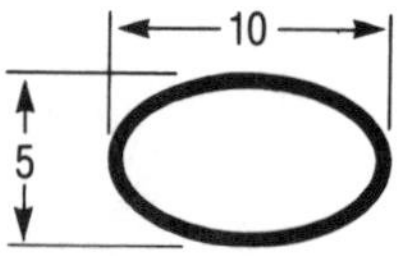

An ellipse with aspect ratio 0.1:

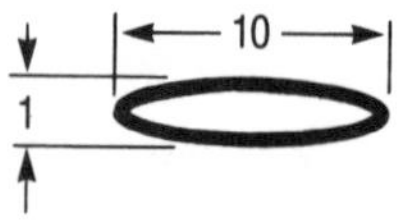

Drawing Ellipses

The CIRCLE statement can also draw ellipses (and arcs of ellipses and sectors of ellipses) if you add the *aspect ratio* that you wish the ellipse to have. The aspect ratio of an ellipse is the ratio between its height and its width. When you ask the computer to draw an ellipse with a certain radius, the width of the resulting ellipse will be the radius, but the height will be the radius times the aspect ratio. An ellipse with an aspect ratio of 1.0, therefore, is a circle (ignoring the problems caused by the fact that your screen doesn't have an aspect ratio of 1.0). An ellipse with an aspect ratio greater than 1.0 is more pixels tall than a circle with the same radius, but the same width. An ellipse with an aspect ratio less than 1.0 is fewer pixels tall than a circle with the same radius, but the same width. See Fig. 3-20.

The aspect ratio is inserted in the CIRCLE statement after the radius, the color, and the start and stop angles. As before, if you leave any of the earlier parameters out, you must still put in the requisite commas so that the computer will recognize the aspect ratio when it finds it and not think that it is a stray angle or color. Here is an example of an ellipse that fills the screen:

501 CIRCLE (160,100) , 159 , 2 , , , 5/8

The ellipse will extend 318 units across the screen (159 times 2) and will be 199 units high (318 times 5/8). Note all the commas where the start and stop angles are left out.

To display something that looks like a true circle, you must give an aspect ratio that is the reciprocal of the aspect ratio of your screen.

A program that draws a whole series of ellipses with various aspect ratios on the screen is shown in Fig. 3-21.

Fig. 3-21   Circles and Ellipses

```
10       ' --- VARIOUS ASPECT RATIOS FOR CIRCLES GIVE ELIPSES
20       '
30       '
40       SCREEN 1,0
50       CLS
60       FOR HUE = 3 TO 0 STEP -1
70          FOR ASPECT = 1 TO .05 STEP -.05
80             CIRCLE (160,100) , 100 , HUE ,,, ASPECT
90          NEXT ASPECT
100      NEXT HUE
110      '
120      END
```

Output from Above Program

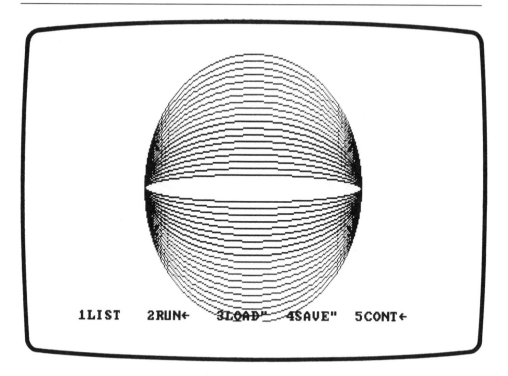

1LIST   2RUN←   3LOAD"   4SAVE"   5CONT←

3.7 FILLING AREAS—THE PAINT STATEMENT

In Section 3.4, while we were doing things the hard way with the PSET statement, we used two nested FOR-NEXT loops to fill an entire block with blue pixels. In Section 3.5, we saw how to fill rectangular areas easily with the box fill option of the LINE statement. In this section, we shall discuss the PAINT statement, which can tell the computer to fill an area of any shape. To use the PAINT statement, you first use the PSET, LINE, and CIRCLE statements (or other statements we will discuss later in this chapter) to draw a boundary for the area to be filled. You then give the PAINT statement a point inside the area, and it colors all the pixels in the area inside the boundary.

Here is a very simple example:

```
10 CIRCLE (100,100) , 20 , 1
20 PAINT (100,100) , 2 , 1
```

We'll now discuss what these two statements do, but typing them into your computer and trying them is quicker and probably more fun. Statement 10 draws a circle whose center is at (100,100) in color number 1. Statement 20 colors the point (100,100) with color number 2, the *fill color,* and then colors adjacent pixels with color number 2 until it cannot color any more pixels without crossing a boundary made up of color number 1, the *boundary color.* Since the circle is made of color number 1 and encloses the point (100,100), statement 20 fills the circle with color number 2 and leaves the rest of the screen black.

Here is a complementary example:

```
10 CIRCLE (100,100) , 20 , 1
20 PAINT (0,0) , 2 , 1
```

Statement 10 again draws a circle with color number 1. The revised statement 20 starts coloring pixels starting in the upper left-hand corner of the screen. Since the circle is in color number 1, the PAINT statement can't get inside it, but all of the screen outside the circle is changed to color number 2.

An example that is complementary in a different sort of way is:

```
10 CIRCLE (100,100) , 20 , 1
20 PAINT (100,100) , 2 , 3
```

Once again, the PAINT statement starts at the center of the circle; but in this example, although the circle is still drawn with color number 1, the PAINT statement has been told that the boundary color is color number 3. The PAINT statement never finds a boundary and fills the entire screen with color number 2, obliterating the circle on its way.

The following example also fills the entire screen, even though the circle has the same color as the color the PAINT statement uses to fill the screen.

```
10 CIRCLE (100,100) , 20 , 2
20 PAINT (100,100) , 2 , 3
```

You can draw more complex outlines, and PAINT will fill them:

```
10 LINE (100,100) - (160,30) , 2
20 LINE - (200,30) , 2
30 LINE - (240,170) , 2
40 LINE - (80,180) , 2
50 LINE - (100,100) , 2
60 PAINT (120,100) , 3 , 2
```

Statements 10 to 50 draw an odd five-sided figure with color number 2. Statement 60 fills it up with color number 3.

The fill color may be the same as the boundary color. For example, if statement 60 above were changed to

60 PAINT (120,100) , 2 , 2

the computer would fill the area with color number 2.

You can omit the fill color or the boundary color from PAINT statements. Colors you omit are assumed to be color number 3.

An area you wish to fill with the PAINT statement must have an airtight boundary. The PAINT process can squeeze through a one-pixel leak and paint all sorts of areas you hadn't intended. The program in Fig. 3-22 was supposed to color the left half of the screen with color number 2. Unfortunately, the line drawn by statement 80 to divide the screen in half stops one pixel short of the bottom of the screen. The PAINT statement at line 90 sneaks through this gap and colors the entire screen, with the exception of statement 80's vertical boundary line. The statement KEY OFF at line 60, incidentally, just turns off the function key labels that normally appear at the bottom of the screen.

You must start painting *inside* the area you wish to fill. Starting on the boundary is not good enough. In fact, a PAINT statement that tries to start on the boundary does nothing. The PAINT statement in line 80 of the program in Fig. 3-23, for example, which tries to start filling on the line drawn by statement 70, has no effect.

Fig. 3-22   Painting the Whole Screen (by Mistake)

```
10      ' --- PROGRAM THAT SHOULD FILL HALF THE SCREEN
20      ' --- (THIS PROGRAM DOESN'T WORK)
30      '
40      '
50          SCREEN 1,0
60          KEY OFF
70          CLS
80          LINE (160,0) - (160,198) , 3
90          PAINT (0,0) , 2 , 3
100         END
```

Fig. 3-23   Painting Nothing (by Mistake)

```
10      ' --- PROGRAM THAT DOESN'T FILL THE SCREEN
20      '
30      '
40          SCREEN 1,0
50          KEY OFF
60          CLS
70          LINE (160,0) - (160,199) , 3
80          PAINT (160,50) , 2 , 3
90          END
```

Fig. 3-24   Painting Again and Again

```
10      ' --- PROGRAM TO FILL A MAZE
20      '
30      '
35          SCREEN 1,0
36          CLS
37      '
40      ' --- DRAW THE MAZE
50          LINE (10,10)-(300,190),2,B
60          FOR I = 20 TO 260 STEP 40
70              LINE (I,10)-(I+10,188),2,BF
80              LINE (I+20,12)-(I+30,190),2,BF
90          NEXT I
100     '
110     ' --- FILL THE MAZE
120         PAINT (15,15),1,2
125     ' --- COVER THE MAZE
130         PAINT (0,199),3,1
135     ' --- COVER THE MAZE AGAIN
139         PAINT (0,199),2,2
140     '
150         END
```

Display Made by Above Program

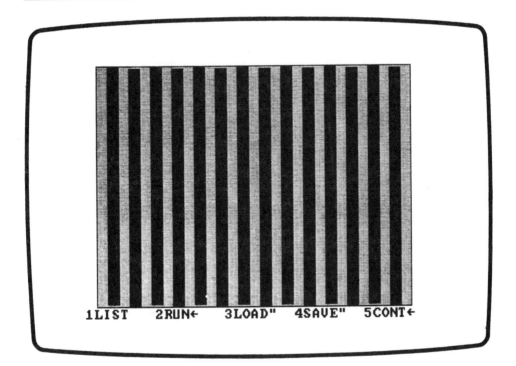

You can paint over areas previously painted. Type the program in Fig. 3-24 into your computer to see this process in action. Statements 50 to 90 draw a complicated figure on the screen with color number 2. Statement 120 fills the interior of this figure with color number 1. The screen now contains pixels with colors number 1 and 2. Statement 130 starts filling the screen in the lower left-hand corner using color number 3. Since color number 1 is its boundary color, it fills the entire screen except those pixels changed to color number 1 by statement 120. Statement 129 looks for a boundary of pixels with color number 2, but since no pixels on the screen have color number 2 when it starts, this statement fills the entire screen with color number 2.

The program in Fig. 3-25 is a rewritten version of the IBM sample program entitled "Circle." To see what this program does without typing it in, run the sample "Circle" program the same way you ran the "Art" program in Section 3.5. (Watching this program provides a puzzle that may interest you.

Fig. 3-25   The IBM Sample Program "Circle" (Rewritten)

```
10  ' --- THIS PROGRAM DRAWS CIRCLES AND PAINTS AROUND THEM
20  '
30  '
40        TWO.PI = 6.28
50        ASPECT = 5/6
60        SCREEN 1,0
70  '
80        FOR I = 1 TO 10
90            ARC.SWEEP = .5 + RND*5
100           ANGLE.STEP = RND * 2
110           CLS
120 '
130          FOR RADIUS = 5 TO 100 STEP 2
140 '
150              LET ANGLE2 = ANGLE + ARC.SWEEP
160              IF ANGLE2 > TWO.PI   THEN
                     LET ANGLE2 = ANGLE2 - TWO.PI
170 '
180              CIRCLE(160,100),RADIUS,2,ANGLE,ANGLE2,ASPECT
190 '
200              LET ANGLE = ANGLE + ANGLE.STEP
210              IF ANGLE > TWO.PI   THEN
                     LET ANGLE = ANGLE - TWO.PI
220 '
230          NEXT RADIUS
240 '
250          PAINT(160,100),3,2
260          FOR DELAY = 0 TO 1000
270          NEXT DELAY
280       NEXT I
290       END
```

Display Made by Program

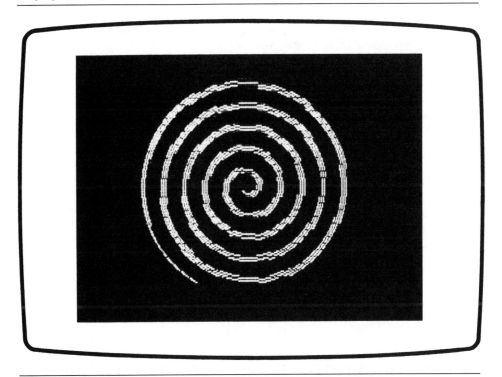

In what order does the PAINT statement color pixels on the screen? The answer to this question is beyond the scope of this book, so if you're interested, you'll have to figure out the answer on your own.) There are only two differences in function between this program and the IBM sample: (1) this one does not print a title page screen, and (2) this one draws ten screenfuls and then quits, whereas the IBM program runs until you press the "escape" key.

Summary of Graphics Statements

A summary of the statements we have discussed so far is presented in Fig. 3-26.

Fig. 3-26 Summary of the Graphics Statements

These rules summarize the graphics statements we have discussed:
1. The syntax for the statements we have discussed is:

```
PSET (x,y) , color
PRESET (x,y) , color
LINE (x,y) – (x2,y2) , color , box option
CIRCLE (x,y) , radius , color , start angle , stop angle , aspect ratio
PAINT (x,y) , fill color , boundary color
```

2. You can always omit a color number. All the statements assume that an omitted color number is a 3, with the exception of the PRESET statement, which assumes that it is a 0.

3. The computer uses commas to figure out how to interpret the numbers given as parts of statements. For example, it decides whether a number in a CIRCLE statement is a radius, a start or stop angle, or an aspect ratio by counting the commas that appear in the statement prior to the number. Whenever you omit a parameter but intend to include a later parameter, you must include all the commas that would be there if you had included all the parameters.

3.8 DRAWING PICTURES—THE DRAW STATEMENT

In this section, we shall discuss the DRAW statement, an alternative to the previously discussed LINE statement. The DRAW statement consists of the word DRAW followed by a string or the name of a string variable. The string or string variable must contain what IBM calls *graphics definition language,* which tells the DRAW statement what to draw. Graphics definition language consists of a series of commands, each of which tells the DRAW statement to do something, such as to draw a line, to draw a subpicture, to scale something, to rotate something, or to draw subsequent items with a different color.

The advantages of a DRAW statement over a series of LINE statements are that complex pictures can be constructed with string functions, that one DRAW statement can draw as complex a figure as can be stored in one string, and that horizontal, vertical, and 45-degree diagonal lines are particularly easy to create with the DRAW statement. The disadvantages are that the DRAW statement hasn't the LINE statement's box or box fill options and that a program must set up a string to draw even a simple picture with the DRAW statement.

Fig. 3-27   Graphics Definition Language Commands

This figure lists the graphics definition language commands and describes the effect of each.

M x,y—Move to the pixel whose coordinates are (x,y). These coordinates are absolute unless the values of x and y are preceded by a plus or minus sign, in which case they are relative. For example,

M +5, −11

moves five pixels to the right and eleven pixels upward from whatever the last referenced location was.

U n—Move n pixels up. This coordinate is always relative.

D n—Move n pixels down.

L n—Move n pixels to the left.

R n—Move n pixels to the right.

E n—Move n pixels up and to the right.

F n—Move n pixels down and to the right.

G n—Move n pixels down and to the left.

H n—Move n pixels up and to the left.

B—Do the following move command (any of the above commands) but do not draw a line to the new location; just move there.

N—Do the following move command, drawing a line, and then come back to this location. This command can be applied to any of the above commands.

S n—Set a scale. Divide the number n by 4 to get the actual scale.

A n—Set an angle. The number n must be one of the numbers 0 to 3, and they correspond to the following rotations:

Number	Rotation
0	No rotation.
1	Rotate 90 degrees counterclockwise.
2	Rotate 180 degrees.
3	Rotate 270 degrees counterclockwise (the same as 90 degrees clockwise).

C n—Set a color. The number n must be from 0 to 3.

X—Execute a variable. The variable must be a string that contains more graphics definition language commands. The name of the variable must be followed by a semicolon.

Any of the above commands that use x, y, or n as parameters may have an equal sign, the name of a numeric variable, and a semicolon substituted for the number. For example:

```
10  LET S99 = 99
20  DRAW "S=S99;"
```

sets the scale to 99. This example (see top of following page):

continued from p. 65

```
10   LET XMOVE = 43
20   LET YPOSITION = 99
30   DRAW "M +=XMOVE;,=YPOSITION;"
```

draws 43 units to the right from wherever it was and draws to a pixel whose y coordinate is 99.

Graphics Definition Language

THE M COMMAND

See Fig. 3-27 for a complete listing of the commands in graphics definition language. The first command we shall discuss tells the DRAW statement to "move" to a particular pixel on the screen. The command consists of the letter M and the x and y coordinates of the pixel to move to, separated by a comma. For example, this command

M 70,60

tells the DRAW statement to move to the pixel at (70,60). The space between the M and the 70 in the command string is optional. Spaces can be inserted anywhere in graphics definition language.

Normally, the M command causes the DRAW statement to draw a line from wherever it was to the new pixel, but you can have the DRAW statement move to a pixel without drawing a line by preceding the above command with a B. For example,

B M 70,60

moves to the pixel (70,60) without drawing a line to it. This allows you to move to the pixel (70,60) in order to start a new line there.

A possible program fragment to draw a rectangle using the DRAW statement is shown below. This is not the easiest way to accomplish the job, as we shall discuss later, but it is a straightforward use of the DRAW statement. Here is the fragment:

```
10  LET GDL$ = "B M 70,60  M 200,60  M 200,90
               M 70,90  M 70,60"
20  DRAW GDL$
```

Statement 20 moves to the pixel (70,60) without drawing a line, then draws lines from there to (200,60), from (200,60) to (200,90), thence to (70,90), and back to (70,60). The program fragment will have the same effect when written this way:

10 DRAW "BM 70,60 M 200,60 M 200,90
        M 70,90 M 70,60"

The coordinates in the M commands above are absolute coordinates, as discussed in Section 3.3. To use relative coordinates in an M command, you put plus or minus signs in front of the numbers. The program fragment below draws the same rectangle as the fragments above using relative coordinates:

10 DRAW "BM 70,60 M +130,+0 M+0,+30
        M −130,+0 M +0,−30"

It is not possible to make the x coordinate relative and the y coordinate absolute or vice versa. For example, this program fragment does not draw a zigzag across the screen:

```
10    DRAW   "BM 100,100"
20    FOR I = 1 TO 10
30        DRAW   "M +10,110  M +10,100"
40    NEXT I
```

The plus signs in front of the x coordinates make the y coordinates relative as well.

THE U, D, L, R, E, F, G, AND H COMMANDS

We can abbreviate the two program fragments in the section above, because graphics definition language includes short commands for drawing horizontal, vertical, and 45-degree diagonal lines. These are the U (up), D (down), L (left), and R (right) commands and the E (up and to the right), F (down and to the right), G (down and to the left), and H (up and to the left) commands. (The first four are, obviously, much easier to remember than the last four.) Each of these commands consists of the letter that indicates the direction of the line to draw and a number, which indicates its length. For example, the rectangle-drawing progam fragment above could be changed to:

10 DRAW "BM 70,60 R 130 D 30 L 130 U 30"

A (now correct) program to draw a zigzag might be:

```
10   DRAW   "BM 100,100"
20   FOR I = 1 TO 10
30       DRAW   "F 10  E 10"
40   NEXT I
```

You can put the B command in front of any of the eight commands discussed in this section to cause them to move to a new location rather than to draw a line to it.

USING VARIABLES IN GRAPHICS DEFINITION LANGUAGE COMMANDS

Graphics definition language allows you to use the value of a numeric variable in place of a number wherever a number is called for. To do this, replace the number with an equal sign, the name of the numeric variable, and a semicolon. For example, the rectangle program fragment could be rewritten as:

```
10   LET   THIRTY = 30
20   LET   HORIZ = 130
30   DRAW   "BM 70,60  R=HORIZ; D=THIRTY; L=HORIZ;
             U=THIRTY; "
```

Statement 30 finds the values of the variables THIRTY and HORIZ in order to draw the lines requested in the string, thereby yielding the same rectangle as before. Do not neglect to insert a semicolon after the variable name, even if the graphics command is the last one in the string. The semicolon after U = THIRTY above, for example, is necessary.

You must be the judge of whether the above program fragment is clearer than the one below that uses the LINE statement:

```
10   LET   THIRTY = 30
20   LET   HORIZ = 130
30   LINE   (70,60) - STEP(HORIZ,THIRTY),,B
```

SUBPICTURES, SCALES, AND ANGLES

The most powerful feature of graphics definition language is its ability to include one picture as a subpicture within another picture. This feature allows you to create one string that draws a very complex picture by referring to other strings that draw simpler pictures. To do this, you use the X command, which consists of the letter X, the name of the string that contains your subpicture, and a semicolon. This example draws three boxes:

```
10   LET BOX$ = "R 130  D 30  L 130  U 30"
20   LET BOXES$ = "BM 50,50  X BOX$;  BM 50,100  X BOX$;
        BM 50,150  X BOX$;"
30   DRAW BOXES$
```

The string BOX$ draws a rectangle 130 pixels wide by 30 pixels high. The string BOXES$ moves to the pixel (50,50), invokes the string BOX$, which draws a box starting at (50,50), moves to the pixel (50,100), invokes BOX$ to draw another box there, and finally moves to the pixel (50,150) and draws a third box.

You can set a scale factor by which all relative coordinates will be multiplied with the graphics definition language scale command. The scale command consists of the letter S and a number from 1 to 255, which represents the new scale factor. For example

S 12

The number given in the scale command is divided by 4, and all subsequent distances given in L, R, U, D, E, F, G, and H commands, and all distances given in terms of relative coordinates in M commands are multiplied by the result. The string above would cause all of the subsequent distances to be multiplied by 3, for example, since 12 divided by 4 is 3. Whenever the program is started, the scale factoring is turned off, but a scale factor set in one DRAW statement applies to all subsequently executed DRAW statements as well until the scale factor is set again.

The most useful application of the scale command is to tell the DRAW statement to draw a subpicture at a scale different from the one at which it was defined. Figure 3-28, which is a variation of a program presented in the IBM BASIC manual, is a good example. The variable STAR$ contains graphics definition language to draw a relatively small five-pointed star. In the loop from statement 90 to statement 110, the star is drawn at scale 1/4, then at scales 3/4, 5/4, 7/4, and so on. As the program proceeds, it draws larger and larger stars on the screen. See also Color Plate 3 for the output from this program.

You can rotate moves given in the M command with relative coordinates, and you can change the directions of lines drawn with the U, D, L, R, E, F, G, and H commands by using the angle command. The angle command consists of the letter A and a number from 0 to 3. When angle is set to 0, subsequent relative moves are interpreted in the usual way. If angle is changed to 1, then all moves are rotated 90 degrees counterclockwise: moves to the right become moves up; moves up become moves left; moves left become moves down; moves down become moves to the right; diagonal moves change correspondingly. When angle is 2, then relative moves are

Fig. 3-28   Using the Scale Command

This figure illustrates the use of the S command to make the shooting star, defined by the string STAR$, appear larger and larger.

```
10      ' --- IBM SHOOTING STAR EXAMPLE
20      '
30      '
40          SCREEN 1,0
50          CLS
60          COLOR 0,0
70          DRAW "BM 300,25"
80          LET STAR$ = "M +7,17   M -17,-12   M +20,0
                M -17,12   M +7,-17"
90          FOR SCALE = 1 TO 40 STEP 2
100             DRAW "S=SCALE; BM -2,0 XSTAR$;"
110         NEXT SCALE
120         END
```

Display Created by Above Program

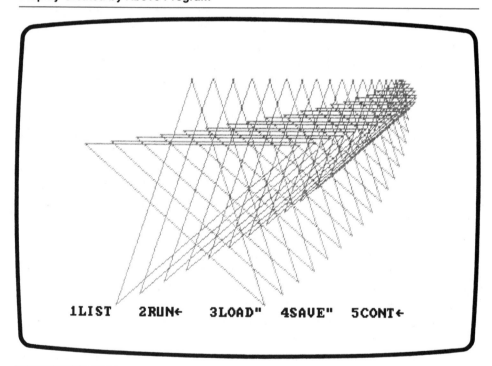

1LIST   2RUN←   3LOAD"   4SAVE"   5CONT←

rotated 180 degrees: moves to the right become moves to the left and vice versa; moves up become moves down and vice versa; diagonal moves change correspondingly. When angle is 3, moves are rotated 270 degrees counterclockwise (or 90 degrees clockwise). Whenever the program is started, the angle defaults to 0, but an angle set in one DRAW statement applies to all subsequently executed DRAW statements as well until angle is set again.

As with the scale, the most useful application for the angle command is just before an X command to draw a subpicture. The program shown in Fig. 3-29 "wanders" around the screen, drawing arrows as it goes. The string ARROW$ draws one arrow pointing to the right. The sequence of commands in ARROW$ ends at the head of the arrow so that when another arrow is drawn, it starts at the head of the previous one. Whenever statement 120 draws an arrow, it first sets the angle using the variable ANGLE, which is set randomly at statement 100. Subsequently, it invokes the variable ARROW$, which then draws an arrow in whichever of the four directions has been selected by the value of ANGLE. All of the drawing commands in the ARROW$ string are rotated by statement 120. The program starts at the center of the screen and draws an arrow randomly either upward, downward, to the right, or to the left. Starting at the head of the first arrow, it draws a second arrow in one of the four directions. At the head of the second arrow, the program draws a third in a random direction, and so on.

You must take care not to use absolute coordinates in any picture to which you intend to apply a scale or angle command. Since locations given with absolute coordinates are not changed by the scale and angle commands, the results will be peculiar if you use them.

COLOR

By using the color command you can change the color with which the lines from the DRAW statement are drawn. The color command consists of the letter C and one of the numbers from 0 to 3. The color defaults to 3, but after the C command is executed, all lines are drawn with the new color until another color command is executed. The program in Fig. 3-30 draws a pattern on the screen using the color given by the user at the beginning of the program. This figure also shows how the execute command can create a complex picture in one string. It is left to you to figure out how that program works.

Fig. 3-29 Using the Angle Command

This figure illustrates the use of the A command to rotate a subpicture.

```
10    ' --- DRAW ARROWS AS YOU MOVE
20    '
30    '
40        CLS
50        SCREEN 1,0
60        SEED = VAL(RIGHT$(TIME$,2))
70        RANDOMIZE(SEED)
80        ARROW$ = "R15 H3 BD6 E3"
90        FOR I = 1 TO 100
100          ANGLE = INT(4*RND)
120          DRAW "A=ANGLE;  X ARROW$;"
130          FOR DELAY = 1 TO 25
140          NEXT DELAY
150       NEXT I
160       END
```

Output of Above Program

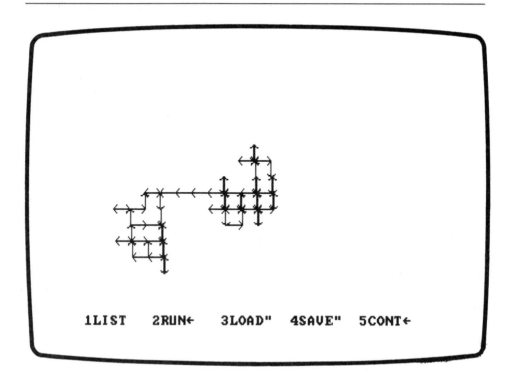

Fig. 3-30   Using the Color Command

This program illustrates the use of the color command to change the color with which the DRAW statement draws lines.

```
10      ' --- FILL A SCREEN WITH ARROWS OF ANY COLOR
20      '
30      '
40          CLS
50          INPUT "WHAT COLOR DISPLAY WOULD YOU LIKE (1,2,3)" ;
                HUE
60            HUE = INT(HUE)
70            IF HUE > 3 GOTO 50
80            IF HUE < 1 GOTO 50
100         CLS
120         SCREEN 1,0
130         LET A$ = "R15 H3 BD6 E3 L15"
140         LET C$ = "XA$;A1 XA$;A2 XA$;A3 XA$;A0"
150         LET R$ = "XC$;BR40 XC$;BR40 XC$;BR40 XC$;BR40 XC$;
                BR40 XC$;BR40 XC$;BL240"
160         LET S$ = "XR$;BD40 XR$;BD40 XR$;BD40 XR$;BD40
                XR$;BU160"
170         PSET (20,20)
180         DRAW "C=HUE;" + S$
```

Output of Above Program

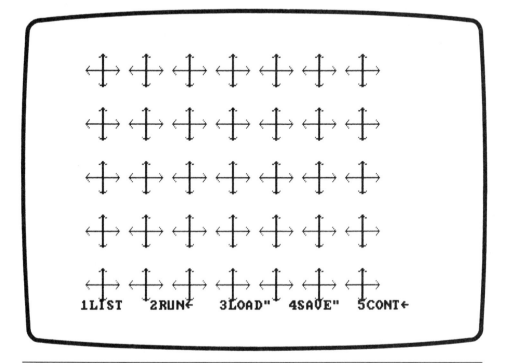

Limitations and Accuracy Considerations

Obviously, for the DRAW statement to draw lines on the screen, the x coordinates you use must lie between 0 and 319, and the y coordinates must lie between 0 and 199. The DRAW statement, however, can keep track of much larger coordinates. The numbers following the U, D, L, R, E, F, G, H, and M commands can be from one to four digits long and can therefore have values up to 9,999, even though lines this long will be mostly or completely off the screen. If you use a number with five or more digits, you will get this error message:

```
Illegal function call
```

DRAW statements keep track of coordinates from −32,767 to 32,767. This program fragment, for example, draws the left end of a very large rectangle on the screen:

```
10  DRAW "BM 50,50"
20  FOR I = 1 TO 32
30      DRAW "R 1000"
40  NEXT I
50  DRAW "D 100"
60  FOR I = 1 TO 32
70      DRAW "L 1000"
80  NEXT I
90  DRAW "U 100"
100 END
```

The rectangle that it draws has corners at:

(50 , 50)   (32,050 , 50)

(50 , 150)   (32,050 , 150)

This, as you can see, is mostly off the screen. However, if you change statement 20 to

20 FOR I = 1 TO 33

and change statement 60 to

60 FOR I = 1 TO 33

the computer loses track of the coordinates, since they will exceed 32,767. Exactly what the computer does when the coordinates get out of range depends on a number of factors, but its response is usually bizarre and useless. Since the computer doesn't check the sizes of your coordinates, you must be sure that they stay in bounds.

If you request the computer to draw a line that lies off the edge of the screen, the DRAW statement draws a line along the edge of the screen closest to where the line really should be. In the sample program fragment given above, the vertical line drawn by statement 50 should run from (32,050 , 50) to (32,050 , 150). Since this is off the right-hand edge of the screen (by about a mile), the computer draws a line along the right-hand edge of the screen.

The scale factors controlled by the scale command work entirely in integers and hence are not entirely accurate. Consider this program fragment:

```
10  DRAW "BM 50,50  R 43  D 21"
20  DRAW "S = 1  L 43  L 43  L 43  L 43
          U 21  U 21  U 21  U 21"
```

This program fragment should draw a rectangle, since setting the scale to 1 (that is, 1/4) at the beginning of statement 20 should be exactly offset by including the L 43 and U 21 commands four times each. However, the scale factor calculation is done with whole numbers. When the 43 in each of the L 43 commands is divided by 4, the computer truncates the exact answer (10.75) to an integer, for a final result of 10. Similarly, when dividing the 21 in the L 21 command, the computer gets 5. The computer therefore moves 10 units to the left four times and 5 units upward four times, for a total of 40 units to the left and 20 units up, instead of the required 43 units left and 21 units up.

The DRAW statement can be intermixed with other graphics statements such as PSET, LINE, CIRCLE, and so on. When this is done, the location and color last used by one of these other graphics statements is used by subsequent DRAW statements.

4 More BASIC Primitives

4.1 CHANGING THE COLORS—THE COLOR STATEMENT

In Chapter 3 we discussed the various BASIC statements that add pictures or parts of pictures to the display. In this chapter, we shall discuss BASIC statements that control other aspects of graphics: controlling the colors on the screen, using a joystick, copying and moving sections of a picture from one place on a screen to another, and so on.

Introduction to Color

In our discussions of the PSET, LINE, CIRCLE, and PAINT statements, we have spoken of drawing on the screen with color number 0, color number 1, color number 2, and color number 3. However, on observing a landscape, a photograph, or a computer display, few people would exclaim, "Look at those wonderful shades of color number two!" Most are far more likely to remark on the reds, blues, and greens. The sample graphics displays in this book so far have all been magenta, cyan, and white on a black background, and all text has been white letters on a black background. Other colors are possible on the IBM Personal Computer, however, and in this section, we shall discuss how to control the process that translates color numbers into colors on the screen. Since colors are treated one way in text mode and very differently in the graphics modes, and since one IBM sample program, "Colorbar," uses the colors in the text mode, we shall discuss both text and graphics modes. This discussion is divided into three parts. The first part discusses considerations that apply both to graphics mode and to text mode. The second and third parts explain how to handle color in graphics and text modes.

General Considerations

The IBM Personal Computer can display the sixteen colors listed in Fig. 4-1. We shall call the number that appears next to a color in this figure the *color index* for that color. Color indexes do *not* relate to the color numbers we have previously discussed; they are used only in the COLOR statement discussed below. The colors in the right-hand column of Fig. 4-1 are the *light* or *high-intensity* colors, since with one exception the colors in the right-hand column are lighter versions of the corresponding colors in the left-hand column. The exception is the pair brown and yellow, the colors with indices 6 and 14. Note that you can always find the index number of the light version of the color by adding 8 to the index number of the regular version of the color.

How the colors look on your monitor depends on what type of monitor you have and how you adjust it. The colors displayed by the IBM Personal Computer Color Display match the list in Fig. 4-1 quite well. The colors displayed by other monitors may or may not. Brown is a particularly tricky color, even on fairly good monitors. A color television set with a Sup-R-Mod may have trouble with several of the colors, especially the high-intensity ones from the right-hand column of Fig. 4-1. We'll discuss one good way to adjust your monitor at the end of this section.

Fig. 4-1   Possible Colors on the IBM Personal Computer

The following list shows the colors that the IBM Personal Computer can display and the index numbers the COLOR statement uses to refer to them. The colors in the right-hand column are the light or high-intensity colors. Note that the numbers shown here are the *color indices* discussed in this section and do *not* have any relationship to the color numbers discussed in other sections of this book.

Regular Colors	*High-Intensity Colors*
0 Black	8 Grey
1 Blue	9 Light Blue
2 Green	10 Light Green
3 Cyan	11 Light Cyan
4 Red	12 Light Red
5 Magenta	13 Light Magenta
6 Brown	14 Yellow
7 White	15 High-Intensity White

COLOR IN MEDIUM RESOLUTION GRAPHICS MODE

In medium resolution graphics mode, you can display up to four colors at a time. (In high resolution graphics mode, as you may remember from our earlier discussion, all pictures are black and white.) You may pick any color from Fig. 4-1 as the *background* color, which is the color the system displays for pixels colored with color number 0. If you pick a color from the left-hand column for your background color, then for pixels colored with the *foreground* colors—colors 1, 2, and 3—you must pick one of two *palettes*. They are:

Color Number	Palette 0		Palette 1	
1	Green	(2)	Cyan	(3)
2	Red	(4)	Magenta	(5)
3	Brown	(6)	White	(7)

The numbers in parentheses indicate the index numbers used in Fig. 4-1. You must choose your foreground colors as a group. You can have either the group of colors on palette 0 or the group of colors on palette 1; you can't have colors from both at the same time. If you use a light color for your background color, then your foreground colors will come from palettes with the lighter versions of the same colors:

Color Number	Palette 0		Palette 1	
1	Light Green	(10)	Light Cyan	(11)
2	Light Red	(12)	Light Magenta	(13)
3	Yellow	(14)	Bright White	(15)

The COLOR statement is used to select the colors used in your display. It consists of the word COLOR followed by the index number of the color you want for your background color, a comma, and the number of the palette you wish to use. This COLOR statement, for example, changes the background color to light blue (color number 9) and the foreground colors to light cyan, light magenta, and bright white (palette 1):

```
20 COLOR 9,1
```

In graphics mode, the COLOR statement affects everything on the screen, even things drawn before the COLOR statement was executed. When the COLOR statement is executed, items already on the screen change to the new colors specified by the COLOR statement. The hardware design of the graphics on the IBM Personal Computer forces this to happen. As explained in Chapter 2, the computer stores one number—0, 1, 2, or 3—for each pixel and decides later what colors these numbers represent. The COLOR statement sends new colors to the piece of hardware that makes this decision; all of the pixels on the screen immediately change to the new colors when you use the COLOR statement.

When text is displayed in graphics mode—which happens whenever you have changed to graphics mode and then use a PRINT statement—the letters are displayed in color number 3. (Letter colors in text mode behave entirely differently and will be discussed below.)

The program in Fig. 4-2 will illustrate the colors that you can get on your screen. Statements 80, 90, and 100 draw filled boxes on the screen, one

Fig. 4-2   The COLOR Statement in Graphics Mode

```
10      ’ --- VARIOUS POSSIBLE COLOR COMBINATIONS
20      ’
30      ’
40      ’ --- DRAW SAMPLE PICTURE
50          SCREEN 1,0
60          CLS
70          COLOR 0,1
80          LINE (50,50)-(100,150) , 1 , BF
90          LINE (135,50)-(185,150) , 2 , BF
100         LINE (220,50)-(270,150) , 3 , BF
105         PRINT "          TEXT ON THE SCREEN"
110     ’
120         FOR DELAY = 1 TO 1500
130         NEXT DELAY
140     ’
150     ’ --- CHANGE THE BACKGROUND COLOR (COLOR 0)
160         FOR HIGH.INTENSITY = 0 TO 1
170            FOR PALETTE = 1 TO 0 STEP -1
180               FOR BACKGROUND = 8*HIGH.INTENSITY TO 7 +
                       8*HIGH.INTENSITY
190                  COLOR BACKGROUND , PALETTE
200                  FOR DELAY = 1 TO 500
210                  NEXT DELAY
220               NEXT BACKGROUND
230               FOR DELAY = 1 TO 1000
240               NEXT DELAY
250            NEXT PALETTE
260         NEXT HIGH.INTENSITY
270     ’ --- SET COLORS BACK TO BLACK AND WHITE
280         COLOR 0,1
290     ’
300         END
```

each with colors number 1, 2, and 3. Statement 105 prints a line of text at the top of the screen, which is printed with color number 3. Since statement 70 previously set the background color to the color with index 0 and the palette to 1, the three boxes initially appear in the three colors from palette 1 (cyan, magenta, and white), and the rest of the screen is the color with index 0 (black). The text at the top of the screen appears white, color number 3 on the chosen palette.

The nested FOR-NEXT loops from statement 160 to statement 260 display each of the possible color combinations one at a time. The COLOR statement at statement 190 changes the colors on the screen, and the delay loop in statements 200 and 210 distracts the computer long enough for you to get a look at the new colors. The order in which this program displays the various color combinations is:

Palette 1—Background color 0
Palette 1—Background color 1
Palette 1—Background color 2
Palette 1—Background color 3
. . .
. . .
Palette 1—Background color 7
Palette 0—Background color 0
Palette 0—Background color 1
Palette 0—Background color 2
Palette 0—Background color 3
. . .
. . .
Palette 0—Background color 7
Palette 1—Background color 8
. . .
. . .
Palette 1—Background color 15
Palette 0—Background color 8
. . .
. . .
Palette 0—Background color 15

Just before the program changes from one palette to another, there is a slightly longer than normal delay.

As your computer executes this program, note three things. First, whenever the background color is the same as one of the palette colors, one of the boxes disappears. Second, when the background colors are running from 8 to 15, the foreground colors all come from the high-intensity side of the chart. (This, incidentally, is not mentioned in the IBM manual.) Third, note that the text is always color number 3.

If you give a number greater than 15 as the index for the background color, the computer will divide your number by 16 and use the remainder as the index for the background color. If you give a palette number that is neither 0 nor 1, the computer will pick palette 0 if your number is even and palette 1 if your number is odd. If either of your numbers is larger than 255, you will get an error message.

Until you give a COLOR statement in graphics mode, black will be the background color, and the foreground colors will be selected from palette 1.

You can use COLOR as a command if you wish.

CHANGING THE COLOR OF TEXT IN GRAPHICS MODE

As mentioned, text appears in color number 3 in graphics mode. You can change this if you wish with one of these statements:

```
35 DEF SEG: POKE &H4E , 1
35 DEF SEG: POKE &H4E , 2
35 DEF SEG: POKE &H4E , 3
```

These statements change the color of *subsequently entered* text to 1, 2, or 3, respectively. *Warning:* Type these statements very carefully. If you mistype one of them and subsequently let the computer execute it, you can cause your computer to crash, after which the computer may not talk to you until you restart it by turning it off and back on again or by using the control-alt-del sequence outlined in the IBM manual. If this happens, the computer will erase your program from the memory. *Second warning:* You may not have your text appear in color 0, and if you put a 0 in the statement shown above, the computer will no longer pay attention to anything you type until you start it up again.

The statements above work rather differently from the COLOR statement in that they do *not* affect lettering already on the screen but only lettering printed after one of them is executed. Text on the screen, however, will still be affected by the COLOR statement. If you use the statement above that changes the color of text to color number 2, then text will be whatever color number 2 happens to be in the foreground palette of colors set with a COLOR statement.

CHANGING THE COLOR OF TEXT IN TEXT MODE

The IBM Personal Computer treats color in text mode quite differently from color in graphics mode. As in graphics mode, where pictures are drawn by changing the colors of the pixels on the screen, letters in text mode are drawn using pixels of one foreground color against a box of pixels drawn in the background color. The letter I, for example, consists of a vertical row of pixels in the foreground color surrounded by lots of other pixels colored with the background color. However, in text mode, each letter on the screen can have its own foreground and background color independent of the rest of the letters on the screen.

The foreground color selected for a letter can be any of the colors listed in Fig. 4-1. The background color can be any of the eight in the left-hand column. In text mode, the COLOR statement is used to select the foreground and background colors for *subsequently inserted* text. It can further decide whether subsequent text will be blinking and can select a color for the area of the screen around the edges outside the area used for graphics and text (the *border color*). The COLOR statement consists of the word COLOR followed by the index numbers for the background color, the foreground color, and the border color, separated by commas. For example:

    128 COLOR 1 , 2 , 3

chooses blue (color number 1) letters on a green (color number 2) background. The border area of the screen will be cyan (color number 3). This statement does not affect letters already on the screen. It affects only letters that are printed after this statement is executed.

The program in Fig. 4-3 illustrates the COLOR statement in text mode. After the COLOR statement at line 260, statement 270 prints the name of the foreground and background colors that have been chosen. As a result, the words BROWN ON WHITE, for example, are printed in brown letters on a white background. This program uses up more than one screenful, by the way, so be prepared to watch it go by when you type RUN. See Color Plate 4 for the output from this program.

When you try this program, you will note that if you specify the foreground and background color to be the same, the text that is printed will be invisible. You will not see YELLOW ON YELLOW, because the yellow letters disappear into the yellow background.

If you specify a number between 16 and 31 as the index of the foreground color, the computer subtracts 16 from that number to find the new foreground color, and any text inserted subsequently will blink. You can modify the program in Fig. 4-3 to give the numbers from 16 to 31 as indices for the

Fig. 4-3   The COLOR Statement in Text Mode

```
100    ' --- COLORING TEXT ON THE TEXT SCREEN
110    '
120    '
130        DIM HUES$(16)
140    '
150        DATA BLACK , BLUE , GREEN , CYAN , RED , MAGENTA ,
               BROWN , WHITE
160        DATA GRAY , LIGHT BLUE , LIGHT GREEN , LIGHT CYAN
170        DATA LIGHT RED , LIGHT MAGENTA , YELLOW , BRIGHT WHITE
180    '
190        SCREEN 0
200        FOR I = 0 TO 15
210            READ HUES$(I)
220        NEXT I
230    '
240        FOR BACKGROUND = 0 TO 7
250            FOR FOREGROUND = 0 TO 15
260                COLOR FOREGROUND , BACKGROUND
270                PRINT "    ";HUES$(FOREGROUND);" ON ";
                         HUES$(BACKGROUND);"    ";
280            NEXT FOREGROUND
290        NEXT BACKGROUND
300        END
```

new foreground color, which will make all the text printed by that program blink—but the experience is blinding.

If you give a number greater than 7 as the index for the background color, the computer will divide your number by 8 and use the remainder as the index for the new background color. If you choose a number greater than 31 as the index for the foreground color, the computer will divide your number by 32, use the remainder as the foreground color, and blink the lettering if the remainder is 16 or greater. If either color you give is greater than 255, you will get an error message.

Until you give a COLOR statement or command in text mode, you will get white (color number 7) letters on black (color 0) background.

The "Colorbar" Program

In Fig. 4-4 you will find a rewritten version of the IBM sample program entitled "Colorbar." Since this program displays all sixteen possible colors, it is very useful for adjusting your monitor. We will discuss the LOCATE and CHR$ features of BASIC in later sections. In the meantime, take it for granted that statements 1230, 1240, 1350, and 1360 print solid blocks of the foreground text color on the screen. The program here functions in the same

Fig. 4-4   The "Colorbar" Program

```
1000  ’ --- COLOR BAR PROGRAM TO PUT COLORED TEXT ON THE SCREEN
1001  ’
1002  ’
1160       KEY OFF
1170       SCREEN 0
1176       COLOR 0,0
1177       CLS
1200  ’
1201  ’ --- PRINT THE TOP ROW OF COLORS
1210       FOR X = 0 TO 7
1220          FOR Y=2 TO 11
1230             LOCATE Y,X*5+1
1235             COLOR X,0
1240             PRINT CHR$(219);CHR$(219);CHR$(219);
1250          NEXT Y
1260       NEXT X
1310  ’
1320  ’ --- PRINT THE BOTTEM ROW OF COLORS
1330       FOR X = 0 TO 7
1340          FOR Y = 14 TO 22
1350             LOCATE Y,X*5+1
1355             COLOR X+8,0
1360             PRINT CHR$(219);CHR$(219);CHR$(219);
1370          NEXT Y
1380       NEXT X
2000       COLOR 15,0
```

manner as the "Colorbar" sample from IBM, except that the IBM version puts the color names under the blocks of color, and it clears the screen and quits when you press the escape key.

Adjusting Your Display

The IBM Personal Computer Color Display is relatively easy to adjust, since it has only brightness and contrast controls. The author found it easiest to adjust his by running the "Colorbar" program from IBM, then adjusting the brightness control until the color grey appeared grey, and finally adjusting the contrast control until the color brown appeared brown. If getting the brown right seemed impossible, turning down the brightness a little solved the problem.

Adjusting a television set can be trickier, because television sets usually have several color controls and some fine-tuning controls; also, the electronics connecting the computer to the television set—a Sup-R-Mod, for example—often has an adjustment on it. The author found this to be the best technique:

1. Tune the television set to a regular station and adjust the colors to look natural. The manufacturers of color television sets advise you to tune in a picture with close-ups of people and adjust them until the flesh tones look normal—that is, until the people look like people and not like fish or aliens or sunburned zombies.

2. Tune the television set to the computer (usually channel 33) and have the computer draw a picture on the screen. The "Colorbar" example that IBM provides is ideal, since it shows all sixteen colors.

3. Adjust the Sup-R-Mod or other electronic interconnection between your computer and your television set. Then adjust the fine tuning on the television set. If you still don't like the colors you get, work some more on these two adjustments but resist the temptation to adjust the color knobs on the television set. Indiscriminate fiddling at this point usually leads to worse colors rather than better.

4.2 ANIMATION—THE GET AND PUT STATEMENTS

You can "copy" the image contained in a rectangular area on the screen into an array, and later "copy" it back onto the screen somewhere else with the GET and PUT statements. The GET and PUT statements allow you to create an image at one location on the screen and then duplicate it at other places without redrawing it, and they allow you to create an illusion of motion.

To store data from a rectangular area in an array, you use the GET statement. You must include in the statement the coordinate pairs of two opposite corners of the rectangle to be stored, separated by a hyphen, a comma, and the name of the array in which the data are to be stored. For example, these statements

```
1000   DIM  PICTURE.SAV(99)
2000   GET (0,0) - (20,20) , PICTURE.SAV
```

copy the part of the screen in the rectangle whose corners are:

(0,0)   (20,0)

(0,20)   (20,20)

into the array PICTURE.SAV.

How big must the array PICTURE.SAV be? To calculate that, find the number of dots across the width of the rectangle and the number of dots of height. In this case, both are 21. Then use this formula:

(7 + INT((2 * width + 7) / 8) * height) / 4

(It's an appalling formula, we agree, but that's how it is.) In our case, the result is

(7 + INT((2 * 21 + 7) / 8) * 21) /4

which is

(7 + INT (49 / 8) * 21) / 4

(7 + 126) / 4

33

PICTURE.SAV must be dimensioned with at least 33 spaces in it. Since array spaces start numbering at 0, we can use a DIM statement with the number 32, which will get us 33 spaces, numbered 0 to 32. Statement 1000 above therefore could be changed to this:

1000 DIM PICTURE.SAV(32)

but not to this:

1000 DIM PICTURE.SAV(31)

To copy an image saved in an array with the GET statement back to the screen, you use the PUT statement, which consists of: the word PUT, the coordinate pair of the point where the upper left-hand corner of the rectangle of data is to be drawn, a comma, the name of the array in which the image is stored, a comma, and an *action*, which tells the computer how the image being copied from the array to the screen should interact with the image already on the screen. The PSET action simply erases whatever is in the rectangle and replaces it with whatever is in the array. For example, if the array PICTURE.SAV contains a green circle in a 20-by-20 black rectangle, then this statement:

1250 PUT (80,30) , PICTURE.SAV , PSET

will put a green circle on a black rectangle in the screen area shown at the top of the following page:

(80,30)   (99,30)

(80,49)   (99,49)

regardless of what was there before.

The PRESET action copies the array onto the screen but "negates" the colors of the picture stored in the array: color 0 becomes color 3 and vice versa, and color 1 becomes color 2 and vice versa.

The other actions—XOR, OR, and AND—look at the colors of the pixels already on the screen and combine them with the colors of the pixels stored in the array to produce the new picture. Figure 4-5 describes what new colors result from previous colors.

Fig. 4-5   AND, OR, and XOR in the PUT Statement

This figure shows how the AND, OR, and XOR actions in the PUT statement combine the color of a pixel already on the screen with the color of a pixel in a stored array to decide on a new color for the pixel on the screen. In all cases, it does not matter which color is in the array and which is on the screen; the resultant color is the same in either case. The PUT statement performs the specified action on a pixel-by-pixel basis. (These actions correspond to the corresponding logical operations on the bit patterns in the pixel memory. You can skip this figure if you understand this concept as a result of other computer work you have done.)

AND

If either the pixel on the screen or the pixel in the array is the background color (color 0), then the resulting pixel on the screen will be the background color. If one of the pixels is color number 3, the resulting pixel will have the color of the other pixel. If both colors are the same, the resulting pixel will be the same also. If one of the pixels is color 1 and the other is color 2, the result will be the background color.

OR

If either the pixel on the screen or the pixel in the array is color 3, the resulting pixel on the screen will also be color 3. If one of the pixels is the background color (color 0), the resulting pixel will have the color of the other pixel. If both colors are the same, the resulting pixel will be the same also. If one of the pixels is color 1 and the other is color 2, the result will be color 3.

continued on p. 88

continued from p. 87

XOR

A table is the easiest way to describe this action:

One input color:	0	1	2	3
Other input color:				
0	0	1	2	3
1	1	0	3	2
2	2	3	0	1
3	3	2	1	0

Find the resulting colors by reading across and down in the table.

The program shown in Fig. 4-6 negates whatever image is on the screen when the program starts by storing rectangular areas of the screen one at a time and then drawing them back at the same location on the screen with the PRESET option. To try out this program, you must put some picture on the screen before you load and run it.

The program shown in Fig. 4-7 first draws a checkerboard on the screen. Then it picks up random rectangles from the checkerboard and moves them to other random locations.

Fig. 4-6 Negating the Screen

This program negates the screen using the PRESET action in the PUT statement.

```
1000 ' --- PROGRAM TO NEGATE THE SCREEN
1010 '
1020 '
1030       DIM ARRAY (300)
1040 '
1050       FOR X = 0 TO 280 STEP 40
1060           FOR Y = 0 TO 180 STEP 20
1070               GET (X,Y)-(X+39,Y+19),ARRAY
1080               PUT (X,Y),ARRAY,PRESET
1090           NEXT Y
1100       NEXT X
1110 '
1120       END
```

Fig. 4-7   Moving Random Rectangles

This program draws a checkerboard on the screen. Then it picks up random areas on the screen and moves them elsewhere.

```
1000 ' --- PROGRAM TO DRAW CHECKERBOARD AND MOVE IT ABOUT
1010 '
1020       DEFINT A-Z
1030       DIM BLOCK(5000)
1040 '
1050       LET HUE = 2
1060       CLS
1070 '
1080 ' --- DRAW THE CHECKERBOARD
1090       FOR X = 0 TO 250 STEP 50
1100          FOR Y = 0 TO 160 STEP 40
1110             LINE (X,Y) - (X+49,Y+39) , HUE , BF
1120             LET HUE = 3 - HUE
1130          NEXT Y
1140       NEXT X
1150 '
1160 '
1170 '
1180       FOR I = 1 TO 25
1190          LOW.X = INT(300*RND)
1200          LOW.Y = INT(180*RND)
1210          X.SIZE = 20 + INT(80*RND)
1220          Y.SIZE = 20 + INT(60*RND)
1230          HI.X = LOW.X + X.SIZE
1240          HI.Y = LOW.Y + Y.SIZE
1250          IF  HI.X > 319  THEN  LET HI.X = 319 :
                     X.SIZE = HI.X - LOW.X
1260          IF  HI.Y > 199  THEN  LET HI.Y = 199 :
                     Y.SIZE = HI.Y - LOW.Y
1270 '
1280          GET (LOW.X,LOW.Y)-(HI.X,HI.Y),BLOCK
1290 '
1300 ' ---   PUT BLOCK IN NEW LOCATION
1310          NEW.X = INT(320*RND)
1320          NEW.Y = INT(200*RND)
1330          IF  NEW.X + X.SIZE > 319  THEN
                     LET NEW.X = 319 - X.SIZE
1340          IF  NEW.Y + Y.SIZE > 199  THEN
                     LET NEW.Y = 199 - Y.SIZE
1350          PUT (NEW.X,NEW.Y),BLOCK,PSET
1360          FOR DELAY = 1 TO 300
1370          NEXT DELAY
1380       NEXT I
1390       END
```

Creating Motion

The PUT statement with the XOR action can be used to move an object around the screen. If the PUT statement with the XOR action is executed twice at the same location on the screen, then the first PUT statement draws the image of the array on the screen (with some interaction with what was previously on the screen), and the second PUT statement erases it and restores the original image on the screen. You can therefore create an illusion of motion by PUTting an array on the screen with the XOR option at one location, then PUTting it at the same location a second time to erase the image, then PUTting it at a slightly different location, and so on.

In Fig. 4-8 you will find the IBM sample program entitled "Ball." There are only three differences between the program presented here and the one on the DOS diskette: (1) the DOS diskette program runs forever until you press the escape key, whereas this one quits after the ball bounces five times back and forth across the screen; (2) this program puts up no title screen; and (3) this program makes no sounds.

The program shown in Fig. 4-8 draws a ball at statements 1080 and 1090 by drawing a circle and then filling it. Statement 1100 stores a rectangle containing the ball in the array BALL. Statements 1110 to 1133 draw a background on the screen in which the bouncing ball will move. The program works by drawing the ball at one location, erasing it, and then drawing it at an adjacent location. Therefore, it is necessary to calculate coordinates for the various locations. The x coordinates of these locations run from 0 to 280 in increments of 4. The y coordinates are calculated and stored in the array HEIGHT in statements 1140 through 1160 with a formula we shall not discuss. (The formula is wrong, incidentally, in that it does not represent the true motion of a bouncing ball, but the result looks good.)

The loop from statement 1200 to statement 1340 bounces the ball back and forth across the screen five times. The variable TIMES counts the number of times it has crossed the screen. The loop from statement 1210 to 1330 bounces the ball back and forth once. When DIRECTION equals 0, the ball bounces from left to right, and when DIRECTION equals 1, the ball bounces back from right to left. The calculations in statements 1220, 1225, and 1230 cause the FOR statement at 1230 to be one of these two statements:

```
FOR X = 4 TO 280 STEP 4
FOR X = 280 TO 4 STEP −4
```

The statement you get depends on whether DIRECTION is 0 or 1. The FOR-NEXT loop starting at 1230 bounces the ball once across the screen.

Fig. 4-8   The IBM Sample Program "Ball"

```
1000 ' --- IBM 'BALL' EXAMPLE, REWRITTEN
1001 '
1002 '
1003 '
1010       DIM HEIGHT(280)
1020       DIM BALL(150)
1030       CLS
1040       SCREEN 1,0
1050       COLOR 8,0
1060       KEY OFF
1065       LET NOT.FIRST.TIME = 0
1070 '
1071 ' --- GET THE IMAGE OF THE BOUNCING BALL IN ARRAY 'BALL'
1080       CIRCLE (160,100),10,2
1090       PAINT (160,100),2,2
1100       GET (150,90)-(170,110),BALL
1101 '
1102 '
1103 ' --- PUT THE BOUNDARY AND THE COLOR BARS ON THE SCREEN
1110       CLS
1120       LINE (19,0)-(299,177),,B
1130       LINE (20,1)-(300,178),,B
1131       LINE (223,3)-(253,175),3,BF
1132       LINE (191,3)-(222,175),2,BF
1133       LINE (160,3)-(190,175),1,BF
1136 '
1137 '
1139 ' --- CALCULATE HEIGHT TO WHICH BALL BOUNCES AT EACH X-VALUE
1140       FOR X=20 TO 280 STEP 4
1150          LET HEIGHT(X) = 159 -CINT(ABS(SIN(X*.0785398)*X)\2)
1160       NEXT X
1170 '
1180 '
1190 ' --- MAKE BALL BOUNCE BACK AND FORTH FIVE TIMES
1200       FOR TIMES = 1 TO 5
1210          FOR DIRECTION = 0 TO 1
1220             LET START = 20 + DIRECTION*260
1225             LET BOUNCE.END = 280 - DIRECTION*260
1230             FOR X = START TO BOUNCE.END STEP 4 - 8*DIRECTION
1240                LET Y = HEIGHT(X)
1260                IF  NOT.FIRST.TIME  THEN PUT(OLDX,OLDY),BALL
1270                PUT (X,Y),BALL
1280                LET OLDX = X
1290                LET OLDY = Y
1300                LET NOT.FIRST.TIME = -1
1310             NEXT X
1330          NEXT DIRECTION
1340       NEXT TIMES
1350       END
```

Screen Display During "Ball"

At each x coordinate in the loop from 1230 to 1310, a y coordinate is found from the array HEIGHT. The very first time through this loop, no previous image of the ball is on the screen (the one that used to GET the array BALL was erased when the CLS statement was executed at statement 1110), and NOT.FIRST.TIME is 0, so statement 1260, whose purpose is to erase a previous image, is skipped. Statement 1270 draws a ball at the location given by the x and y coordinates just found. Since XOR is the default action with the PUT statement, the ball is put on the screen with the XOR action. The x and y coordinates where the ball was just drawn are saved in OLD.X and OLD.Y.

On the second and subsequent times through the loop, variables X and Y are set to values slightly different from the previous time through the loop. Statement 1260 erases the image of the ball put on the screen the previous time through the loop using the values of OLD.X and OLD.Y. Statement 1270 draws a new ball on the screen a little distance away.

4.3 READING BACK WHAT IS ON THE SCREEN—THE POINT FUNCTION

To find the color of a pixel on the screen, you can use the POINT function. To use it, pass it the coordinates of a pixel, and it will return one of the numbers 0, 1, 2, or 3, indicating the color of that pixel. For example,

10 LET X = POINT(33,49)

sets the value of the variable X to be the color of the pixel whose coordinates are (33,49).

If you send the POINT function a pair of coordinates not on the screen, it returns the value −1.

The program in Fig. 4-9 negates the image on the screen by examining each pixel with the POINT function and then changing its color with the PSET statement. Pixels with color 3 are changed to color 0 and vice versa; pixels with color 1 are changed to color 2 and vice versa. This program, incidentally, runs much more slowly than the one in Section 4.2, because the POINT function and the PSET statement are not as fast as the GET and PUT statements.

The program in Fig. 4-10 finds the number of pixels of each color in the upper half of the screen. To try this program, first run another program to draw a picture on the screen; then load this program and run it. This program erases the lower half of the screen and then examines each point in the upper half to count the number of pixels of each color. It prints its results periodically near the bottom of the screen. This program is also not very fast.

Fig. 4-9   Program to Negate the Screen (Slowly)

```
10      ' --- PROGRAM TO NEGATE THE SCREEN
20      ' _
30      '
40          FOR X = 0 TO 319
50            FOR Y = 0 TO 199
60              HUE = POINT(X,Y)
70              LET NEWHUE = 3 - HUE
80              PSET (X,Y),NEWHUE
90            NEXT Y
100         NEXT X
110     '
120     '
130         END
```

Fig. 4-10   Counting the Number of Pixels of Each Color

```
10     ' --- PROGRAM TO FIND OUT HOW MANY PIXELS OF EACH COLOR
            ARE ON THE SCREEN
20     '
30     '
40     '
50         LINE (0,0)-(319,100),,B
60         LINE (0,101)-(319,199),0,BF
70         LOCATE 22,1 : PRINT "   0       1       2       3   "
80     '
90         FORMAT$ = "###### ###### ###### ######"
100        COUNT(1) = 0
110        COUNT(2) = 0
120        COUNT(3) = 0
130        COUNT(4) = 0
140    '
150        FOR X = 1 TO 318
160           FOR Y = 1 TO 99
170              HUE = POINT(X,Y) + 1
180              COUNT(HUE) = COUNT(HUE) + 1
190           NEXT Y
200           LOCATE 23,1
210           PRINT USING FORMAT$ ; COUNT(1),COUNT(2),
                    COUNT(3),COUNT(4)
220        NEXT X
230    '
240    '
250        END
```

4.4 TEXT AND GRAPHICS—THE LOCATE STATEMENT

The regular PRINT and PRINT USING statements print text and variable values on displays in graphics modes just as they do in text mode. The comma and semicolon in the PRINT statement and the image strings in the PRINT USING statement place information in position on the display as usual. Below, we shall discuss the LOCATE statement, a more powerful way of determining where on the display your programs print their output. We shall also discuss aligning text material with graphics on the screen, a technique made harder because the coordinates used with the LOCATE statement are different from those used for graphics.

Letters Printed in Graphics Modes

Graphics and text share one set of pixels in graphics modes. To draw letters with a PRINT statement, the computer first erases whatever graphics are in the area to make way for them. Similarly, graphics drawn on top of letters already on the screen partly or entirely erases those letters.

Whenever the PRINT statement prints a letter, it first clears an area eight pixels high and eight pixels wide by changing all of the pixels in that area to the background color; then it draws the letter inside the cleared area by setting selected pixels to color number 3. (You can change the color with which the letters are drawn to any of the three foreground colors, as described in Section 4.1, but the area around the letters is always the background color.) Any graphics image previously in the eight-by-eight area is erased.

If a letter is printed at the very upper left-hand corner of the screen, the area whose coordinates are shown here is cleared to the background color:

(0,0)   (7,0)

(0,7)   (7,7)

Most letters and symbols, with the exceptions noted below, do not use the right-most column or the bottom-most row of pixels in the eight-by-eight area. Although the entire eight-by-eight area is cleared, the letter at the upper left-hand corner of the screen will actually be drawn entirely within this seven-by-seven area:

(0,0)   (6,0)

(0,6)   (6,6)

An unused column of blank pixels is therefore left along the right-hand edge of the area, and a row of blank pixels is left at the bottom of the area. These blank pixels serve to separate one letter from its neighbors to the right and below.

The letters that use the bottom pixel in the eight-by-eight area are the lower-case letters g, j, p, and q, which have *descenders* (parts that extend below the line). The asterisk (*) and the underline (_) use the right-most pixel. (The underline is the shifted version of the hyphen key.) These letters and symbols may well bump into letters printed directly below or to the right of them: there may be no blank pixel separating the pixels that make up one of these symbols from the pixels that make up an adjacent letter. This is one of the things that make text harder to read in graphics mode than in text mode.

For narrow letters like I the eight-pixel area leaves the computer a lot of room to draw the letter. For wide letters like W the computer must squeeze to make the letter fit.

Using the LOCATE Statement

The IBM Personal Computer maintains a text *cursor,* a location on the screen at which to print text. Whenever it comes to a PRINT or PRINT USING statement, the computer prints at the cursor's location. Some BASIC programs simply print wherever on the screen the cursor happens to be when the computer gets to the PRINT statement, but with graphics on the screen it is usually important to put the text in the proper location. You must therefore know how to move the cursor to any location on the display before printing.

The screen has twenty-five *rows,* numbered 1 to 25 from top to bottom of the screen. Each row has forty character positions, or *columns,* numbered 1 to 40 from left to right. (The monochrome display has eighty columns rather than forty.) The bottom row, number 25, is taken up by the *soft key display* that appears when you start up BASIC (unless you turn that display off with a KEY OFF statement; see the IBM BASIC manual). To move the cursor to a particular location on the screen, you tell the computer to which row and column to move it with a LOCATE statement. Here is an example:

    20 LOCATE 10,14

This tells the computer to put the cursor on the screen in the tenth row (from the top) at the fourteenth column (from the left). If the next statement in the program is:

    30 PRINT "URGENT MESSAGE"

then the U of URGENT will be printed in column 14 of row 10, and the rest of the message will be to the right of that, in columns 15, 16, 17, etc.

The LOCATE statement is quite intolerant of requests to place the cursor at nonexistent locations: at rows not between 1 and 25 or columns not between 1 and 40. You can use variables as row and column numbers in the LOCATE statement, but be careful that their values are in the required ranges to avoid the "Illegal function call" error that you otherwise will get.

COORDINATING COORDINATES

With the LOCATE statement, row and column numbers determine the location of the text on the screen. Row and column numbers correspond roughly to the x and y coordinates that determine the positions of graphics entities. When you wish to align text with graphics, you face two problems: (1) the column and row numbers run from 1 to 40 and from 1 to 25, respectively, whereas x and y coordinates run from 0 to 320 and from 0 to 200, and (2) the "coordinates" in a LOCATE statement are in reverse order. *Note well: The first number in the LOCATE statement is the row number, which is the analog of the y coordinate; the second number in the LOCATE statement is the column number, the analog of the x coordinate.* This is exactly backwards from the graphics way of doing things, but you just have to deal with this perversity. Your programs must convert from the one set of coordinates to the other.

Consider this program fragment:

```
10 LOCATE 1,1
20 PRINT "A"
```

As discussed above, it draws a letter in this box:

(0,0)   (7,0)

(0,7)   (7,7)

This program fragment

```
10 LOCATE 1,2
20 PRINT "A"
```

draws a letter in this box:

(8,0)   (15,0)

(8,7)   (15,7)

Other letters positioned with the LOCATE command land in boxes whose coordinates are shown in Fig. 4-11.

Given the column and row numbers used in a LOCATE statement to place a letter on the screen, the easiest way to find the graphics coordinates of the upper left-hand corner of the letter is to subtract 1 from the column and row numbers and then multiply each result by 8. As a formula, it looks like this:

graphics x coordinate of upper left corner of letter =
    8 ∗ (column number −1)

graphics y coordinate of upper left corner of letter =
    8 ∗ (row number −1)

For example, let us find the graphics coordinates of the letter W printed by this program fragment:

```
10 LOCATE 23,11
20 PRINT "W"
```

To find the x coordinate of the upper left-hand corner of the W, subtract 1 from 11 (not from 23, remember), leaving 10, and then multiply by 8, giving 80. Similarly, to find the y coordinate, subtract 1 from 23, leaving 22, and multiply by 8, giving 176. The coordinates of the upper left-hand corner of the letter are therefore (80,176). You can find coordinates of the other corners by adding 7 appropriately. The W printed by the program fragment above is therefore printed in this area:

(80,176)   (87,176)

(80,183)   (87,183)

Fig. 4-11   Graphic Coordinates of Letters on the Screen

Each letter on the screen fits into an eight-pixel-square box, as shown below. Most letters leave the right-most and bottom-most row of pixels in the box blank, but lower-case g, j, p, and q and the asterisk and underline are exceptions.

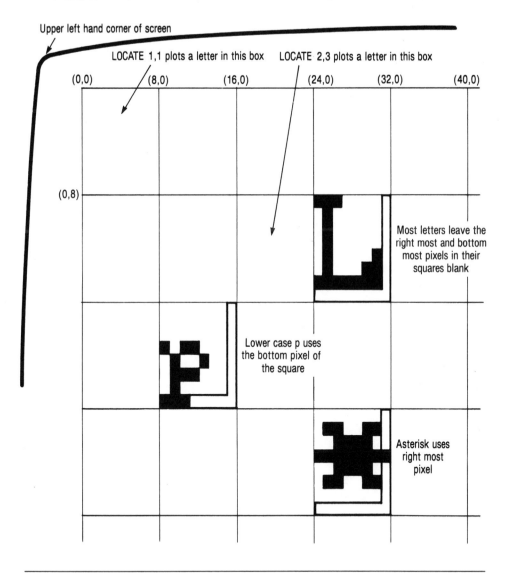

A new problem arises in translating from graphics coordinates to row and column numbers for the LOCATE statement: the LOCATE statement can print letters only at every eighth pixel in each direction on the screen, and you cannot draw letters at the pixels in between. Therefore, you must often print letters a little away from the ideal location. No exact formula can tell you how best to do this, but dividing the graphics x and y coordinates by 8, ignoring the remainder, and then adding 1 gives results that are at least close. Be prepared for text to end up one row or one column away from where you want it and to have to adjust your program accordingly.

EXAMPLES

The program in Fig. 4-12 draws four boxes, one each of the colors 0, 1, 2, and 3, and labels them according to what color they are filled with. The output from that program and some corresponding coordinates are shown in Fig. 4-13.

Fig. 4-12   Program to Draw Four Colored Boxes and Label Them

```
100    ' --- THIS PROGRAM DRAWS FOUR BOXES AND LABELS
110    ' --- THEIR COLORS
120    '
130         SCREEN 1,0
140    '
150    ' --- DRAW THE BOXES
160         LINE (80,64) - (87,71) , 3 , BF
170         LINE (80,80) - (87,87) , 2 , BF
180         LINE (80,96) - (87,103), 1 , BF
190    '
200    ' --- OUTLINE THE BOXES
210         LINE (80,80) - (87,87) , 3 , B
220         LINE (80,96) - (87,103), 3 , B
230         LINE (80,112)- (87,119), 3 , B
240    '
250    ' --- LABEL THE BOXES
260         LOCATE 9, 13 : PRINT "COLOR 3 -- WHITE"
270         LOCATE 11,13 : PRINT "COLOR 2 -- MAGENTA"
280         LOCATE 13,13 : PRINT "COLOR 1 -- CYAN"
290         LOCATE 15,13 : PRINT "COLOR 0 -- BLACK"
300    '
310         LOCATE 20,1
320    '
330         END
```

Screen Display from Program

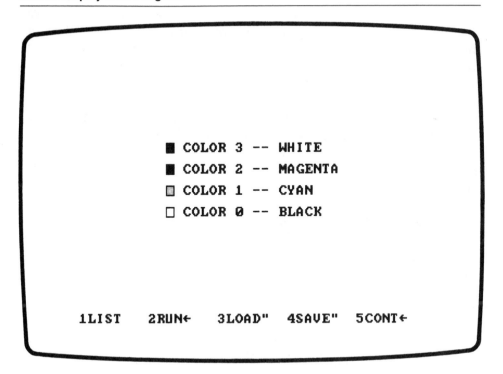

Fig. 4-13   Coordinates Used by Box Labeling Program

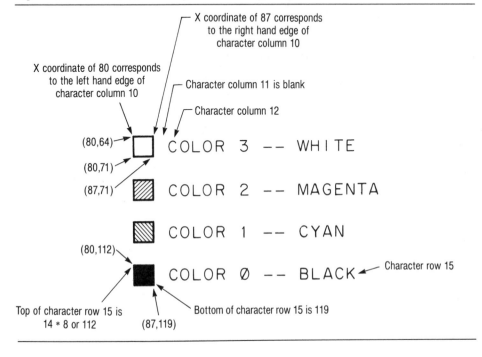

The program in Fig. 4-14 inputs a word and row and column numbers; then it prints the given word at the given location and draws a rectangle around it. To draw the rectangle, the program must use the LINE statement, and to use the LINE statement, the program must find graphics x and y coordinates of the corners of the rectangle. To find these coordinates from the input row and column numbers, the program uses the formulas discussed above. The system finds y coordinates of the top-most and bottom-most pixels used in the letters at statements 210 and 220. At statement 240, the LEN function returns the number of letters in WORD$, which the program uses to find the column number of the last letter of the word. Statement 250 finds the left-hand edge of that letter, and statement 260 finds the right-hand edge of that letter.

Fig. 4-14 Drawing a Box around a Word

This program prints a word input by the user at a location input by the user and then draws the smallest possible rectangle around it.

```
100     ' --- PROGRAM TO ALIGN A RECTANGLE WITH TEXT
110     '
120     '
130         PRINT "INPUT COLUMN AND ROW FOR LOCATE STATEMENT
                PLUS A WORD TO PRINT"
140         INPUT COLUMN , ROW , WORD$
150         CLS
160         SCREEN 1,0
170         LOCATE ROW,COLUMN
180         PRINT WORD$
190     '
200     ' --- FIND RELEVANT COORDINATES OF BOX
210         LET Y.OF.TOP.OF.LETTERS = 8 * (ROW - 1)
220         LET Y.OF.BOTTOM.OF.LETTERS = Y.OF.TOP.OF.LETTERS + 7
230         LET X.OF.LEFT.OF.FIRST.LETTER = 8 * (COLUMN - 1)
240         LET COLUMN.OF.LAST.LETTER =
                COLUMN + LEN(WORD$) - 1
250         LET X.OF.LEFT.OF.LAST.LETTER =
                8 * (COLUMN.OF.LAST.LETTER - 1)
260         LET X.OF.RIGHT.OF.LAST.LETTER =
                X.OF.LEFT.OF.LAST.LETTER + 7
270         LET LEFT.OF.BOX = X.OF.LEFT.OF.FIRST.LETTER - 2
280         LET RIGHT.OF.BOX = X.OF.RIGHT.OF.LAST.LETTER + 1
290         LET TOP.OF.BOX = Y.OF.TOP.OF.LETTERS - 2
300         LET BOTTEM.OF.BOX = Y.OF.BOTTOM.OF.LETTERS + 1
310     '
320         LINE (LEFT.OF.BOX,TOP.OF.BOX) -
                (RIGHT.OF.BOX,BOTTEM.OF.BOX) ,, B
330         END
```

Statements 270 to 300 find the coordinates of the corners of the rectangle. Because the rectangle must not use the top-most pixel of the letters (that would obliterate the tops of the letters), and because it is desirable for readability to leave a blank pixel between the top of the letter and the rectangle, statement 270 subtracts 2 from the y coordinate of the top pixel used by the letters to find the y coordinate of the top of the rectangle. Similarly, statement 290 subtracts 2 from the x coordinate of the word's left-most pixel to find the left-hand edge of the rectangle. Statements 280 and 300 add only one to their respective coordinates, since the bottom-most and right-most pixels of most letters are already blank. Obviously, if the input word contains one of the characters that uses the right-most or bottom-most pixel of the letter square, then the rectangle will bump into those letters.

Note that this program fails if ROW or COLUMN is 1 because one edge of the rectangle will be off the screen.

When you use text and graphics in the same program, you will find it helpful to make a graph-paper diagram of the intended display before you start to program. Otherwise, Murphy's Law dictates that graphics will be at one location on the display and text will be somewhere else.

4.5 SOUND AND MUSIC—THE SOUND STATEMENT

In this and the next sections, we shall discuss programming the speaker/noisemaker in the IBM Personal Computer to make sounds or "music." This section discusses the SOUND statement, which produces a single tone of any pitch and any duration. The next section discusses the PLAY statement, which interprets a string to produce a series of notes on the speaker in much the same way that the DRAW statement interprets a string to draw lines. The SOUND statement has two advantages over the PLAY statement: (1) the SOUND statement allows you to specify any pitch whereas the PLAY statement restricts you to notes found on a piano, and (2) it is easier to specify arbitrary durations for tones with the SOUND statement. The strings used by the PLAY statement, on the other hand, are more similar to regular musical notation than are the frequencies and durations required for the SOUND statement. Concepts such as sharps, flats, quarter notes, legato, and so on can be represented in those strings. Furthermore, one PLAY statement can play as complex a tune as one string can store.

The SOUND statement needs two parameters: the frequency (or pitch) of the tone and the length of time that the tone is to last. Here is one possible SOUND statement:

10 SOUND 440 , 5

This statement plays a tone whose frequency is 440 and whose duration is 5.

Frequency is measured in *hertz* or *cycles per second,* the number of times per second that the speaker must vibrate to produce the given tone. The IBM Personal Computer SOUND statement plays frequencies from 37 hertz to 32,767 hertz; your ear hears frequencies from somewhat lower than 37 to somewhere between 7,000 and 15,000, depending on how good your hearing is. More traditional musical instruments play notes with frequencies from about 40 hertz to about 2,000 hertz. The A to which orchestras tune is 440 cyles per second. Middle C on the piano is the C below that, which vibrates at 294 cycles per second (contrary to what it says in the IBM manual). All musical instruments, including the speaker in the IBM Personal Computer, also produce *overtones,* notes at much higher frequencies. Your ear distinguishes different musical instruments by recognizing the patterns of these overtones.

Duration is measured in units 0.0549 seconds long. (The IBM manual defines the unit of duration as 1.0 divided by 18.2, which is 0.0549.) The SOUND statement above, for example, produces a tone five times as long as 0.0549 seconds, or 0.2747 seconds. This peculiar unit of duration, found only in the SOUND statement, stems from the speed of certain internal signals in the Personal Computer, which are beyond the scope of this book. Duration must be a number between 0 and 65,535. A tone with duration of 0, however, can't be heard because it doesn't last for any time. A tone with duration 65,535 lasts the better part of an hour.

Fig. 4-15   Playing Random "Music" with the SOUND Statement

```
100    ' --- THIS PROGRAM PUTS 'RANDOM SOUNDS' ON THE SPEAKER
110    '
120           CLS
130           LOCATE 7,20 :
                   PRINT "THE SOUND STATEMENT"
140           LOCATE 9,10 :
                   PRINT "FREQUENCY   (HERTZ)     DURATION (SECONDS)"
150           LET FORMAT$ =        "     ####.#              #.###"
160    '      ---
170             LET FREQ = RND(1) * 2000 + 37
180             LET DURATION = 5 * RND(1)
190             SOUND FREQ , DURATION
200             LET DURATION = DURATION / 18.2
210             LOCATE 10,10 : PRINT USING FORMAT$ ; FREQ,DURATION
220           GOTO 160
230           END
```

The program fragment in Fig. 4-15 produces "music" by playing tones with random frequencies and durations. Statement 170 picks a random frequency between 37 and 2,037, a frequency in the range of regular musical instruments, and statement 180 picks a random duration between 0 and 5, which translates into a tone that lasts for between 0 and 0.2747 seconds. Statement 190 plays the tone. Statement 200 divides the number chosen for the duration by 18.2, which converts it into seconds, and statement 210 prints the frequency (in hertz) and the duration (in seconds). Note that a tone with duration of 0 will be over before its frequency and duration have been printed on the screen and the random frequency and duration for the next tone have been calculated. In this case, there will be a very short pause between tones while the computer works.

The "music" from the program fragment in Fig. 4-15 can be modified by changing the constants in statements 170 and 180. Increasing or decreasing the 2,000 increases or decreases the range of pitches played. Increasing the 37 raises the pitches of all the tones. The "music" can be speeded up or slowed down by decreasing or increasing the 5 in statement 180. If you change these parameters, be sure that the frequencies and durations that the program will use in the SOUND statement will fall within the legal ranges.

The program in Fig. 4-16 plays a series of tones starting with low frequencies and continuing to high. Statement 170 increases the frequency of the tone to be played by multiplying the old frequency by 1.01. After the

Fig. 4-16   Program to Play an Ascending Musical "Scale"

```
100    ' --- THIS PROGRAM PUTS SOUNDS OF INCREASING PITCH
110    '
120          CLS
125          LET FREQ = 200
130          LOCATE 7,20 : PRINT "THE SOUND STATEMENT"
140          LOCATE 9,10 :
                  PRINT "FREQUENCY   (HERTZ)      DURATION (SECONDS)"
150          LET FORMAT$ =        "      #####.#              #.###"
160    '     ---
170             FREQ = FREQ * 1.01
180             DURATION = .01
190             SOUND FREQ , DURATION
200             LET DURATION = DURATION / 18.2
210             LOCATE 10,10 : PRINT USING FORMAT$ ; FREQ,DURATION
220          GOTO 160
230          END
```

tone with frequency 200 hertz is played, the next tone played will have frequency 202, an increase of 2 hertz; after a tone with frequency 5,000 hertz is played, the next tone will have frequency 5,050, an increase of 50 hertz; and so on. Your ear, however, perceives this sort of frequency increase as steady. If you change statement 170 from a multiplicative operation to an additive one, perhaps to

    170 LET FREQ = FREQ + 5

your ear will perceive that the pitch increases at one speed to begin with and then slows down as the program continues.

    This program eventually crashes, because FREQ becomes larger than the legal limit of 32,767. When it does, the error message you get is

```
Overflow in statement 190
```

If you watch the display and listen to the tones while this program runs, you will get some idea of the highest pitch you can hear. As the frequency becomes higher and higher, you will eventually be unable to hear the tones.

    You can modify the program in Fig. 4-16 to play a *chromatic scale,* the scale you get by playing all of the notes on a piano, both white and black. Change statement 170 to

    170 LET FREQ = FREQ * 2 $^\wedge$ (1/12)

The frequency of each note on the piano differs from that of the adjacent notes by a factor of about 2 to the 1/12 power, which is approximately 1.0595. According to physics, each note on the piano should differ from the adjacent notes by a factor of *exactly* 2 to the 1/12 power. However, pianos are usually tuned with the notes a little farther apart than this, especially at the very ends of the keyboard, because most people think pianos sound better tuned that way. Notes played by orchestral instruments have no such neat relationship to one another.

    Figure 4-17 is a modification of the IBM sample program "Music." It differs from the original IBM program in the usual ways: it has no title screen, for example. Furthermore, the program here does not produce the elaborate display that the original IBM program does. (We will revisit this program in Section 4.8 to discuss how the display is done.) An error in IBM's version of Mozart's Symphony No. 40 has been corrected in this version in statements 3780, 3790, and 3800.

Statements 1030 to 1300 print the music choices on the screen as does the original program. At statements 1364 to 1371, the program inserts values in the array FREQ to correspond to all but the bottom-most 6 of the 88 keys on a piano keyboard. It does this by using 36.8 hertz as the frequency for the seventh key on the keyboard and then multiplying this number by 2 to the 1/12 to find the frequency for the eighth key, and again to find the frequency for the ninth key, and so on. Music is stored in DATA statements in the program according to which of the 88 piano keys should be played and in what order. The FREQ array allows the program to translate quickly from the number of a key found in a DATA statement to the corresponding frequency for the SOUND statement. To play key 48, the program looks up the frequency in FREQ(48).

The loop from statement 1630 to statement 1830 interprets the user's input. If you press the escape key, the program goes to statement 1850 and ends. If you press a key that does not represent one of the musical selections, the program just waits for you to press another key. When you press a key that represents one of the musical selections, the program executes a RESTORE statement to the DATA statement containing the notes for the tune you have requested; then it calls the subroutine at statement 1490.

The subroutine at statement 1490 plays the tune. The loop from 1490 to 1620 first reads J and K from whichever of the DATA statements was RESTORED to before the subroutine was called. If J is −1, the subroutine has reached the end of the tune, so it returns. If J is not −1, then J is the note number to be played, and K is the duration of that note. The frequency for the note is found in FREQ(J). After the SOUND statement plays this one note, statement 1595 plays a tone of frequency 32,767. Since no one can hear a tone of such a high frequency, the result is a silence that lasts for 0.0549 seconds. The subroutine then goes back to statement 1490 to repeat the loop.

The mass of DATA statements at the bottom of the program contains the names of the musical selections (so that they can be printed on the screen by statement 1805) and then the note numbers and durations for the tones that make up the selections. Here are the first two DATA statements for the Dvořák *Humoresque:*

```
3500   DATA −2, "Humoresque by Dvorak"
3510   DATA 47,3,0,2,49,1,47,3,0,2,49,1,51,3,0,2,54,1,56,
       3,0,2,54,1
```

The first statement tells the system that the name of this piece is *Humoresque* by Dvořák. The second DATA statement tells the system to play note number 47 for duration 3, then to play note 0 (silence) for duration 2, then to play note 49 for duration 1, and so on.

One problem this program shares with other music-playing programs is that even though the durations in the DATA statements are correct, the rhythm of the music is not perfect because of the delay caused by computing time.

Fig. 4-17   IBM Sample Program "Music"

The program shown here is an abridged version of the IBM sample program entitled "Music." It does not produce the elaborate screen display that the IBM version provides. See Section 4.8 for a discussion of the display created by "Music."

```
1000 ' --- IBM 'MUSIC' PROGRAM WITHOUT A DISPLAY
1010 '
1020 '
1030 ' --- PRINT THE MENU OF MUSIC THAT CAN BE PLAYED
1150      SCREEN 0,1:WIDTH 40:COLOR 15,1,1:CLS:DEFINT A-Z
1160      LOCATE 15,7,0:PRINT " ------- selections -------"
1170      LOCATE 16,7:PRINT " A-MARCH   E-HUMOR   I-SAKURA"
1180      LOCATE 17,7:PRINT " B-STARS   F-BUG     J-BLUE   "
1190      LOCATE 18,7:PRINT " C-FORTY   G-POP     K-SCALES"
1191      LOCATE 19,7:PRINT " D-HAT     H-DANDY   ESC KEY-EXIT"
1200      COLOR 15,0
1363 '
1364 ' --- SET UP THE FREQUENCIES FOR THE SOUND STATEMENT
1365      DIM FREQ(88)
1366      FOR I = 0 TO 6
1367         FREQ(I) = 32767
1368      NEXT I
1369      FOR I = 7 TO 88
1370         FREQ(I) =  36.8*(2^(1/12))^(I-6)
1371      NEXT I
1480      GOTO 1630
1488 '
1489 ' --- SUBROUTINE TO PLAY ONE TUNE
1490         READ J,K
1539 '
1540         IF J = -1  THEN RETURN
1541 '
1590         SOUND FREQ(J),K
1595         IF  J <> 0 OR K <> 1  THEN SOUND 32767,1
1626      GOTO 1490
1627 '
```

continued on p. 109

continued from p. 108

```
1628  ' --- LOOP TO GET A SELECTION OF A TUNE AND PLAY IT
1630          LOCATE 21,5 :
                     PRINT "                                    ";
1640          LOCATE 21,5 : PRINT "ENTER SELECTION ==>";
1650  '       --- LOOP TO GET VALID SELECTION
1660           SL$=INKEY$
1670           IF SL$ = CHR$(27)   THEN 1850
1680           IF SL$="A" OR SL$="a" THEN S$="MARCH ":
                     RESTORE 4000:GOTO 1770
1690             IF SL$="B" OR SL$="b" THEN S$="STARS ":
                     RESTORE 4100:GOTO 1770
1700             IF SL$="C" OR SL$="c" THEN S$="FORTY ":
                     RESTORE 3700:GOTO 1770
1710             IF SL$="D" OR SL$="d" THEN S$="HAT   ":
                     RESTORE 4300:GOTO 1770
1720             IF SL$="E" OR SL$="e" THEN S$="HUMOR ":
                     RESTORE 3500:GOTO 1770
1730             IF SL$="F" OR SL$="f" THEN S$="BUG   ":
                     RESTORE 3200:GOTO 1770
1740             IF SL$="G" OR SL$="g" THEN S$="POP   ":
                     RESTORE 3600:GOTO 1770
1750             IF SL$="H" OR SL$="h" THEN S$="DANDY ":
                     RESTORE 3900:GOTO 1770
1755             IF SL$="I" OR SL$="i" THEN S$="SAKURA":
                     RESTORE 4500:GOTO 1770
1757             IF SL$="J" OR SL$="j" THEN S$="BLUE  ":
                     RESTORE 3300:GOTO 1770
1761             IF SL$="K" OR SL$="k" THEN S$="SCALES":
                     RESTORE 4400:GOTO 1770
1769           GOTO 1650
1770           PRINT " ";SL$;"-";S$
1780           READ D
1800           READ S$ : LOCATE 23,1+(40.5-LEN(S$))/2
1805           COLOR 15,4 : PRINT S$; : COLOR 0,7
1810           GOSUB 1490
1820           S$=STRING$(39," ") : LOCATE 23,1 :
                     COLOR 4,1 : PRINT S$ : COLOR 0,7
1830          GOTO 1630
1840          END
1845  '
1850  ' --- EXIT FROM PROGRAM
1860         SCREEN 0,1 : COLOR 7,0,0 : CLS : WIDTH 80 : END
2998  '
2999  '
3000  ' --- The IBM Personal Computer Music Scroll
3010  ' --- Version 1.00 (C)Copyright IBM Corp 1981
3020  ' --- Licensed Material - Program Property of IBM
3200          DATA -2,"La Cucaracha - Mexican Folk Song"
3210          DATA 42,1,0,1,42,1,0,1,42,1,0,1,47,1,0,5,51,1,0,3,
                     42,1,0,1,42,1,0,1
3220          DATA 42,1,0,1,47,1,0,5,51,1,0,5,30,1,0,1,30,1,0,1,
                     35,1,0,3,47,1,0,1
3230          DATA 47,1,0,1,46,1,0,1,46,1,0,1,44,1,0,1,44,1,0,1,
                     42,8,0,2,42,1,0,1
```

continued on p. 110

continued from p. 109

```
3240      DATA 42,1,0,1,42,1,0,1,46,1,0,5,49,1,0,3,42,1,0,1,
               42,1,0,1,42,1,0,1
3250      DATA 46,1,0,5,49,1,0,5,37,1,0,1,37,1,0,1,30,1,0,3,
               54,2,56,2,54,2,52,2
3260      DATA 51,2,49,2,47,8
3270      DATA -1,-1
3300      DATA -2,"Blue Danube Waltz by J.S.Strauss"
3310      DATA 42,4,46,4,49,4,49,4,0,4,61,2,0,2,61,2,0,6,58,2,
               0,2,58,2,0,6,42,4,42,4
3320      DATA 46,4,49,4
3330      DATA 49,4,0,4,61,2,0,2,61,2,0,6,59,2,0,2,59,2,0,6,
               41,4,41,4,44,4,51,4,51,4
3340      DATA 0,4,63,2,0,2,63,2,0,6,59,2,0,2
3350      DATA 59,2,0,6,41,4,41,4,44,4,51,4,51,4,0,4,63,2,0,2,
               63,2,0,6,58,2,0,2,58,2
3360      DATA 0,6,42,4
3370      DATA 42,4,46,4,49,4,54,4,0,4,66,2,0,2,66,2,0,6,61,2,
               0,2,61,2,0,6,42,4
3380      DATA 42,4,46,4,49,4,54,4,0,4,66,2,0,2
3390      DATA 66,2,0,6,63,2,0,2,63,2,0,6,44,4,44,4,47,4,51,2,
               0,2,51,14,0,2,48,4
3400      DATA 49,4,58,16
3410      DATA 54,4,46,4,46,8,44,4,51,8,49,4,42,4,0,2,42,2,
               42,4,0,8,49,2,0,2,47,2
3420      DATA 0,6,49,2,0,2
3430      DATA 47,2,0,6,49,4,58,16,56,4,49,2,0,2,46,2,0,6,49,2,
               0,2,46,2,0,6,49,4
3440      DATA 56,16,54,4,49,2,0,2,47,2,0,6,49,2,0,2,47,2,0,6,
               49,4,58,16
3450      DATA 56,4,49,4,54,4,56,4,58,4,61,8,59,4,58,2,58,2,
               58,4,56,2,0,2,54,4,0,8
3460      DATA -1,-1
3500      DATA -2,"Humoresque by Dvorak"
3510      DATA 47,3,0,2,49,1,47,3,0,2,49,1,51,3,0,2,54,1,56,3,
               0,2,54,1
3520      DATA 59,3,0,2,58,1,61,3,0,2,59,1,58,3,0,2,61,1,59,3,
               0,2,56,1
3530      DATA 54,3,0,2,54,1,56,3,0,2,54,1,59,3,0,2,56,1,54,3,
               0,2,51,1
3540      DATA 49,24,47,3,0,2,49,1,47,3,0,2,49,1,51,3,0,2,54,1,
               56,3,0,2,54,1
3550      DATA 56,3,0,2,58,1,61,3,0,2,59,1,58,3,0,2,61,1,59,3,
               0,2,56,1
3560      DATA 54,3,0,2,54,1,59,3,0,2,47,1,49,6,54,6,47,18
3570      DATA -1,-1
3600      DATA -2,"Pop! Goes the Weasel - Anonymous"
3610      DATA 47,2,0,2,47,2,49,2,0,2,49,2,51,2,54,2,51,2,
               47,2,0,2,42,2
3620      DATA 47,2,0,2,47,2,49,2,0,2,49,2,51,6,47,2,0,2,42,2,
               47,2,0,2,47,2,49,2
3630      DATA 0,2,49,2,51,2,54,2,51,2,47,2,0,4,56,2,0,4,49,2,
               0,2,52,2,51,6,47,2
3640      DATA 0,4,59,2,0,2,59,2,56,2,0,2,59,2,58,2,61,2,58,2,
               54,2,0,4,59,2,0,2
```

continued on p. 111

continued from p. 110

```
3650      DATA 59,2,56,2,0,2,59,2,58,6,54,2,0,2,51,2,52,2,0,2,
          51,2,52,2,0,2,54,2
3660      DATA 56,2,0,2,58,2,59,2,0,4,56,2,0,4,49,2,0,2,52,2,
          51,6,47,2
3670      DATA -1,-1
3700      DATA -2,"Symphony #40 by Mozart"
3710      DATA 55,2,54,2,54,4,55,2,54,2,54,4,55,2,54,2,54,4,
          62,4,0,4
3720      DATA 62,2,61,2,59,4,59,2,57,2,55,4,55,2,54,2
3730      DATA 52,4,52,4,0,4,54,2,52,2,52,4,54,2,52,2,52,4,
          54,2,52,2
3740      DATA 52,4,61,4,0,4,61,2,59,2,58,4,58,2,55,2,54,4,
          54,2,52,2
3750      DATA 50,4,50,4,0,4,62,2,61,2,61,4,64,4,58,4,61,4
3760      DATA 59,4,54,4,0,4,62,2,61,2,61,4,64,4,58,4,61,4
3770      DATA 59,4,62,4,61,2,59,2,57,2,55,2,54,4,46,4,47,4,49,4
3780      DATA 50,4,52,2,50,2,49,4,47,4,54,4,0,4,65,8
3790      DATA 66,2,0,6,65,8,66,2,0,6,65,8
3800      DATA 66,4,65,4,66,4,65,4,66,4
3810      DATA -1,-1
3900      DATA -2,"Yankee Doodle - Anonymous "
3910      DATA 50,3,50,3,52,3,54,3,50,3,54,3,52,3,45,3,50,3,
          50,3,52,3,54,3,50,6
3920      DATA 49,3,0,3
3930      DATA 50,3,50,3,52,3,54,3,55,3,54,3,52,3,50,3,49,3,
          45,3,47,3,49,3,50,6
3940      DATA 50,3,0,3
3950      DATA 47,5,49,1,47,3,45,3,47,3,49,3,50,3,0,3,45,5,
          47,1,45,3,43,3,42,6
3960      DATA 45,3,0,3
3970      DATA 47,5,49,1,47,3,45,3,47,3,49,3,50,3,47,3,45,3,
          50,3,49,3,52,3,50,6
3980      DATA 50,6
3990      DATA -1,-1
4000      DATA -2,"FUNERAL MARCH OF A MARIONETTE - GOUNOD"
4010      DATA 37,1,0,2,30,1,0,5,42,3,42,3,41,3,39,3,41,3,0,3,
          42,3,44,3,0,3,37,1,0,2
4020      DATA 30,1,0,5,42,3,42,3,41,3,39,3,41,3,0,3,42,3,44,3,
          0,3,37,3,42,3,0,3,45,3
4030      DATA 49,6,47,3,45,3,0,3,49,3,52,6,50,3,49,3,0,3,53,3,
          56,6,54,3,53,3,50,3
4040      DATA 49,3,47,3,45,3,44,3,30,1,0,5,42,3,42,3,41,3,
          39,3,41,3,0,3,42,3,44,3
4050      DATA 0,3,37,1,0,2,30,1,0,5,42,3,42,3,41,3,39,3,41,3,
          0,3,42,3,44,3,0,
4060      DATA 37,3,45,3,0,3,49,3,52,6,50,3,49,3,47,3,45,3,
          43,3,47,3,50,3,42,3
4070      DATA 41,3,42,3,44,3,0,3,45,1,0,2,44,9,42,1
4080      DATA -1,-1
4100      DATA -2,"STARS AND STRIPES FOREVER - SOUSA "
4110      DATA 54,6,54,6,52,3,51,3,51,6,50,3,51,3,51,16,0,2,50,3
4120      DATA 51,3,51,6,50,3,51,3
4130      DATA 54,6,51,3,54,3,52,12,49,6,0,3,49,3,49,6,48,3,49,3
4140      DATA 49,6,48,3,49,3
```

continued on p. 112

continued from p. 111

```
4150      DATA 52,16,0,2,51,3,49,3,51,3,54,9,56,9,56,3,49,16,
          0,2,54,6
4160      DATA 54,6,52,3,51,3,51,6,50,3,51,3,51,16,0,2,50,3,
          51,3,51,6,50,3 ,51,3
4170      DATA 52,3,51,3,49,5,46,1,49,12,47,6,0,3,47,3,47,6,
          46,3,47,3,50,6,49,3,47,3
4180      DATA 59,15,0,3,47,3,49,3,51,3,54,1,0,2,47,3,49,3,
          51,3,54,1,0,2,42,3,44,5
4190      DATA 51,1,49,12,47,1
4200      DATA -1,-1
4300      DATA -2,"Mexican Hat Dance - Traditional "
4310      DATA 52,2,57,2,0,2,52,2,57,2,0,2,52,2,57,6,0,4,52,2,
          57,2,59,2,57,2,56,4
4320      DATA 57,2,59,2,0,8,52,2,56,2,0,2,52,2,56,2,0,2,52,2,
          56,6,0,4,52,2
4330      DATA 56,2,57,2,56,2,54,4,56,2,57,2,0,6,64,2,63,2,
          64,2,61,2,60,2,61,2
4340      DATA 57,2,56,2,57,2,52,2,0,4,49,2,50,2,52,2,54,2,
          56,2,57,2,59,2,61,2
4350      DATA 62,2,59,2,0,4,62,2,61,2,62,2,59,2,58,2,59,2,
          56,2,55,2,56,2,52,2
4360      DATA 0,4,64,2,63,2,64,2,66,2,64,2,62,2,61,2,
          59,2,57,2
4370      DATA -1,-1
4400      DATA -2,"SCALES                            "
4410      DATA 38,1,39,1,40,1,41,1,42,1,43,1,44,1,45,1,46,1,47,1
4420      DATA 48,1,49,1,50,1,51,1,52,1,53,1,54,1,55,1,56,1
4430      DATA 57,1,58,1,59,1,60,1,61,1,62,1,63,1,64,1,65,8,0,4
4440      DATA 65,8,64,1,63,1,62,1,61,1,60,1,59,1,58,1,57,1
4450      DATA 56,1,55,1,54,1,53,1,52,1,51,1,50,1,49,1,48,1
4460      DATA 47,1,46,1,45,1,44,1,43,1,42,1,41,1,40,1,39,1,38,8
4470      DATA -1,-1
4500      DATA -2,"Sakura - Japanese Folk Melody "
4510      DATA 49,8,49,8,51,12,0,4,49,8,49,8,51,12,0,4,49,8,
          51,8,52,8,51,8
4520      DATA 49,8,51,4,49,4,45,16,44,8,40,8,44,8,45,8
4530      DATA 44,8,44,4,40,4,39,16,49,8,49,8,51,12,0,4,
          49,8,49,8,51,12,0,4
4540      DATA 40,8,44,8,45,8,49,8,51,4,49,4,45,8,44,16
4550      DATA -1,-1
```

Music Running in Background

The IBM Personal Computer plays tones and does other computing simultaneously. As soon as the speaker starts playing a tone, the computer goes on to the subsequent statements in your program. The computer continues the program indefinitely unless it comes to another SOUND statement while the speaker is still playing the first tone. If it is in the default mode—*music foreground mode*—the computer must wait for the first tone to finish before it can start the second tone and continue with the program. You can, however, change the computer to *music background mode,* in which the computer stores the second tone and continues with the program immediately. The speaker will finish playing the first tone; then it will find the second tone the computer stored for it and play that. If the computer comes to further SOUND statements, it just stores the tones and continues on. This continues indefinitely unless the program manages to get more than 32 tones ahead of the speaker. Since the speaker can only remember 32 tones, the computer must then wait until one tone finishes. Then only 31 tones will be waiting, and the program will store the new tone as the thirty-second in line and go on computing.

Music background mode is useful, for example, for game programs in which the game action must continue even though a little tune is playing to indicate that something has happened. In music foreground mode, the game would have to stop until the last note of the tune was started. In music background mode, as long as the little tune is shorter than 32 notes, the game can continue and the speaker will catch up.

The program in Fig. 4-18 illustrates the possibilities. As the loop from statement 170 to statement 240 executes, statement 180 plays an ascending chromatic scale. The loop from statement 190 to statement 230 provides other "computing" for the computer to do. Since this "computing" prints results on the screen, you can observe whether the computer is proceeding with the program while the tones of the scale are being played.

Fig. 4-18 Music That Plays While Computing Continues

This program illustrates the various possibilities of the "music background" feature of the IBM Personal Computer.

```
100   ' --- THIS PROGRAM DEMONSTRATES THE BACKGROUND CAPABILITY
110   ' --- OF THE SOUND STATEMENT
120   '
130        PLAY "MF"
135        CLS
140   '
160        COUNT = 0
170        FOR I = 1 TO 60
180           SOUND 74 * 2^(I/12) , 10
190           FOR J = 1 TO 5
200              COUNT = COUNT + 2
210              LOCATE 10,10
220              PRINT USING "#######" ; COUNT
230           NEXT J
240        NEXT I
250   '
255        SOUND 100,0
260        END
```

Statement 130 tells the computer to run in music foreground mode. (This is just one feature of the PLAY statement, which is discussed thoroughly in Section 4.6.) The computer plays one tone and counts to 10 the first time through the loop. Since in music foreground mode the computer does not store tones to be played, you will see the counting pause when the computer has counted to 10, gets to statement 170 for the second time, and has to wait for the first tone to finish before it can start the second tone and continue the program. When the first tone finishes, the computer starts the second tone and counts to 20. Then there will be another pause as the computer is ready to play the third tone, but the speaker has not finished with the second. When the speaker finishes with the second tone, the computer starts the third tone and counts to 30. During each tone, the computer counts another 10 and then pauses while it waits for the tone to finish. Incidentally, statement 130 could just be left out of the program and the result would be the same.

If you change statement 130 to read

130 PLAY "MB"

then the program will play tones in music background mode. You will see it count continuously to about 400 while playing just the first few tones. At that point the program will get 32 tones ahead of the speaker, and you will see it count in tens and then pause; during each pause, the computer waits for a tone to finish so that it can store another without overflowing the 32 memory spaces for tones. When the program "finishes," that is, when it stops counting and prints

Ok

the speaker has 32 tones to go. It will go right ahead and play those 32 tones, even though the program is "over."

You can cut off the speaker when the program is done by inserting the statement

245 SOUND 100,0

This causes the speaker to stop the tone it is playing and to forget about the stored tones. When you are in music background mode, any SOUND statement with duration of 0 (and a legal frequency) cuts off whatever tone is being played, if any, and erases the stored tones, if any.

4.6 MORE SOUND AND MUSIC—THE PLAY STATEMENT

In this section, we shall discuss the PLAY statement, which interprets a string representing a tune and sends tones to the speaker. The PLAY statement is to the SOUND statement what the DRAW statement is to the other graphics statements: it allows you to do about the same things, but more easily. As we mentioned in Section 4.5, the advantages of the PLAY statement over the SOUND statement are that one PLAY statement can play as complex a tune as can be stored in one string and that the notation used in PLAY statement strings to store lists of notes to play is easier to deal with than the frequencies and durations used in the SOUND statement.

The PLAY statement consists of the word PLAY followed by a string or the name of a string variable. The string of string variable must contain what IBM calls *tune definition language,* which tells the PLAY statement what notes to play, how fast to play them, and so on. Tune definition language consists of a series of commands, each of which tells the PLAY statement to play a note, to change the tempo, to change articulation, and so forth.

Tune Definition Language

Since tune definition language uses musical notation and terminology, this section assumes that you have some familiarity with that notation and terminology. If you are not familiar with musical notation and terminology, examine Fig. 4-20, where you will find BASIC programs that play several useful snippets of music; you can copy any that are appropriate for programs you are writing.

Figure 4-19 contains a complete listing of the commands in tune definition language.

THE C, D, E, F, G, A, AND B COMMANDS

The C, D, E, F, G, A, and B commands tell the PLAY statement to play one note. For example,

    10 PLAY "CEG"

plays the notes C, E, and G, one after the other in that order. Later in this section, we shall discuss how to control what octave the notes are played in

Fig. 4-19 Summary of Commands in Tune Definition Language

The following summarizes the various commands in tune definition language.

COMMANDS TO PLAY NOTES AND RESTS

C, D, E, F, G, A, B, C#, D#, F#, G#, A#, D−, E−, G−, A−, and B−—play the various notes. If a number follows the note, it is the time value for the note, as explained in the discussion of the L command.

On—chooses octave number n as the current octave, where n is a number from 0 to 6. All subsequent notes are played in this octave. Octave 0 is the lowest octave; octave 6, the highest. Until an O command is given, the default octave is octave 4, which begins with the C above middle C and continues to the B above that.

Nn—plays note n, where n is a number from 1 to 84. Note 1 is the low C in octave 0, three octaves below middle C. Note 37 is middle C. If n is 0, then the computer plays a rest.

Pn—plays a rest ("pause") whose length is determined by the number n. See the discussion of the L command for an explanation of how the length of a rest is determined from the number n.

NOTE LENGTHS AND TEMPOS

Ln—chooses the length of the following notes. The number n represents the fraction of a whole note that the following notes should be. L4, for example, means that the following notes should be quarter notes.

Tn—chooses the tempo; n is the number of quarter notes per minute.

MISCELLANEOUS

MN, ML, and MS—set the music to normal, legato, and staccato. In normal music, each note is held to 7/8 of its length and is followed by a rest that is 1/8 of the length. In legato music, each note is held to its full value. In staccato music, each note is held to only 3/4 of its value.

MB and MF—set the music into foreground and background, either forbidding or allowing the computer to continue computing while the speaker is playing the music.

X—executes a variable. The variable must contain a string with more tune definition language commands. The name of the variable must be followed by a semicolon.

Any of the above commands that use n as a parameter may have an equal sign, the name of a numeric variable, and a semicolon substituted for the number. This command, for example, plays note 99:

```
10 LET S99 = 99
20 PLAY "N = S99;"
```

and the lengths of the notes. A sharp sign (#) or a plus sign (+) following a letter indicates a sharp; a minus sign (−) indicates a flat. The following therefore plays up and down a one-octave chromatic scale:

    20 PLAY "C C# D D# E F F# G G# A A# B B− A A− G G−
        F E E− D D− C"

Sharps and flats that do not correspond to black keys on a piano—that is, B#, E#, F−, C−, and all double sharps and double flats—are not allowed. Such notes have to be written as their piano equivalents. Note that spaces are allowed within tune definition language.

OCTAVES: THE O COMMAND

The O command lets you choose the octave in which notes are to be played. The range of the PLAY statement is seven octaves, numbered 0 to 6, each one extending from a C to the B above it. Octave number 0 is the lowest octave; octave 6, the highest. Octave number 3 starts with middle C and ends with the B on the middle line in treble clef (the B above middle C). To choose an octave, insert the letter O and the number of the octave you wish to select in the tune definition. All subsesquent notes will be played in that octave until another O command is given. The following PLAY statement plays an ascending A-flat major scale starting in the third octave and ending in the fourth:

    30 PLAY "O3 A− B− O4 C D− E− F G A−"

Until you give an O command, all notes will be played in octave number 4.

The computer remembers your most recent octave command from one PLAY statement to the next. The following two statements, for example, will play a descending D major scale:

    10 PLAY "O4 D C # O3 B A"
    20 PLAY "G F# E D"

The O3 command in the first PLAY statement applies to the notes in statement 20.

NOTE LENGTHS AND TEMPOS

Unless you tell the computer otherwise, all notes are quarter notes. The letter L followed by an integer is the command that tells the computer to do otherwise. The integer is the fraction of a whole note that the following notes are to be. For example, "L2" makes all the following notes into half notes. "L8" makes all subsequent notes into eighth notes. "L16," "L32," and "L64" indicate sixteenth notes, thirty-second notes, and sixty-fourth notes. Since eighth-note triplets occur twelve to the whole note, notes after an L12 command are eighth-note triplets. And so on. The following sequence of statements plays the bugle call "Charge":

```
1000 ' --- CHARGE!!
1010     LET  CHARGE$ = "L8 O3 G O4 C E L4 G L8 E L2 G"
1020     PLAY CHARGE$
```

The first three notes are eighth notes. The first high G is a quarter note. The E following that is another eighth, and the final G is a half note. Figure 4-21 contains the music for this call.

A note can be given a value different from the value the most recent L command would give it by following the name of the note with its time value. For example, "Charge" could be rewritten as follows:

```
1000 ' --- CHARGE!!
1010     LET  CHARGE$ = "L8 O3 G O4 C E G4 E G2"
1020     PLAY CHARGE$
```

As before, all of the notes are eighth notes except the first high G, which is a quarter note, and the last G, which is a half note.

Dots work as they do in musical notation: they increase the time value of a note by half. This statement, for example, plays dotted eighths followed by sixteenths:

```
10  PLAY  "O3 L8 G.   G16 G.   G16 G.   G16"
```

Double dotted notes are allowed in tune definition language, but they are different from double dots in musical notation. Whereas in musical notation the second dot increases the time value only of the first dot, the second dot in tune definition language increases the value of the entire note-and-first-dot combination. A double dotted half note in tune definition language, for example, comes out as a whole plus an eighth note, which is longer than a standard double-dotted half.

You can set the tempo with the T command by inserting the letter T and a metronome marking. The metronome marking is assumed to apply to quarter notes. For example,

```
10 PLAY "T68"
```

tells the computer to play all subsequent notes at the rate of 68 quarter notes per minute. This tempo applies until a new tempo is set. If you give no tempo indication, the computer uses metronome marking 120.

THE N COMMAND: AN ALTERNATE WAY TO SPECIFY NOTES

Instead of specifying notes by name with the C, D, E, F, G, A, and B commands, you can specify notes by number with the N command. Notes are numbered from 1 to 84, starting with the C three octaves below middle C and continuing on up the chromatic scale. Middle C is note number 37, for example. Since the notes 44, 49, 53, and 56 correspond to the G, C, E, and high G that we used in "Charge" before, the bugle call can be rewritten this way:

```
1000  ' --- CHARGE!!
1010       LET  CHARGE$ = "T150  L8 N44 N49 N53 L4 N56
                 L8 N53 L2 N56"
1020       PLAY CHARGE$
```

RESTS

Rests can be specified in two ways in tune definition language. First, you can specify note number 0 with the N command. Second, you can use the P (Pause) command. The P command consists of the letter P followed by an integer that represents the length of the rest in the same way that the integer after an L command specifies the lengths of the notes that follow. Either of these two statements plays a quarter-note rest:

```
10  PLAY "L4 N0"
10  PLAY "P4"
```

ARTICULATION: LEGATO, STACCATO, AND "NORMAL"

Unless you tell it otherwise, the PLAY statement plays each note for 7/8 of its time value and follows it with a rest 1/8 of its value. The effect of this is to separate the notes slightly from one another. The IBM BASIC manual refers to this articulation as "Music Normal." The ML and MS commands change subsequent notes to "Music Legato" and "Music Staccato." A note played in Music Legato is held to its full value. A note played in Music Staccato is held to 3/4 of its value and is followed by a rest of 1/4 its value. This is not a sharp staccato, but it creates a definite separation between notes. The MN command causes subsequent notes to be played in "Music Normal." Here, once again, is "Charge," with legato and staccato thrown in:

```
'1000 ' --- CHARGE!!
 1010        LET   CHARGE$ = "T150   L8 O3 G O4 C E MS L4 G
                        MN L8 E L2 G"
 1020        PLAY CHARGE$
```

This is the most faithful rendition of the bugle call.

In Music Legato, two adjacent notes of the same pitch have no articulation between them; it is the equivalent of a tie.

USING VARIABLES IN TUNE DEFINITION LANGUAGE COMMANDS

Tune definition language, like graphics definition language, allows you to insert the name of a numeric variable in place of a numeric parameter. As in graphics definition language, you replace the number with an equal sign, the name of the numeric variable you wish to use, and a semicolon. For example, this fragment plays the same A-flat major scale as the example we considered earlier in the discussion of octaves:

```
10  LET OCT3 = 3
20  LET OCT4 = 4
30  PLAY "O=OCT3; A- B- O=OCT4; C D- E- F G A-"
```

The PLAY statement at statement 30 looks up the values of OCT3 and OCT4. Since OCT3 equals 3, the command "O = OCT3;" has the same effect as did "O3" in the previous example, and since OCT4 equals 4, the command "O = OCT4;" has the same effect as did "O4". The following two fragments both play a seven-octave ascending chromatic scale:

```
10  FOR OCT = 0 TO 6
20     PLAY "O=OCT; C C# D D# E F F# G G# A A# B"
30  NEXT OCT
```

```
10  FOR CHROMATIC.NOTE = 1 TO 84
20     PLAY "N=CHROMATIC.NOTE;"
30  NEXT CHROMATIC.NOTE
```

The first fragment plays the scale an octave at a time. Each time through the loop, the variable OCT is incremented and the next octave higher is played. In the second fragment, each PLAY statement plays the next higher note as the value of CHROMATIC.NOTE runs from 1 to 84.

The following example is yet another alternative way to play "Charge":

```
1110          LET   NOTE.CHARGE$ = "T150   L8
                    N=NT(1); N=NT(2); N=NT(3);"
1120          LET   NOTE.CHARGE$ = NOTE.CHARGE$ +
                    "MS L4 N=NT(4); MN L8 N=NT(3);"
1130          LET   NOTE.CHARGE$ = NOTE.CHARGE$ +
                    "L2 N=NT(4);"
1140          LET   NT(1) = 44
1150          LET   NT(2) = NT(1) + 5
1160          LET   NT(3) = NT(2) + 4
1170          LET   NT(4) = NT(3) + 3
1190          PLAY NOTE.CHARGE$
```

Instead of the actual note numbers we used before, we have inserted references to array variable NT. This is a little clumsy, but it allows easy transposition to a new key. This program fragment plays "Charge" as it is sometimes played at sports events: the call is played several times, each time in a key a half step above the preceding time:

```
1100  ' --- CHARGE AGAIN
1110          LET   NOTE.CHARGE$ = "T150   L8
                    N=NT(1); N=NT(2); N=NT(3);"
1120          LET   NOTE.CHARGE$ = NOTE.CHARGE$ +
                    "MSL4N=NT(4); MNL8N=NT(3);"
1130          LET   NOTE.CHARGE$ = NOTE.CHARGE$ +
                    "L2N=NT(4);"
1140          LET   NT(1) = 44
1150          LET   NT(2) = NT(1) + 5
1160          LET   NT(3) = NT(2) + 4
1170          LET   NT(4) = NT(3) + 3
1180          FOR I = 1 TO 4
1190             PLAY NOTE.CHARGE$
1200             FOR J = 1 TO 4
1210                LET NT(J) = NT(J) + 1
1220             NEXT J
1230          NEXT I
```

Each time through the loop that starts at statement 1180, the subloop starting at 1200 increments each of the elements in NT; when the string is played again at statement 1190, all of the notes have been moved up a half step.

Do not neglect to insert a semicolon after the variable name, even if the command is the last one in the string. The semicolon after N=NT(4) in statement 1130 is necessary for the program to work.

SUBTUNES

Tune definition language allows you to include one string of tune definition language as a "subtune" within another such string. You can therefore write a simple string that plays a complex tune by referring to other strings. To do this, use the X command, which consists of the letter X, the name of the subtune string, and a semicolon. Try out the example below if you cannot figure out what it does:

```
10 LET DOODLE$ = "CGEG"
20 PLAY "L16 XDOODLE$; XDOODLE$; XDOODLE$;
        XDOODLE$;"
```

The following example plays "Taps":

```
1300  ' --- TAPS
1310       LET TAPS1$ = "T60 L8 O3G L16NO G L2 O4C L4NO"
1320       LET TAPS2$ = "L8 O3G L16NO O4C L2 E L4NO"
1330       LET TAPS3$ = "L8 O3G L16NO O4C L4 E"
1340       LET TAPS4$ = "L8 O3G L16NO O4C MLL2EMN L4C"
1350       LET TAPS5$ = "L8 C L16NO E MLL2G L4E C O3L2GMN L4NO"
1360       LET TAPS$ = "XTAPS1$; XTAPS2$; XTAPS3$; XTAPS3$;
                    XTAPS4$; XTAPS5$; XTAPS1$;"
1370       PLAY TAPS$
```

The strings TAPS1$, TAPS2$, . . ., TAPS5$ play various phrases of the bugle call. The string TAPS$ refers to each of the phrases in turn to play the whole bugle call. Note that phrases 1 and 3, which are repeated in "Taps," can be repeated in the string TAPS$ without writing out the notes again.

Music Foreground and Background

As discussed in the section on the SOUND statement, a program can get up to 32 notes ahead of the speaker. This feature can be enabled and disabled for the PLAY statement in the same way as for the SOUND statement with the MB and MF commands in tune definition language. The statement

```
10 PLAY "MB"
```

puts the music in background mode so that the computer can go on computing while the music is playing. The statement

```
10 PLAY "MF"
```

puts the music back in foreground mode so that the computer waits while the music plays. Music background mode allows the program to get only 32 *notes* ahead of the speaker, not 32 *PLAY statements*.

RITARDS, VIBRATO, DYNAMICS, PHRASING

Sorry. These features do not exist in tune definition language. The piano, violin, French horn, and bassoon are in no danger of being replaced by the IBM Personal Computer.

Examples

Figure 4-20 contains several sample tunes, some of which we have discussed in the text. They also illustrate the various techniques we have discussed in this section. Figure 4-21 contains the music played by the program examples in Fig. 4-20.

Fig. 4-20   Programs to Play Various Tunes

```
1000  '
1005  ' --- CHARGE!!
1010        LET   CHARGE$ = "T150   L8 O3G O4 C E MSL4G MNL8E L2 G."
1020        PLAY CHARGE$
1100  '
1105  ' --- CHARGE AGAIN!!
1110        LET   NOTE.CHARGE$ = "T150   L8
                     N=NT(1); N=NT(2); N=NT(3);"
1120        LET   NOTE.CHARGE$ = NOTE.CHARGE$ +
                     "MSL4N=NT(4); MNL8N=NT(3);"
1130        LET   NOTE.CHARGE$ = NOTE.CHARGE$ +
                     "L2N=NT(4);."
1140        LET   NT(1) = 44
1150        LET   NT(2) = NT(1) + 5
1160        LET   NT(3) = NT(2) + 4
1170        LET   NT(4) = NT(3) + 3
1180        FOR I = 1 TO 4
1190           PLAY NOTE.CHARGE$
1200           FOR J = 1 TO 4
1210              LET NT(J) = NT(J) + 1
1220           NEXT J
1230        NEXT I
1300  '
1305  ' --- TAPS
1310        LET TAPS1$ = "T60 L8 O3G L16NO G L2 O4C L4NO"
1320        LET TAPS2$ = "L8 O3G L16NO O4C L2 E L4NO"
1330        LET TAPS3$ = "L8 O3G L16NO O4C L4 E"
1340        LET TAPS4$ = "L8 O3G L16NO O4C MLL2EMN L4C"
1350        LET TAPS5$ = "L8 C L16NO E MLL2G L4E C O3L2GMN L4NO"
1360        LET TAPS$ = "XTAPS1$; XTAPS2$; XTAPS3$; XTAPS3$;
                     XTAPS4$; XTAPS5$; XTAPS1$;"
1370        PLAY TAPS$
```

continued on p. 124

continued from p. 123

```
1400 '
1405 ' --- CHROMATIC SCALE
1410       LET CHROMATIC$ = "O3 L8 C C# D D# E F F# G
              G# A A# B O4 C"
1420       PLAY CHROMATIC$
1500 '
1505 ' --- BACH E MAJOR PRELUDE
1510       LET BACH1$ = "T130 O4 L16 E D# MS E8 O3 B8 G#8 B8
              MN E F# E D#"
1520       LET BACH2$ = "MS E8 O2 B8 G#8 B8 MN"
1530       LET BACH3$ = 'E B F# B G# B A B G# B F# B"
1540       LET BACH4$ = "E O3 E D# C# O2 B O3 E D# C#
              O2 B A G# F#"
1545       LET BACH5$ = "E F# G# A B O3 C# D# E F# G# A F#"
1546       LET BACH6$ = "G# B E F# G# A B O4 C# D# E C# D# L1 E"
1550       LET BACH$ = BACH1$ + BACH2$ + BACH3$ + BACH4$
1560       LET BACH$ = BACH$ + "XBACH3$; XBACH4$; XBACH5$;
              XBACH6$;"
1570       PLAY BACH$
1600 '
1605 ' --- STARS AND STRIPES FOREVER
1610       LET STARS$(1) ="T120 L4 O3 D D C8 O2 B8 B A#8 B8 B2."
1620       LET STARS$(2) ="A#8 B8 B A#8 B8 O3 D"
1630       LET STARS$(3) ="O2 B8 O3 D8 C2 O2 ML L4A L8 MN NO"
1640       LET STARS$(4) ="A L4 A G#8 A8 A G#8 A8
              O3 MLL2 C L8C MN NO"
1650       LET STARS$(5) ="O2 B8 A8 B8 O3 MLD MN L4 D MLE MNL8 E"
1660       LET STARS$(6) ="E O2 L2 A L4 NO"
1670       LET STARS$(7) =STARS$(1)
1680       LET STARS$(8) ="L8 A# B B4 A# B O3 C O2 B A. F#16
              A2 G4 P8"
1690       LET STARS$(9) ="G G4 F# G B-4 A G O3 G2 P8"
1700       LET STARS$(10)="O2 G A B O3 D16 P16 MN
              O2 G A B O3 D16 P16 MN O2 D E. B16 A2 MS G8 P8 G8"
1720       FOR I = 1 TO 10
1730          PLAY STARS$(I)
1740       NEXT I
1800 '
1805 ' --- YOU BLEW IT!
1810       PLAY "T120 ML O3 L5 G C#8"
```

Fig. 4-21 Music Played by Programs in Fig. 4-20

continued on p. 126

continued from p. 125

A Special Note on IBM's Sample Program "Music"

One of the examples in Fig. 4-20 is the Sousa march, "Stars and Stripes Forever," which was also programmed using the SOUND statement and many DATA statements in the IBM sample program "Music" discussed in the previous section. After you compare the PLAY statements here with the DATA statements in the previous program, you may have doubts about the sanity of the programmer who wrote "Music," but do not judge too hastily. "Music," in addition to playing the music, draws a fancy little picture of a piano keyboard with a bouncing note symbol that moves from key to key as the tunes are played. The difficulty with the PLAY statement is that no way exists to synchronize the music with the picture, since the PLAY statement starts a whole series of notes. Using the SOUND statement, however, the programmer could start each note and then have the program take care of the graphics.

4.7 USING A JOYSTICK—THE STICK AND STRIG FUNCTIONS

So far, typing things at the keyboard is the only input technique we have used. In this section, we shall discuss writing programs that use a *joystick* to indicate locations on the screen. A joystick is a lever or stick mounted in a box in such a way that you can use your hand to move the stick forward, backward, left, and right. The joystick sends signals to the computer indicating the location at which the stick is being held.

Buying Joystick Hardware

To plug a joystick into the IBM Personal Computer, you must have a *Game Control Adapter.* This is a circuit board that fits inside the IBM Personal Computer. IBM sells one, as do several other manufacturers. The one IBM sells has a fifteen-wire connector on the back, and various manufacturers sell joysticks with fifteen-pin plugs that fit into this connector. Be sure that the joystick you buy is compatible with your Game Control Adapter. Not all joysticks with fifteen-pin plugs on them are compatible with all Game Control Adapters, because the adapters expect signals on certain pins to mean certain things, and joysticks can be wired up in different ways.

The IBM Personal Computer can handle two joysticks, but the Game Control Adapter has only one fifteen-pin connector. To use two joysticks, you must arrange that they be wired together so that both send their signals into one fifteen-pin plug. You can buy joystick pairs already wired up this way. The author has not seen for sale a y connector for wiring two regular joysticks together, but an electronics wizard of modest talents could easily build one, given a few dollars' worth of parts and the information available in the IBM *Technical Reference Manual* for the Personal Computer.

If a joystick has one or two buttons on it, the IBM Personal Computer can detect whether or not they have been pressed.

Two special features are available on some joysticks. First, most joy-sticks have a spring that makes the joystick point straight up out of its box whenever you aren't pushing it in some direction. On some joysticks, you can disengage the spring, after which the stick stays where you put it instead of snapping back to the center. Second, on some joysticks, you can adjust the signals that are sent to the computer. We shall discuss these features later in this section, and you can decide if they are important to you.

Joysticks are sold in wide variety: large, small, fat, skinny, attached to big boxes, attached to small boxes, with a button on top of the stick, with buttons on the box beside the stick, in various colors, with different lengths of cord, and so on. Choose one you like.

Joystick Coordinates—The STICK Function

The Game Control Adapter turns the signals from each joystick into two numbers: an x coordinate, which indicates where the joystick is in the left to right sense, and a y coordinate, which indicates where the joystick is in the forward and back sense. Most joysticks send larger x coordinates when the stick is farther to the right and larger y coordinates when the stick is farther back (toward the user). Moving the stick to the right, therefore, corresponds to farther to the right on the screen, and pulling the stick back corresponds to lower on the screen. BASIC refers to the two joysticks as joystick A and joystick B. If you have only one, then it is joystick A. The STICK function returns the coordinates of each joystick. You tell the STICK function which coordinate of which joystick you want by passing one of the numbers 0, 1, 2, or 3 to the STICK function. The following four statements get the x and y coordinates of the two joysticks:

```
10  LET  X.COORD.OF.JOYSTICK.A = STICK(0)
20  LET  Y.COORD.OF.JOYSTICK.A = STICK(1)
30  LET  X.COORD.OF.JOYSTICK.B = STICK(2)
40  LET  Y.COORD.OF.JOYSTICK.B = STICK(3)
```

You might expect that the STICK function would check the joystick's positions whenever it is used, but it doesn't. When you use STICK(0), the computer gets *all four* joystick coordinates, and when you ask for one of the other coordinates with STICK(1), STICK(2), or STICK(3), the computer tells you what they were when you last used STICK(0) without bothering to see if they have changed since. Therefore, whenever you are interested in the current position of either joystick, you must first use STICK(0) to force the computer to go look. If you happen not to be interested in the x coordinate of joystick A, that's too bad; you have to find it out anyway.

Joystick Buttons—the STRIG Function

The STRIG (*Stick TRIG*ger) function allows a program to find out which, if any, of the joystick buttons are currently pressed, and which, if any, have ever been pressed since you last asked. BASIC calls the two buttons on joystick A "A1" and "A2" and the two buttons on joystick B "B1" and "B2."

You tell the STRIG function which of the buttons interests you by passing it a number between 0 and 7. The STRIG function always returns -1 or 0; -1 means yes, and 0 means no. The following eight statements get information about the joystick buttons:

```
10  LET  A1.DOWN.EVER = STRIG(0)
20  LET  A1.DOWN.NOW  = STRIG(1)
30  LET  B1.DOWN.EVER = STRIG(2)
40  LET  B1.DOWN.NOW  = STRIG(3)
50  LET  A2.DOWN.EVER = STRIG(4)
60  LET  A2.DOWN.NOW  = STRIG(5)
70  LET  B2.DOWN.EVER = STRIG(6)
80  LET  B2.DOWN.NOW  = STRIG(7)
```

Whenever you call the STRIG function, the computer checks the relevent button, unlike the STICK function. If you use the STRIG function to ask whether a button has been pressed since you last asked, it means whether it has been pressed since the last time you asked *about that button*. If you have asked about other buttons in the meantime, that makes no difference.

Before you can use the STRIG function, you must execute this statement:

5 STRIG ON

This enables the joystick buttons. If you want, you can disable the buttons later with this statement:

15 STRIG OFF

Why might you want to disable the buttons? Because whenever the joystick buttons are enabled, in order to be able to tell you if a joystick button has ever been pressed, the computer must continually check which joystick buttons are pressed. This checking takes a little time, and hence programs slow down a little when the joystick buttons are enabled. In most circumstances, the speed difference is negligible, but if your program happens to be the exception, the STRIG OFF statement may solve your problem.

Calibrating Your Joysticks

With a Game Control Adapter plugged into your Personal Computer and a joystick or two plugged into that, you are ready to try out the program in Fig. 4-22. We urge you to type it in and run it. The reason you should actually try this one out rather than just read about it (as we certainly hope

Fig. 4-22 Joystick Calibration Program

Type this into your computer and try it out with your joystick to find out how your joystick works.

```
1000 ' --- PROGRAM TO TRY OUT JOYSTICK
1010 '
1020 '
1030 '
1040       STRIG ON
1050       LET FORM.A$ = "A: ###.##   ###.##   A1 ##    A2 ##"
1060       LET FORM.B$ = "B: ###.##   ###.##   B1 ##    B2 ##"
1070       LET FORM$ = FORM.A$ + "           " + FORM.B$
1080 ' --- LOOP TO READ JOYSTICK AND PRINT COORDS ON THE SCREEN
1090       IF   INKEY$ <> ""   GOTO 1230
1100 '     --- SAMPLE THE JOYSTICK
1110       LET X.STICK.A = STICK(0)
1120       LET Y.STICK.A = STICK(1)
1130       LET X.STICK.B = STICK(2)
1140       LET Y.STICK.B = STICK(3)
1150       LET A1.BUTTON = STRIG(0)
1160       LET B1.BUTTON = STRIG(2)
1170       LET A2.BUTTON = STRIG(4)
1180       LET B2.BUTTON = STRIG(6)
1190       PRINT USING FORM$ ; X.STICK.A,Y.STICK.A,
                A1.BUTTON,A2.BUTTON,
                X.STICK.B,Y.STICK.B,B1.BUTTON,B2.BUTTON
1200       GOTO 1080
1210 '
1220 '
1230       END
```

you have felt free to do with at least some of the other program examples in this book) is that joysticks from different manufacturers behave differently, and this program is a handy way to find out how yours behaves.

The program in Fig. 4-22 checks the joystick coordinates, checks the buttons, and prints what it finds on the screen. Statement 1040 turns on the joystick buttons. Statements 1050, 1060, and 1070 set up a format for printing on the screen. Statements 1110 to 1180 gather all of the values from each of two joysticks and their buttons, and these values are printed at statement 1190. Statement 1090 just checks if you have pressed a key on the keyboard; when you do, the program ends.

If the x and y coordinates for a joystick are always 0, it means that the joystick isn't working or that it isn't plugged in properly. Get defective joysticks repaired, but first check to see that they were really plugged into the computer. The x and y coordinates printed on the screen should vary as you move the joystick around. Push your joystick to the right and check to see that the x coordinate gets bigger. Push it to the left, forward, and back and note how the coordinates change. Find out the maximum and minimum x and y coordinates your joysticks send. If you have a joystick with buttons, press them and note the computer's response. Push your joystick away from its center and let its spring snap it back to the center and note the coordinates you get. If your joystick can be adjusted, adjust it while the program is running and note the changes.

The author discovered that his joystick returns x and y coordinates that range from 3 to about 250. Its two buttons work, and he knows which one is button A1 and which is A2. When the spring centers the stick, the x and y coordinates are approximately 150, although this varies by up to 20 in either direction depending on how far in which direction the joystick was pushed before the spring was allowed to bring it back to the center. The adjustments on his joystick allow him to change the coordinates when the spring centers the stick by about 25 in any direction.

If your joystick is wildly different from the author's, you may have to modify the example programs slightly to make them work well.

Moving a Dot around the Screen—Position and Motion Control

The program in Fig. 4-23 allows a joystick to control the position of a dot on the screen. The loop from statement 1040 to statement 1210 gets coordinates from the joystick and puts a dot on the screen at the location indicated by those coordinates. The x and y coordinates of the joystick are found and stored in X.CURRENT and Y.CURRENT by statements 1070 and 1080. Statements 1090 to 1120 check that these coordinates are actually on the screen. The author's joystick, for example, can send y coordinates larger than 199, the largest that can be displayed on the screen. Statement 1140 determines if the joystick has been moved since the last time around the loop. If it has, statement 1150 erases the dot on the screen that was drawn to indicate the old joystick location, statements 1160 and 1170 copy the location of the new dot to be drawn into the variables X.CURRENT.LAST and Y.CURRENT.LAST (for later erasing at statement 1150), and statement 1080 puts a new dot on the screen. Statement 1200 ends the program if the user presses any key on the regular keyboard.

You can simplify this program slightly by removing statement 1140, after which the program erases the old dot and puts in the new one whether or not the joystick has moved. This, however, makes for an irritating program, because the dot on the screen flickers even when it isn't moving.

Fig. 4-23   Moving a Dot—Position Control

```
1000 ' --- DOT MOVING (ABSOLUTE JOYSTICK POSITION)
1010 '
1020 '
1030 '
1040 ' --- LOOP TO MOVE CURSOR ACCORDING TO JOYSTICK LOCATION
1070          X.CURRENT = STICK(0)
1080          Y.CURRENT = STICK(1)
1090      IF  X.CURRENT > 310   THEN LET X.CURRENT = 310
1100      IF  X.CURRENT < 10    THEN LET X.CURRENT = 10
1110      IF  Y.CURRENT > 190   THEN LET Y.CURRENT = 190
1120      IF  Y.CURRENT < 10    THEN LET Y.CURRENT = 10
1130 '
1140      IF  X.CURRENT = X.CURRENT.LAST   AND
                  Y.CURRENT = Y.CURRENT.LAST   GOTO 1200
1150          PSET (X.CURRENT.LAST,Y.CURRENT.LAST) , 0
1160          X.CURRENT.LAST = X.CURRENT
1170          Y.CURRENT.LAST = Y.CURRENT
1180          PSET (X.CURRENT,Y.CURRENT) , 2
1200      IF  INKEY$ <> ""   GOTO 1220
1210      GOTO 1040
1220      END
1230 '
1240 '
```

You can complicate this program slightly by making it capable of moving the dot to any location on the screen. The largest x coordinate that your joystick sends back—which you know if you tried out the program in Fig. 4-22—is undoubtedly less than 319, the largest possible x coordinate on the screen, because the largest coordinate that any joystick can send back is 255. To get the program to move the dot to locations all the way across the screen, one possible program change is to have statements 1070 and 1080 multiply the joystick coordinates by a constant slightly larger than 1.0 to obtain screen coordinates slightly larger than the joystick coordinates. If you do this, there will be some points in the middle of the screen that you can't hit (why?), but you probably won't notice that when you run the program.

The program in Fig. 4-23 draws the dot at a position on the screen that corresponds to the position of the joystick. Whenever the joystick is in a particular position, the dot on the screen is in the position on the screen that corresponds to that position of the joystick. The joystick position controls the *position* of the dot. Alternatively, a joystick can control the *motion* of a dot: if you hold the joystick to the right, the dot moves to the right; if you hold the joystick forward, the dot moves up; if you hold the joystick in the center position, then the dot stays put; and so on.

In the program in Fig. 4-24, the joystick controls the motion of the dot rather than its position, but the program is otherwise like the one in Fig. 4-23.

Fig. 4-24   Moving a Dot—Motion Control

```
1000 ' --- DOT MOVING (RELATIVE JOYSTICK POSITION)
1010 '
1020 '
1030 '
1040 ' --- SET JOYSTICK PARAMETERS
1050       X.CENTER = 150
1060       Y.CENTER = 150
1070       SLOP     = 30
1080       LET X.RIGHT = X.CENTER + SLOP
1090       LET X.LEFT  = X.CENTER - SLOP
1100       LET Y.UP    = Y.CENTER - SLOP
1110       LET Y.DOWN  = Y.CENTER + SLOP
1120 '
1130 '
1140 ' --- SET OTHER PARAMETERS
1150       X.CURRENT = 160
1160       Y.CURRENT = 100
1170       X.CURRENT.LAST = 160
1180       Y.CURRENT.LAST = 100
1200 '
1210 ' --- LOOP TO MOVE CURSOR ACCORDING TO JOYSTICK LOCATION
1220         X.STICK = STICK(0)
1230        .Y.STICK = STICK(1)
1240       IF  X.STICK > X.RIGHT  THEN LET X.CURRENT =
                X.CURRENT + (X.STICK-X.RIGHT+10)/10 : MOVE = 1
1250       IF  Y.STICK > Y.DOWN   THEN LET Y.CURRENT =
                Y.CURRENT + (Y.STICK-Y.DOWN+10)/10 : MOVE = 1
1260       IF  X.STICK < X.LEFT   THEN LET X.CURRENT =
                X.CURRENT + (X.STICK-X.LEFT+10)/10 : MOVE = 1
1270       IF  Y.STICK < Y.UP   THEN LET Y.CURRENT =
                Y.CURRENT + (Y.STICK-Y.UP+10)/10 : MOVE = 1
1280       IF  X.CURRENT > 310   THEN LET X.CURRENT = 310
1290       IF  X.CURRENT < 10    THEN LET X.CURRENT = 10
1300       IF  Y.CURRENT > 190   THEN LET Y.CURRENT = 190
1310       IF  Y.CURRENT < 10    THEN LET Y.CURRENT = 10
1320 '
1330       IF MOVE = 0   GOTO 1390
1340          PSET (X.CURRENT.LAST,Y.CURRENT.LAST) , 0
1350          X.CURRENT.LAST = X.CURRENT
1360          Y.CURRENT.LAST = Y.CURRENT
1370          PSET (X.CURRENT,Y.CURRENT) , 3
1380          MOVE = 0
1390       IF  INKEY$ <> ""  GOTO 1410
1400     GOTO 1210
1410     END
1420 '
1430 '
```

The program first initializes several variables that reflect the characteristics of the particular joystick being used: X.CENTER, Y.CENTER, and SLOP. The variables X.CENTER and Y.CENTER are the average x and y coordinates the joystick sends when the joystick's spring has centered it; SLOP is the amount by which the coordinates coming from the centered joystick might differ from X.CENTER and Y.CENTER. In Fig. 4-24, these variables are set to correspond to the observed characteristics of the author's joystick, which, when centered, sets both coordinates to 150 plus or minus 20 to 30. If your joystick is different, change statements 1050, 1060, and 1070 accordingly.

The main loop from statement 1210 to statement 1400 samples the joystick position and moves the dot accordingly. If the joystick is far enough to the right of center so that the program knows that the user is holding it there (and not just because of the slop in the joystick), then statement 1240 increases X.CURRENT, which will move the dot to the right, and sets MOVE to 1 to indicate that the dot has moved. Similarly, if the joystick is held in other positions, statements 1250, 1260, and 1270 move the dot accordingly. As in Fig. 4-23, if the dot has moved, statement 1340 erases the old one and statement 1370 draws in the new one.

Joystick Hardware Options Revisited

When the joystick controls the position of an item on the screen, it is helpful to disengage the joystick spring if you can. With the spring engaged, the joystick will center itself whenever you let go, and when it does this, the item whose position you are controlling jumps obediently back to the center of the screen (more or less). With the spring disengaged, the joystick and the item on the screen tend to stay put when you let go of the joystick. When the joystick controls the motion of the item, however, the spring is helpful, because when you let go of the joystick, it will center itself, and the item will stop moving. When the joystick controls motion, on the one hand, it is helpful to be able to adjust the coordinates that the joystick sends. If the item always moves slowly in a certain direction when the joystick is centered, you can adjust the joystick to make the item stand still. On the other hand, when a joystick controls a position, the adjustments have no such obvious use.

The Etch-A-Sketch Program

The Etch-A-Sketch program in Fig. 4-25 allows you to sketch line drawings on the screen in much the same way as you could with the Etch-A-

Sketch toy. The joystick controls the motion of a small square cursor. By pressing button A1, you can change the cursor's color. It is initially blue but changes to magenta, then to white, then back to blue, and so on each time you press the button. Whenever you press button A2, the program draws a line from wherever the cursor was when you last pressed either of the buttons to wherever the cursor is now. The color of the line matches that of the cursor. If you press any key on the keyboard, the program will end.

The subroutine at statement 1500 saves the three different colored cursors in the arrays CURSOR1, CURSOR2, and CURSOR3. The program always displays CURSOR1. If you press button A1 to change to a differently colored cursor, the subroutine at statement 3000 shuffles the three arrays so that the new cursor is stored in CURSOR1. If you press button A2, the subroutine at statement 4000 draws a line from (X.OLD,Y.OLD) to (X.CURRENT,Y.CURRENT).

The variables X.OLD and Y.OLD store the coordinates of the cursor's screen location the last time that the user pressed one of the joystick buttons. They are updated by the two button-handling subroutines at statements 3000 and 4000. The variables X.CURRENT and Y.CURRENT contain the coordinates of the cursor's current location. The variables X.CURRENT.LAST and Y.CURRENT.LAST contain the coordinates of the cursor's previous location on the screen, which are used to erase the old cursor when you move it with your joystick.

The program displays the cursor on the screen without erasing any of the picture that you have drawn by using a PUT statement with the XOR action.

You can modify the program in Fig. 4-25 so that the joystick will control the cursor position. To do this, replace statements 1240 to 1400 with this sequence of statements:

```
1240            X.CURRENT = STICK(0)
1250            Y.CURRENT = STICK(1)
1260            IF  X.CURRENT > 310    THEN LET X.CURRENT = 310
1270            IF  X.CURRENT < 10     THEN LET X.CURRENT = 10
1280            IF  Y.CURRENT > 190    THEN LET Y.CURRENT = 190
1290            IF  Y.CURRENT < 10     THEN LET Y.CURRENT = 10
1300  '
1310            IF X.CURRENT = X.CURRENT.LAST   AND
                    Y.CURRENT = Y.CURRENT.LAST   GOTO 1400
1320            PUT (X.CURRENT.LAST-2,Y.CURRENT.LAST-2) ,
                    CURSOR1 , XOR
1330            X.CURRENT.LAST = X.CURRENT
1340            Y.CURRENT.LAST = Y.CURRENT
1350            PUT (X.CURRENT-2,Y.CURRENT-2) , CURSOR1 , XOR
1370  '
1380  '
1390  '
1400  '
```

Fig. 4-25   Etch-A-Sketch Program

```
1000 ' --- ETCHASKETCH PROGRAM
1010 '
1030 '
1040 ' --- SET JOYSTICK PARAMETERS
1050       X.CENTER = 150
1060       Y.CENTER = 150
1070       SLOP    = 30
1080       LET X.RIGHT = X.CENTER + SLOP
1090       LET X.LEFT  = X.CENTER - SLOP
1100       LET Y.UP    = Y.CENTER - SLOP
1110       LET Y.DOWN  = Y.CENTER + SLOP
1120 '
1130 '
1140 ' --- SET OTHER PARAMETERS
1150       X.OLD = 160
1160       Y.OLD = 100
1170       X.CURRENT = 160
1180       Y.CURRENT = 100
1190       X.CURRENT.LAST = 160
1200       Y.CURRENT.LAST = 100
1210       GOSUB 1500
1220 '
1230 ' --- LOOP TO MOVE CURSOR ACCORDING TO JOYSTICK LOCATION
1240          X.STICK = STICK(0)
1250          Y.STICK = STICK(1)
1260       IF  X.STICK > X.RIGHT  THEN LET X.CURRENT =
                 X.CURRENT + (X.STICK-X.RIGHT+10)/10 : MOVE = 1
1270       IF  Y.STICK > Y.DOWN   THEN LET Y.CURRENT =
                 Y.CURRENT + (Y.STICK-Y.DOWN+10)/10 : MOVE = 1
1280       IF  X.STICK < X.LEFT   THEN LET X.CURRENT =
                 X.CURRENT + (X.STICK-X.LEFT+10)/10 : MOVE = 1
1290       IF  Y.STICK < Y.UP   THEN LET Y.CURRENT =
                 Y.CURRENT + (Y.STICK-Y.UP+10)/10 : MOVE = 1
1300       IF  X.CURRENT > 310   THEN LET X.CURRENT = 310
1310       IF  X.CURRENT < 10    THEN LET X.CURRENT = 10
1320       IF  Y.CURRENT > 190   THEN LET Y.CURRENT = 190
1330       IF  Y.CURRENT < 10    THEN LET Y.CURRENT = 10
1340 '
1350       IF MOVE = 0   GOTO 1410
1360          PUT (X.CURRENT.LAST-2,Y.CURRENT.LAST-2) ,
                 CURSOR1 , XOR
1370          X.CURRENT.LAST = X.CURRENT
1380          Y.CURRENT.LAST = Y.CURRENT
1390          PUT (X.CURRENT-2,Y.CURRENT-2) , CURSOR1 , XOR
1400          MOVE = 0
1410       IF  INKEY$ <> ""   GOTO 1470
1420       TEMP = STRIG(0)
1430       IF  TEMP <> 0   THEN GOSUB 3000
1440       TEMP = STRIG(4)
1450       IF TEMP <> 0   THEN GOSUB 4000
1460       GOTO 1230
1470       END
```

continued on p. 137

continued from p. 136

```
1480 '
1490 '
1500 ' --- INITIALIZE CURSOR SQUARES
1510      DIM CURSOR1(10)
1520      DIM CURSOR2(10)
1530      DIM CURSOR3(10)
1540 '
1560      LINE (1,1) - (5,5) , 1 , BF
1570      LINE (1,3) - (5,3) , 3
1580      LINE (3,1) - (3,5) , 3
1590      GET (1,1) - (5,5) , CURSOR1
1600 '
1610      LINE (1,1) - (5,5) , 2 , BF
1620      LINE (1,3) - (5,3) , 3
1630      LINE (3,1) - (3,5) , 3
1640      GET (1,1) - (5,5) , CURSOR2
1650 '
1660      LINE (1,1) - (5,5) , 3 , BF
1670      LINE (1,3) - (5,3) , 0
1680      LINE (3,1) - (3,5) , 0
1690      GET (1,1) - (5,5) , CURSOR3
1700 '
2000 ' --- INITIALIZE OTHER VARIABLES
2010      HUE = 1
2020      CLS
2030      PUT (158,98) , CURSOR1
2040      KEY OFF
2050      STRIG ON
2070 '
2080      RETURN
2090 '
2100 '
3000 ' --- SUBROUTINE TO CHANGE COLOR OF CURSOR
3010      FOR I = 1 TO 10
3020         TEMP.ARRAY(I) = CURSOR1(I)
3030         CURSOR1(I) = CURSOR2(I)
3040         CURSOR2(I) = CURSOR3(I)
3050         CURSOR3(I) = TEMP.ARRAY(I)
3060      NEXT I
3070      PUT (X.CURRENT-2,Y.CURRENT-2) , CURSOR3 , XOR
3080      PUT (X.CURRENT-2,Y.CURRENT-2) , CURSOR1 , XOR
3090      TEMP = STRIG(0)
3100      HUE = HUE + 1
3110      IF  HUE = 4  THEN LET HUE = 1
3120      LET X.OLD = X.CURRENT
3130      LET Y.OLD = Y.CURRENT
3140      RETURN
3150 '
3160 '
4000 ' --- DRAW A LINE ON THE SCREEN
4010      PUT (X.CURRENT-2,Y.CURRENT-2) , CURSOR1 , XOR
4020      LINE (X.OLD,Y.OLD) - (X.CURRENT,Y.CURRENT) , HUE
4030      PUT (X.CURRENT-2,Y.CURRENT-2) , CURSOR1 , XOR
4040      LET X.OLD = X.CURRENT
4050      LET Y.OLD = Y.CURRENT
4060      RETURN
```

4.8 GRAPHICS IN TEXT MODE—THE CHR$ AND STRING$ FUNCTIONS

There are sensible reasons for writing a program to do graphics using either the Monochrome Display Adapter or text mode on the Color/Graphics Monitor Adapter: (1) your program is going to run on a computer that has only a Monochrome Adapter; (2) your program needs to use more than four colors—whereas in graphics mode you can have only four, in text mode, you can have sixteen; and (3) your program's text output is more important than its graphics output, and you want the more readable lettering you get in text mode.

One sensible reason for not writing a program to do graphics either using the Monochrome Display Adapter or using text mode on the Color/Graphics Monitor Adapter is that many graphics things can't be done in text mode: for example, only horizontal and vertical lines are possible; items can be positioned in character spaces with the LOCATE statement but not at arbitrary x and y locations; and circles are out of the question.

At each text location on the screen, both the Monochrome and the Color/Graphics adapters can print upper- and lower-case letters, numbers, various symbols shown on the keys of the keyboard, and other characters that do not even appear on the keyboard. The available characters include horizontal and vertical line segments, corners, T intersections, and crossovers for single and double lines, characters that fill or partially fill the character space in several darknesses, dots, arrows, and various additional characters such as those for the four suits from a deck of cards, smiling faces, dots, arrows, and so on. Figure 4-26 contains most of these characters. A complete list is found in Appendix G of the IBM BASIC manual.

The CHR$ ("character") and STRING$ functions allow you to print any of these characters using the PRINT statement. In conjunction with the LOCATE statement discussed in Section 4.4, these two functions can display graphics images adequate for many programming purposes. Figure 4-26 and Appendix G of the IBM BASIC manual associate each character with an *ASCII value*. (*ASCII* stands for American Standard Code for Information Interchange. The ASCII codes for the letters, numbers, and other regular keyboard characters are relatively standard throughout the computer industry, but nothing whatsoever about the special characters under discussion is standard.) If you present an ASCII value to the CHR$ function in a PRINT statement, the character corresponding to that ASCII value will be printed on the screen. For example, since ASCII value 26 represents a right-pointing arrow, this program fragment prints a right-pointing arrow in the tenth space of the tenth row of the screen:

```
10 LOCATE 10,10
20 PRINT CHR$(26)
```

If you present a number and an ASCII value to the STRING$ function in a PRINT statement, the character corresponding to that ASCII value will be printed on the screen as many times as the number indicates. For example, since ASCII value 127 represents a house, this program fragment prints a row of thirteen houses starting in the tenth space of the tenth row of the screen and extending to the right from there:

```
10 LOCATE 10,10
20 PRINT STRING$(13,127)
```

Fig. 4-26 Special Characters Available in Text Mode

The following table summarizes most of the special characters useful for graphics on the IBM Personal Computer and gives the ASCII values for each. In addition to the characters listed here, the IBM Personal Computer can also draw some of the Greek letters, letters with umlauts and accents, a cent sign, a pound sign, the dipthong ae, an inverted question mark, the fractions 1/2 and 1/4, and certain other characters more reminiscent of text than of graphics.

DESCRIPTION	DRAWING	ASCII VALUE
Single Lines		
Horizontal	—	196
Vertical			179
Corners	¬	191
	⌐	218
	∟	192
	⌐	217

continued on p. 140

continued from p. 139

T Intersections	├	195
	┴	193
	┤	180
	┬	194
Cross	┼	197
Double Lines		
Horizontal	═	205
Vertical	║	186
Corners	╗	187
	╔	201
	╚	200
	╝	188
T Intersections	╠	204
	╩	202
	╣	185
	╦	203
Cross	╬	206
Single/Double Mixed Symbols		
Corners	╕	184
	╓	214

continued on p. 141

continued from p. 140

	⊫	212
	⊐⊔	189
	⊐	183
	⊨	213
	⊪	211
	⊒	190
T Intersection with Single Stem/Double Cross Bar	⊩	199
	⊥	207
	⊣	182
	⊤	209
T Intersection with Double Stem/Single Cross Bar	⊨	198
	⊥	208
	⊣	181
	⊤	210
Single/Double Crossovers	⧻	215
	⧾	216
Area-Filling Characters		
Full-Character Space	■	219

continued on p. 142

continued from p. 141

Left Half	▮	221
Right Half	▮	222
Top Half	▬	223
Bottom Half	▬	220
Lower Left Quadrant	▪	254
Lower Left Quadrant with Hole	▫	8
Bottom Quarter	▬	22

Shading

Darkest Shading	■	219
Medium Dark	▓	178
Medium Light	▒	177
Lightest Shading	░	176
No Shading (blank)		32

Dots

Small (centered)	·	250
Medium (centered)	•	249
Medium with Hole (at top of space)	°	248

Arrows

Right-Pointing	→	26
Left-Pointing	←	27

continued on p. 143

continued from p. 142

Upward-Pointing	↑	24
Downward-Pointing	↓	25
Right-Pointing Arrowhead with no shaft	►	16
Left-Pointing Arrowhead with no shaft	◄	17
Double arrow pointing up and down	↕	18
Double arrow pointing up and down with bar beneath	↨	23

Special Characters

Clubs	♣	5
Spades	♠	6
Hearts	♥	3
Diamonds	♦	4
Smiling face	☺	1
Negative smiling face	☻	2
Musical note	♫	14
Sun	☼	15
House	⌂	127

The program in Fig. 4-27 fills most of the screen with smiling faces. Statement 180 sets the value of the variable FACE to either 1 or 2. The ASCII value 1 corresponds to a smiling face made of bright pixels on a dark background and the ASCII value 2 corresponds to a smiling face made of dark pixels on a bright background. Statement 200 prints whichever of these two characters was chosen at statement 180. The nested loops therefore result in a screenful of smiling faces. Note that this program expects the screen to be 80 characters wide, as it is if you are using the Monochrome Display Adapter. If you are using text mode on the Color/Graphics Monitor Adapter, you must change statement 170 to

170 FOR X.LOCATE = 2 TO 39

Fig. 4-27   Program to Fill the Screen with Smiling Faces

```
100   ' --- PROGRAM TO DRAW A POPULATION OF SMILING FACES
110   '
120   '
130       CLS
140       KEY OFF
150   '
160       FOR Y.LOCATE = 2 TO 20
170          FOR X.LOCATE = 2 TO 79
180             FACE = INT(1.3*RND(1)) + 1
190             LOCATE Y.LOCATE,X.LOCATE
200             PRINT CHR$(FACE) ;
210          NEXT X.LOCATE
220       NEXT Y.LOCATE
230   '
240       END
```

Screen Display from Above Program

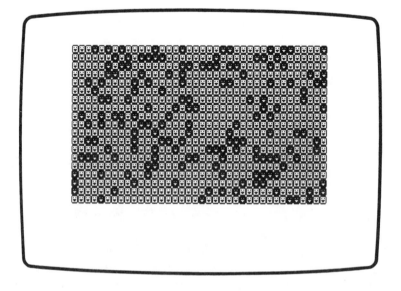

The program in Fig. 4-28 displays a "sunset" on the screen by printing one row each of the characters whose ASCII values are 176, 177, 178, and 219—the four shading characters. This program can also be made to run on the Color/Graphics Monitor Adapter, but it looks better on the monochrome display.

Fig. 4-28   Program to Draw a Sunset

```
100   ' --- PROGRAM TO DRAW A SUNSET
110   '
120   '
130       CLS
140       KEY OFF
150   '
160       FOR Y.LOCATE = 16 TO 19
170           SHADE = Y.LOCATE + 160
180           IF  SHADE = 179  THEN LET SHADE = 219
190           LOCATE Y.LOCATE,2
200           PRINT STRING$(78,SHADE)
210       NEXT Y.LOCATE
220   '
230       END
```

The program fragment in Fig. 4-29 displays the IBM title screen—slightly modified—that comes up at the beginning of each IBM sample program. (This program fragment has been left off the versions of the IBM sample programs discussed in this book.) Some of the line drawing characters are used in this program fragment to draw a box around the letters printed in the title. See Color Plate 5 for the output from this program.

"Music"

The program in Fig. 4-30 is the IBM sample program "Music" (with most of the DATA statements left off this time—they haven't changed since Section 4.5). This version draws the screen display as does the original program. The white keys are drawn first in statements 1210 to 1230. Each consists of a filled character space, CHR$(219), and a space whose left half is filled, CHR$(221). See Fig. 4-31. After the white keys are drawn, the black keys are drawn on top of them by statements 1240 to 1270. Each consists of a blank, CHR$(32), and a space whose left half is blank and whose right half is filled, CHR$(222). Statements 1272 to 1350 draw an outline around the entire keyboard.

Fig. 4-29   IBM Sample Title Screen

```
1000 ' --- PROGRAM TO PRINT TITLE SCREEN
1001 '
1002 '
1003 '
1010        KEY OFF
1020        SCREEN 0,1
1030        COLOR 15,0,0
1040        WIDTH 40
1050        CLS
1055 '
1060        LOCATE 5,19
1070        PRINT "IBM"
1080        LOCATE 7,12,0 : PRINT "Personal Computer"
1084 '
1085        COLOR 10,0
1090        LOCATE 10,9,0
1110        PRINT CHR$(213)+     STRING$(21,205)     +CHR$(184)
1120        LOCATE 11,9,0
1130        PRINT CHR$(179)+"     NEW   EXAMPLE     "+CHR$(179)
1140        LOCATE 12,9,0
1150        PRINT CHR$(179)+     STRING$(21,32)     +CHR$(179)
1160        LOCATE 13,9,0
1170        PRINT CHR$(179)+"     Version 1.10     "+CHR$(179)
1180        LOCATE 14,9,0
1190        PRINT CHR$(212)+     STRING$(21,205)     +CHR$(190)
1199 '
1200        COLOR 15,0
1210        LOCATE 17,4,0
1220        PRINT "(C) Copyright David E. Simon 1983
1229 '
1230        COLOR 14,0
1240        LOCATE 23,9,0
1250        PRINT "Press space bar to quit"
1259 '
1260        IF INKEY$<>"" THEN GOTO 1260
1270            CMD$ = INKEY$
1275 '
1280            IF CMD$ = " " THEN CLS : END
1285 '
1290        GOTO 1260
```

Whenever the computer plays a note, statement 1560 determines whether that note is on the piano keyboard displayed on the screen. If it is, then the column number in which the note should be printed on the screen is found by statement 1550 from the array X.KEY. The array X.KEY is initialized in statements 1390 to 1470 just for this purpose. The computer next determines whether this note is a white key or a black key by examining the character on the screen in row 5 at the column number found in statement 1550. The SCREEN function returns the ASCII value of whatever character is on the screen at the location sent to it. If this character is a blank, then the note being played is a black key and should print in row 7; otherwise, the note being played is a white key and should print in row 11. See Fig. 4-31. After the tone is played, similar logic in statements 1600 to 1625 erases the note by replacing it either with a filled space for a white key or a blank for a black key.

Miscellaneous Observations

1. Characters on the Monochrome Adapter differ subtly from those on the Color/Graphics Adapter. One general difference is that there is less space between characters when you are using the Color/Graphics Adapter rather than the Monochrome Adapter. For example, a small space appears between adjacent characters whose ASCII values are 176, 177, and 178 on the Monochrome Adapter, but these characters are flush against one another with the Color/Graphics Adapter.

2. In graphics modes, characters with ASCII values of 128 or greater do not work properly. Some of them print peculiar patterns of dots on the screen; some of them print nothing. Characters with ASCII values of 0 to 127 work fine in both text and graphics modes.

Further Examples

You might review the IBM sample program "Colorbar," which was introduced in Section 4.1 but not discussed completely. That program uses the CHR$ function to print blocks of color in text mode.

The program in Section 5.2, the "Worm" game, also uses graphics in text mode.

Fig. 4-30   IBM Sample Program "Music" with Screen Display

```
1000 ' --- IBM 'MUSIC' PROGRAM
1010 '
1020 '
1030 ' --- PRINT THE SCREEN
1150      SCREEN 0,1:WIDTH 40:COLOR 15,1,1:CLS:DEFINT A-Z
1160      LOCATE 15,7,0:PRINT " ------- selections -------"
1170      LOCATE 16,7:PRINT " A-MARCH   E-HUMOR   I-SAKURA"
1180      LOCATE 17,7:PRINT " B-STARS   F-BUG     J-BLUE   "
1190      LOCATE 18,7:PRINT " C-FORTY   G-POP     K-SCALES"
1191      LOCATE 19,7:PRINT " D-HAT     H-DANDY   ESC KEY-EXIT"
1200      COLOR 15,0
1201 '
1202 ' --- PRINT THE WHITE KEYS
1210      FOR PIANO.KEY = 0 TO 15
1215 '        --- PRINT EACH KEY
1216         FOR Y = 5 TO 13
1220            LOCATE Y , PIANO.KEY*2 + 5 :
                   PRINT CHR$(219);CHR$(221);
1225         NEXT Y
1230      NEXT PIANO.KEY
1231 '
1232 ' --- PRINT THE BLACK KEYS
1240      FOR PIANO.KEY = 0 TO 12
1245         FOR Y = 5 TO 9
1250            IF PIANO.KEY=2 OR PIANO.KEY=6 OR PIANO.KEY=9
                   THEN 1270
1260               LOCATE Y,PIANO.KEY*2 + 8 :
                      PRINT CHR$(32);CHR$(222);
1265         NEXT Y
1270      NEXT PIANO.KEY
1271 '
1272 ' --- OUTLINE THE KEYBOARD
1280      FOR Y=5 TO 13
1290         LOCATE Y,4  : COLOR 4,0 : PRINT CHR$(221);
1300         LOCATE Y,37 : COLOR 4,1 : PRINT CHR$(221);
1310      NEXT Y
1320      COLOR 4,1 : TEMP$ = STRING$(33,219) + CHR$(221)
1330      LOCATE 4,4  : PRINT TEMP$
1350      LOCATE 13,4 : PRINT TEMP$
1360      COLOR 0,7
1363 '
1364 ' --- SET UP THE FREQUENCIES FOR THE SOUND STATEMENT
1365      DIM FREQ(88),X.KEY(78)
1366      FOR I = 0 TO 6
1367         FREQ(I) = 32767
1368      NEXT I
1369      FOR I = 7 TO 88
1370         FREQ(I) =   36.8*(2^(1/12))^(I-6)
1371      NEXT I
```

continued on p. 149

continued from p. 148

```
1380 '
1381 ' --- SET UP THE X COORDINATES OF THE KEYS ON THE KEYBOARD
1390      X.KEY(0) = 0
1400      X.KEY(39)=5 :X.KEY(40)=7 :X.KEY(41)=8 :X.KEY(42)=9
1410      X.KEY(43)=10:X.KEY(44)=11:X.KEY(45)=13:X.KEY(46)=14
1420      X.KEY(47)=15:X.KEY(48)=16:X.KEY(49)=17:X.KEY(50)=18
1430      X.KEY(51)=19:X.KEY(52)=21:X.KEY(53)=22:X.KEY(54)=23
1440      X.KEY(55)=24:X.KEY(56)=25:X.KEY(57)=27:X.KEY(58)=28
1450      X.KEY(59)=29:X.KEY(60)=30:X.KEY(61)=31:X.KEY(62)=32
1460      X.KEY(63)=33:X.KEY(64)=35:X.KEY(65)=36:X.KEY(66)=37
1470      X.KEY(67)=38:X.KEY(68)=39:X.KEY(69)=40:X.KEY(70)=42
1480      GOTO 1630
1488 '
1489 ' --- SUBROUTINE TO PLAY ONE TUNE
1490         READ J,K
1539 '
1540         IF J = -1   THEN RETURN
1541 '
1550         X.THIS.KEY = X.KEY(J)
1560         IF J>64 OR J<39 THEN 1590
1561 '          --- NOTE IS ON SCREEN.  SHOW IT ON KEYBOARD
1570           IF SCREEN(5,X.THIS.KEY)=32 GOTO 1580
1571 '             --- THIS IS A WHITE KEY
1572              COLOR 0,7
1573              LOCATE 11,X.THIS.KEY
1574              PRINT CHR$(14);
1575              COLOR 15,0
1576              GOTO 1589
1580 '
1581 '             --- THIS IS A BLACK KEY
1582              COLOR 15,0
1583              LOCATE 7,X.THIS.KEY
1584              PRINT CHR$(14) ;
1585              COLOR 0,7
1586              GOTO 1589
1589 '          ---
1590         SOUND FREQ(J),K
1595         IF  J <> 0 OR K <> 1   THEN SOUND 32767,1
1600         IF J>64 OR J<39 THEN 1626
1601 '          --- NOTE IS ON SCREEN.  ERASE IT FROM KEYBOARD
1610           IF SCREEN(5,X.THIS.KEY) <> 32 GOTO 1620
1611 '             --- ERASE FROM A BLACK KEY
1612              COLOR 15,0
1613              LOCATE 7,X.THIS.KEY
1614              PRINT CHR$(32) ;
1615              GOTO 1626
1620 '          ---
1621 '             --- ERASE FROM A WHITE KEY
1622              COLOR 15,0
1623              LOCATE 11,X.THIS.KEY
1624              PRINT CHR$(219) ;
1625              GOTO 1626
1626      GOTO 1490
```

continued on p. 150

continued from p. 149

```
1627 '
1628 ' --- LOOP TO GET A SELECTION OF A TUNE AND PLAY IT
1630           LOCATE 21,5 : PRINT "                              ";
1640           LOCATE 21,5 : PRINT "ENTER SELECTION ==>";
1650 '         --- LOOP TO GET VALID SELECTION
1660             SL$=INKEY$
1670           IF SL$ = CHR$(27)   THEN 1850
1680           IF SL$="A" OR SL$="a" THEN S$="MARCH ":
                    RESTORE 4000:GOTO 1770
1690           IF SL$="B" OR SL$="b" THEN S$="STARS ":
                    RESTORE 4100:GOTO 1770
1700           IF SL$="C" OR SL$="c" THEN S$="FORTY ":
                    RESTORE 3700:GOTO 1770
1710           IF SL$="D" OR SL$="d" THEN S$="HAT   ":
                    RESTORE 4300:GOTO 1770
1720           IF SL$="E" OR SL$="e" THEN S$="HUMOR ":
                    RESTORE 3500:GOTO 1770
1730           IF SL$="F" OR SL$="f" THEN S$="BUG   ":
                    RESTORE 3200:GOTO 1770
1740           IF SL$="G" OR SL$="g" THEN S$="POP   ":
                    RESTORE 3600:GOTO 1770
1750           IF SL$="H" OR SL$="h" THEN S$="DANDY ":
                    RESTORE 3900:GOTO 1770
1755           IF SL$="I" OR SL$="i" THEN S$="SAKURA":
                    RESTORE 4500:GOTO 1770
1757           IF SL$="J" OR SL$="j" THEN S$="BLUE  ":
                    RESTORE 3300:GOTO 1770
1761           IF SL$="K" OR SL$="k" THEN S$="SCALES":
                    RESTORE 4400:GOTO 1770
1769         GOTO 1650
1770         PRINT " ";SL$;"-";S$
1780         READ D
1800         READ S$ : LOCATE 23,1+(40.5-LEN(S$))/2
1805         COLOR 15,4 : PRINT S$; : COLOR 0,7
1810         GOSUB 1490
1820         S$=STRING$(39," ") : LOCATE 23,1 : COLOR 4,1 :
                    PRINT S$ : COLOR 0,7
1830         GOTO 1630
1840         END
1845 '
1850 ' --- EXIT FROM PROGRAM
1860       SCREEN 0,1 : COLOR 7,0,0 : CLS : WIDTH 80 : END
2998 '
2999 '
3000 ' --- The IBM Personal Computer Music Scroll
3010 ' --- Version 1.00 (C)Copyright IBM Corp 1981
3020 ' --- Licensed Material - Program Property of IBM
```

Here follow all of the DATA statements, which we shall not repeat.

Fig. 4-31 Piano Keyboard Drawn by the Sample Program "Music"

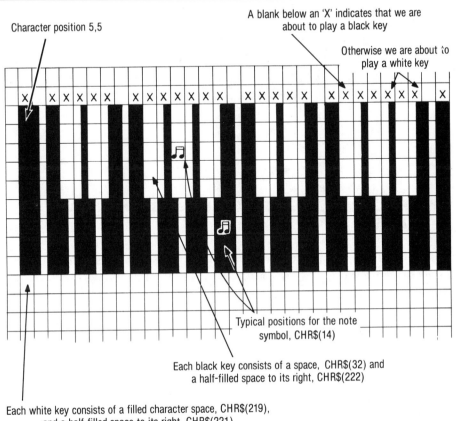

Character position 5,5

A blank below an 'X' indicates that we are about to play a black key

Otherwise we are about to play a white key

Typical positions for the note symbol, CHR$(14)

Each black key consists of a space, CHR$(32) and a half-filled space to its right, CHR$(222)

Each white key consists of a filled character space, CHR$(219), and a half-filled space to its right, CHR$(221)

5 Recreational Applications and Games

5.1 PROGRAMMING ACTION GAMES: THE ERASE GAME

Programs to play action games involve three new considerations. First, since such games depend on your reactions to what is going on, computing speed is important. The tempo of the game makes for the fun and challenge. Second, you can spice up the games considerably with appropriate sounds, and since the IBM Personal Computer can do far more than just beep, you can put it to work. Third, the computer must not only keep the action going continuously but must also simultaneously monitor your input and take it into account. In other words, the computer must keep track of the action in the game and of your reaction to it as well.

Erase

The program in Fig. 5.1 plays the game of Erase, whose title will become clear momentarily. When the game starts, the playing area on the screen is entirely white; your goal is to color as much of it magenta as possible before your time limit expires. During the game, three small squares move around the playing area. One is the erase square. Wherever this square goes, the playing area changes to black. The second square is white. Wherever it passes, the playing area turns to white. The third square is magenta. It can turn black areas to magenta, but it cannot change white areas. The white square always moves randomly about the playing area. You can control the motion of either the erase square or the magenta square. Whichever one you are not controlling moves randomly about the playing area. At any time, you may change which of the two you control.

Fig. 5-1 Program to Play the Erase Game

```
1000 ' --- PROGRAM TO PLAY THE ERASE GAME
1010 '
1020 '
1030 ' --- DIMENSION THE ARRAYS
1040       DIM ERASE.SQ(70),BAD.SQ(70),GOOD.SQ(70),SHOW.SQ(70)
1050       GOSUB 8010
1060 '
1070 '
1080 ' --- INITIALIZE THE THREE SQUARES ON THE SCREEN
1090       LINE (67,75)-(74,82),2,BF
1100       LINE (67,91)-(74,98),3,BF
1110       LINE (67,107)-(74,114),1,B
1120 '
1130 ' --- GET THE SQUARES INTO ARRAYS
1140       GET (67,52)-(74,59),ERASE.SQ
1150       GET (67,91)-(74,98),BAD.SQ
1160       GET (67,75)-(74,82),GOOD.SQ
1170       GET (67,107)-(74,114),SHOW.SQ
1180 '
1190 ' --- INITIALIZE THE PLAYING FIELD
1200       LINE(50,50)-(251,147),1,B
1210       PAINT (0,0),1,1
1220       LINE (51,51)-(250,146),3,BF
1230       LOCATE 3,4
1240       PRINT "TIME   SCORE    CONTROLLING"
1250       LOCATE 4,10
1260       PRINT "   O "
1270       PUT (67,107),ERASE.SQ,PSET
1280 '
2000 ' --- INITIALIZE VARIABLES
2010       SPEED = 8
2020       TEMP = VAL(RIGHT$(TIME$,2))
2030       RANDOMIZE TEMP
2040       GOOD.X = 67
2050       GOOD.Y = 75
2060       BAD.X = 67
2070       BAD.Y = 91
2080       CHANGEDIRC = .25
2090       ERS.X = 67
2100       ERS.Y = 107
2110       CYCLES = 300
2120       LET CNTRL.SQ$ = "ERASE"
2130       LET GOOD.DIRC = 0
2140       LET BAD.DIRC = 0
2150       LET ERS.DIRC = 0
2160       LET CNTRL.DIRC = 0
2170       PUT (176,26),ERASE.SQ,PSET
2180
2190       ON KEY(9) GOSUB 6600
2210       ON KEY(11) GOSUB 6100
2220       ON KEY(12) GOSUB 6200
2230       ON KEY(13) GOSUB 6300
2240       ON KEY(14) GOSUB 6400
2250       KEY (9) ON
2270       KEY (11) ON
2280       KEY (12) ON
2290       KEY (13) ON
2300       KEY (14) ON
```

continued on p. 154

continued from p. 153

```
2310 '
2320 '
3000 ' --- LOOP TO PLAY THE GAME
3010 '
3020 '          --- SET DIRECTION OF CONTROLLED SQUARE
3030          IF  CNTRL.SQ$ = "ERASE"  GOTO 3060
3040             GOOD.DIRC = CNTRL.DIRC
3050             GOTO 3090
3060 '          ---
3070             ERS.DIRC = CNTRL.DIRC
3080             GOTO 3090
3090 '          ---
3100          RANDOM = RND
3110          IF RANDOM > CHANGEDIRC GOTO 3210
3120 '          --- CHANGE DIRECTION OF GOOD OR ERASE,
3130 '          WHICHEVER IS CURRENTLY NOT CONTROLLED BY PLAYER
3140             IF  CNTRL.SQ$ = "ERASE"  GOTO 3170
3150                ERS.DIRC = (793*RANDOM) MOD 4
3160                GOTO 3200
3170 '             ---
3180                GOOD.DIRC = (793*RANDOM) MOD 4
3190                GOTO 3200
3200 '
3210          IF RANDOM < 1-CHANGEDIRC GOTO 3240
3220 '          --- CHANGE DIRECTION OF BAD
3230             BAD.DIRC = (427*RANDOM) MOD 4
3240          KEY (11) ON
3250          KEY (12) ON
3260          KEY (13) ON
3270          KEY (14) ON
3300          ON GOOD.DIRC+1 GOTO 3310,3350,3390,3430
3310             GOOD.X = GOOD.X + SPEED
3320             IF GOOD.X > 245 THEN  GOOD.X = GOOD.X - SPEED :
                    GOOD.DIRC = 3
3330             IF GOOD.X=ERS.X AND GOOD.Y=ERS.Y THEN
                    GOOD.X = GOOD.X-SPEED
3340             GOTO 3500
3350             GOOD.Y = GOOD.Y + SPEED
3360             IF GOOD.Y > 145 THEN  GOOD.Y = GOOD.Y - SPEED :
                    GOOD.DIRC = 0
3370             IF GOOD.X=ERS.X AND GOOD.Y=ERS.Y THEN
                    GOOD.Y = GOOD.Y-SPEED
3380             GOTO 3500
3390             GOOD.X = GOOD.X - SPEED
3400             IF GOOD.X < 51  THEN  GOOD.X = GOOD.X + SPEED :
                    GOOD.DIRC = 1
3410             IF GOOD.X=ERS.X AND GOOD.Y=ERS.Y THEN
                    GOOD.X = GOOD.X+SPEED
3420             GOTO 3500
3430             GOOD.Y = GOOD.Y - SPEED
3440             IF GOOD.Y < 51  THEN  GOOD.Y = GOOD.Y + SPEED :
                    GOOD.DIRC = 2
3450             IF GOOD.X=ERS.X AND GOOD.Y=ERS.Y THEN
                    GOOD.Y = GOOD.Y+SPEED
3460             GOTO 3500
```

continued on p. 155

continued from p. 154

```
3470  '
3500          ON BAD.DIRC+1 GOTO 3510,3550,3590,3630
3510          BAD.X = BAD.X + SPEED
3520          IF BAD.X > 245 THEN  BAD.X = BAD.X - SPEED :
                    BAD.DIRC = 3
3530          IF BAD.X=ERS.X AND BAD.Y=ERS.Y THEN
                    BAD.X = BAD.X-SPEED
3540          GOTO 3670
3550          BAD.Y = BAD.Y + SPEED
3560          IF BAD.Y > 145 THEN  BAD.Y = BAD.Y - SPEED :
                    BAD.DIRC = 0
3570          IF BAD.X=ERS.X AND BAD.Y=ERS.Y THEN
                    BAD.Y = BAD.Y-SPEED
3580          GOTO 3670
3590          BAD.X = BAD.X - SPEED
3600          IF BAD.X < 51  THEN  BAD.X = BAD.X + SPEED  :
                    BAD.DIRC = 1
3610          IF BAD.X=ERS.X AND BAD.Y=ERS.Y THEN
                    BAD.X = BAD.X+SPEED
3620          GOTO 3670
3630          BAD.Y = BAD.Y - SPEED
3640          IF BAD.Y < 51  THEN  BAD.Y = BAD.Y + SPEED  :
                    BAD.DIRC = 2
3650          IF BAD.X=ERS.X AND BAD.Y=ERS.Y THEN
                    BAD.Y = BAD.Y+SPEED
3660          GOTO 3670
3670  '
3700          ON ERS.DIRC+1 GOTO 3710,3740,3770,3800
3710          ERS.X = ERS.X + SPEED
3720          IF ERS.X > 245 THEN  ERS.X = ERS.X - SPEED :
                    ERS.DIRC = 3
3730          GOTO 3830
3740          ERS.Y = ERS.Y + SPEED
3750          IF ERS.Y > 145 THEN  ERS.Y = ERS.Y - SPEED :
                    ERS.DIRC = 0
3760          GOTO 3830
3770          ERS.X = ERS.X - SPEED
3780          IF ERS.X < 51  THEN  ERS.X = ERS.X + SPEED  :
                    ERS.DIRC = 1
3790          GOTO 3830
3800          ERS.Y = ERS.Y - SPEED
3810          IF ERS.Y < 51  THEN  ERS.Y = ERS.Y + SPEED  :
                    ERS.DIRC = 2
3820          GOTO 3830
```

continued on p. 156

continued from p. 155

```
3830 '
4000 '      --- PUT NEW ITEM ON SCREEN
4010        PUT (GOOD.X,GOOD.Y),GOOD.SQ,XOR
4020        PUT (BAD.X,BAD.Y),BAD.SQ,XOR
4030        PUT (ERS.X,ERS.Y),SHOW.SQ,PSET
4040        FOR DELAY = 1 TO 10
4050        NEXT DELAY
4060        PUT (GOOD.X,GOOD.Y),GOOD.SQ,XOR
4070        PUT (GOOD.X,GOOD.Y),GOOD.SQ,OR
4080        PUT (BAD.X,BAD.Y),BAD.SQ,PSET
4090        PUT (ERS.X,ERS.Y),ERASE.SQ,PSET
4100        CYCLES = CYCLES - 1
4110        LET NOTE = 880
4120        IF  CYCLES < 60  THEN  LET NOTE = 440
4130        SOUND NOTE,1
4140        LOCATE 4,4
4150        PRINT USING "####" ; CYCLES
4160        IF CYCLES > 0 GOTO 3000
4170 '
4180 '
4190 '
5000 ' --- LOOP TO SCORE GAME
5010        PLAY "L32"
5020        FOR X = 51 TO 243 STEP 8
5030          FOR Y = 51 TO 149 STEP 8
5040            IF  POINT(X,Y) = 2  THEN  SCORE = SCORE + 16
5050          NEXT Y
5060          LOCATE 4,10
5070          PRINT SCORE
5080          LINE (X,43)-(X,50),2
5090          LET NOTE = X/8 + 30
5100          PLAY "N=NOTE;"
5110        NEXT X
5120        GOSUB 8110
5130        END
5140 '
6100 ' --- HANDLE UP ARROW KEY
6105        GOSUB 6800
6110        CNTRL.DIRC = 3
6120        RETURN
6130 '
6140 '
6200 ' --- HANDLE LEFT ARROW KEY
6205        GOSUB 6800
6210        CNTRL.DIRC = 2
6220        RETURN
6230 '
6240 '
6300 ' --- HANDLE RIGHT ARROW KEY
6305        GOSUB 6800
6310        CNTRL.DIRC = 0
6320        RETURN
```

continued on p. 157

continued from p. 156

```
6330 '
6340 '
6400 ' --- HANDLE DOWN ARROW KEY
6405       GOSUB 6800
6410       CNTRL.DIRC = 1
6420       RETURN
6430 '
6440 '
6600 ' --- HANDLE F9 KEY (CHANGE WHICH SQUARE IS CONTROLLED)
6610       IF  CNTRL.SQ$ = "ERASE"   GOTO 6660
6620          CNTRL.SQ$ = "ERASE"
6630          PUT (176,26),ERASE.SQ,PSET
6640          CNTRL.DIRC = ERS.DIRC
6650          GOTO 6710
6660 '     ---
6670          CNTRL.SQ$ = "GOOD"
6680          PUT (176,26),GOOD.SQ,PSET
6690          CNTRL.DIRC = GOOD.DIRC
6700          GOTO 6710
6710       RETURN
6720 '
6730 '
6800 ' --- DISABLE KEYS FOR ONE CYCLE
6810       KEY (11) STOP
6820       KEY (12) STOP
6830       KEY (13) STOP
6840       KEY (14) STOP
6850       RETURN
6860 '
6870 '
6880 '
8000 ' --- CHANGE SCREENS TO GRAPHIC
8010       DEF SEG = 0
8020       POKE &H410, (PEEK(&H410) AND &HCF) OR &H10
8030       SCREEN 1,0,0,0
8040       SCREEN 0
8050       SCREEN 1,0,0,0
8060       WIDTH 40
8070       RETURN
8080 '
8090 '
8100 ' --- CHANGE SCREENS BACK TO MONOCHROME
8110       DEF SEG = 0
8120       POKE &H410, (PEEK(&H410) OR &H30)
8130       SCREEN 0
8140       WIDTH 40
8150       WIDTH 80
8160       RETURN
```

Figure 5-2 shows how the screen might look during the game. The time entry starts at 300 and counts down to 0, at which point the game ends. Afterward, the computer counts up the magenta area on the screen and prints the score in the appropriate space. Under the word "CONTROL" the computer maintains either a black or a magenta square, depending on whether the player is currently controlling the erase square or the magenta square.

When the game first starts, you control the erase square. Whenever you press one of the arrow keys at the right-hand side of the keyboard, the erase square begins to move in that direction and continues in that direction until you press another of the arrow keys. You use the erase square to erase some of the white in the playing area to allow the magenta square later to color that area magenta. Meanwhile, the magenta square moves randomly. It does nothing to the white areas when it traverses them, but when it wanders into an area that you have turned black with the erase square, it turns that area magenta, and you score points. All this time, the white square roams the playing area turning everything it touches back to white.

Fig. 5-2 Screen Appearance during Erase

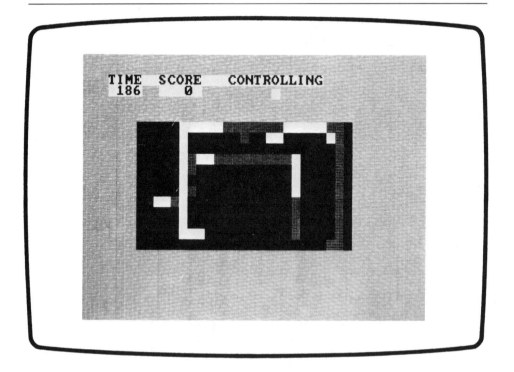

When some of the playing area is black, you may want to steer the magenta square into the black area in order to turn it magenta. You get control of the magenta square by pressing the F9 key at the lower left-hand corner of the keyboard. After you do this, the four arrow keys will change the direction of the magenta square. As you steer the magenta square into areas you have previously erased, they turn magenta, scoring points for you. Meanwhile, the erase square roams the screen, erasing both white and magenta areas. As before, the white square still roams randomly, covering up black and magenta areas indiscriminately.

To again take control of the erase square, you press the F9 key again, after which the magenta square wanders freely and you control the erase square.

Here are some other miscellaneous facts about the game:

1. If a randomly moving square hits the edge of the playing area, it turns left and moves along the edge. If the square you control hits the edge, it stays put until you change its direction with an arrow key.

2. When the erase square traverses ground that is already black, it flashes momentarily as a black square with a blue outline, so that you can see it. Similarly, when the magenta square is in white territory, it appears briefly as a blue square, and the white square in white territory appears briefly black.

3. The game emits a high-pitched beep after every game cycle. When only 60 cycles remain, the pitch drops lower. While the computer is scoring the game, it plays a series of rising beeps that form a chromatic scale.

How the Program Works

Try not to panic. The complexity of the program in Fig. 5-1 is less than its length, and we shall discuss how it works in detail. Figure 5-3 shows coordinates of points that are important in the Erase game program. Refer to it as necessary. Figure 5-4 explains the uses of the variables in the program, from which you can figure out a fair amount about how the program works. Refer to that, also. The sections of the program are as follows:

Function	Statement Numbers
Initialization	1000–2300
Determine Direction to Move Squares	3000–3230
Calculate New Locations of Squares	3300–3820
Draw New Squares	4000–4090
Score the Game	5000–5130
Handle Player Input of Arrow Keys	6000–6710
Change Screens	8000–8160

Fig. 5-3 Screen Coordinates Used in Erase

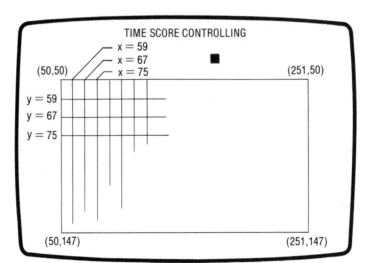

Fig. 5-4 Variables in the Erase Game

This figure describes the uses of the significant variables in the Erase game program, in order of appearance. Variables not in this list are used only to store a value of immediate interest in a short piece of the code.

ERASE.SQ stores the image of the erase square in an array for use with the PUT statement. The array is loaded at statement 1140 and is used during the game to turn square sections of the screen black at statement 4090.

BAD.SQ stores the image of the white square in the same way as ERASE.SQ stores the erase square. It is set at statement 1150 and is used in statements 4080 and 4020.

GOOD.SQ stores the image of the magenta square. It is set at statement 1160 and used in statements 4010, 4060, and 4070.

SHOW.SQ stores the image of a black square with a blue outline. It is set at statement 1170 and used at statement 4030.

SPEED is the distance that each of the three squares moves at each cycle. It is set to the value 8 at statement 2010 and never changes. It is used frequently in the statements from 3300 to 3820, which determine the new locations for the squares at each cycle.

GOOD.X and GOOD.Y are the screen coordinates of the upper left-hand corner of the magenta square. They are initialized in the statements following statement 2000; they are reset in the statements following statement 3300, which calculates a new location for the magenta square; and they are used in the statements following statement 4000, which draw the new squares on the screen.

continued on p. 161

continued from p. 160

BAD.X and BAD.Y are the screen coordinates of the upper left-hand corner of the white square. They are set and used similarly to GOOD.X and GOOD.Y.

ERS.X and ERS.Y are the screen coordinates of the upper left-hand corner of the erase square. They are set and used similarly to GOOD.X and GOOD.Y.

CHANGEDIRC is the probability that one of the randomly moving squares changes the direction of its travel. It is set to 0.25 at statement 2080 and is never changed. It is used at statements 3110 and 3210 to decide whether or not to change the directions of the squares.

CYCLES is the number of remaining game cycles. During each cycle, each square moves once. CYCLES is set to 300 at statement 2110. It is decremented at statement 4100, and when it reaches 0, statement 4160 ends the game.

CNTRL.SQ$ keeps track of which of the two squares—the erase square and the magenta square—you are controlling. This string has one of the values ERASE and GOOD. It is initialized to ERASE following statement 2000, and it is toggled between its two legal values in the subroutine following statement 6600. It is used at statements 3030 and 3140 to determine which of the two squares you are controlling and which the computer is moving randomly.

GOOD.DIRC, BAD.DIRC, and ERS.DIRC control the direction that these three squares are moving (regardless of which square you are controlling). They are initialized to 0 at statements 2130, 2140, and 2150, and they are reset either randomly or under your control in the statements between 3000 and 3300. The values of these variables correspond to directions as shown in this table:

Value	Direction
0	Right
1	Up
2	Left
3	Down
4	Stopped

Direction 4 occurs only when the square you control bumps into the edge of the playing area.

CNTRL.DIRC represents the direction that you want the square you are controlling to move. It is initialized to 0 at the beginning of the program, and it is reset in the subroutines at statements 6100, 6200, 6300, and 6400 whenever you press one of the arrow keys. The values this variable may have are identical to those for GOOD.DIRC, BAD.DIRC, and ERS.DIRC. CNTRL.DIRC is used in the statements between 3000 and 3300 to set GOOD.DIRC or ERS.DIRC, whichever corresponds to the direction of the square you are controlling.

NOTE is the tone to play. It is set at statements 4110 and 4120 to be used at statement 4130. Its value is the frequency of the tone to play. It is also set at statement 5090 for use at statement 5100. In this case, its value is the note number to play.

SCORE is your score.

In the initialization section, the program sets up the arrays it uses later to draw on the screen, prepares the screen for the game, and initializes its variables. The statement GOSUB 8010 at line 1050 changes to the graphics screen—if the system is not already using the graphics screen—and clears it. (This could be replaced by a CLS statement if you do not need to change screens.) Statements 1090 to 1110 draw three squares—white, magenta, and black with blue boundary—and the GET statements at 1150, 1160, and 1170 store them in the arrays BAD.SQ, GOOD.SQ, and SHOW.SQ. Statement 1140, which gets the erase square in ERASE.SQ, grabs a blank area of the screen to make up a black square. The array SHOW.SQ is used to let the player know where the erase square is when it is traversing black territory. During play, the PUT statement and these arrays color areas on the screen.

The statements from line 1200 to line 1270 draw the playing area on the screen. Statements 2000 to 2170 initialize the variables needed during the course of the game. Glance at Fig. 5-4, which tells what the variables represent, to understand this. Statements 2190 to 2300 activate the arrow keys and the F9 key, with which you control the progress of the game. These statements are explained below in the discussion of event trapping.

The loop to play the game, which starts at statement 3000, is executed 300 times; the variable CYCLES keeps count. The loop has three parts. The first part, statements 3000 to 3230, decides which direction to move each square. The second part, statements 3300 to 3830, calculates new coordinates for each square from the old coordinates and from the directions determined in the first part. The third part, statements 4000 to 4160, draws the squares on the screen at the new locations calculated in the second part.

To determine directions for the squares, the program first checks which square you control (variable CNTRL.SQ$) and sets the direction of that square to the direction you have chosen (statements 3030 to 3090). Next, the program gets a random number at statement 3100. At statement 3110, the program decides whether or not to change the direction of whichever of the magenta or erase squares you do not control. If the random number is less than 0.25, then the program picks a new random direction for the square in statements 3140 to 3190. If the random number is greater than 0.25, the program skips these statements and the square continues in its old direction. In statements 3210 to 3230, the program similarly decides whether to change the white square's direction (if the random number is greater than 0.75), and if necessary decides what the new direction is to be (statement 3230).

The second part of the loop determines new coordinates for the squares. The statements following 3300 find coordinates for the magenta square;

those following 3500, for the white square; and those following 3700, for the erase square. Since these three subparts are almost identical, we shall discuss the subpart at 3500 and leave you to figure out how the other two work. The statements following 3510 move the white square to the right (direction 1). The statements following 3550, 3590, and 3630 move the white square down, to the left, or up (directions 2, 3, and 4). These four sub-subparts are almost identical; we shall discuss the sub-subpart that begins at 3550, duplicated here from Fig. 5-1:

```
3550    BAD.Y = BAD.Y + SPEED
3560    IF BAD.Y > 145   THEN   BAD.Y = BAD.Y - SPEED :
          BAD.DIRC = 0
3570    IF BAD.X = ERS.X AND BAD.Y = ERS.Y   THEN
          BAD.Y = BAD.Y-SPEED
3580    GOTO 3670
```

Statement 3550 increments the y coordinate of the white square by the value of SPEED, which is always 8. This moves the white square down the screen. Statement 3560 checks that the new y coordinate is not off the bottom of the playing area. If it is, then statement 3560 changes it back to its old value (at the bottom of the playing area) and changes the value of BAD.DIRC to 0, so that the next time through the loop, the white square will move to the right along the bottom of the playing area (unless its direction is changed by statements 3210 to 3230). If the white square is trying to run over the erase square, then statement 3570 moves it back to its old location.

Eleven other similar series of statements deal with each of the directions for each of the squares.

The third part of the loop, statements 4000 to 4090, draws the squares to show what happened in the first two sections. Statements 4010 to 4030 display temporary images of the squares to allow you to see the erase square moving through the black area, the white square moving through the white area, or the magenta square moving through either the magenta or the white area. Statements 4040 to 4050 delay the program briefly, giving you a chance to see the temporary squares. Statements 4060 to 4090 replace the temporaries with the new colors for each area. Review the use of the OR, XOR, and PSET actions for the PUT statement in Section 4.2 and the summary in Fig. 5-5.

The subroutine starting at statement 5000 scores the game by using the POINT function to find out which parts of the playing area are magenta at the end of the game. At the end of that subroutine, the call to subroutine 8110 sets the system back to using the monochrome display. Delete this call if your computer has no monochrome display.

Fig. 5-5 Colors of Squares in the Erase Game

This figure shows the changes that occur when variously colored squares move over variously colored screen areas as the game progresses. The previous area color is the color that the area has before the square gets there. The intermediate color is the color that it has after statements 4010, 4020, and 4030 are executed. The final color is the color that the area has after statements 4060 to 4090 have been executed.

Square Color	Previous Area Color	Intermediate Area Color	Final Area Color
Black	Black	Outline	Black
	Magenta	Outline	Black
	White	Outline	Black
Magenta	Black	Magenta	Magenta
	Magenta	Black	Magenta
	White	Blue	White
White	Black	White	White
	Magenta	Blue	White
	White	Black	White

These results are achieved by the use of the OR, XOR, and PSET actions with the PUT statement.

Event Traps

For this game to work, the computer must continue to execute the loop from statement 3000 to statement 4160 whether you are busy wearing out the arrow keys on your keyboard or whether you are sitting like a lump on your chair. An INPUT statement to find out if you have pressed a key is out of the question, since an INPUT statement would stop the program. However, the computer must let you change the direction of the square you are controlling whenever you want to. In the ideal arrangement, the computer would listen continuously to the arrow and F9 keys and would GOSUB to one of 6100, 6200, 6300, 6400, or 6600 when you pressed one of them. When you were idle, the computer would concentrate on moving all the squares around the screen. When you were active with the keys, the computer would spend the necessary time to process your commands.

You may by now have noticed that this program contains no GOSUBs to the subroutines at statements 6100, 6200, 6300, 6400, and 6600. This is because it uses *event traps* to GOSUB to these routines. When you press one of the arrow keys or the F9 key (an *event*), the computer drops whatever it is doing and performs a GOSUB to one of the routines. When the routine is over, the computer picks up its regular work wherever it left off. Event traps are like floating GOSUB statements that are performed whenever the event that triggers them occurs. On the one hand, if you never press one of the keys, then the program never gets to the subroutines at 6100, 6200, 6300, 6400, or 6600. If, on the other hand, you have very nimble fingers, the computer may GOSUB to these statements many times during the course of the program. The computer executes the loop from statement 3000 to statement 4160 continuously, but it will pay attention whenever you press a key.

The events that you can trap in BASIC are the *soft keys* from "F1" to "F10" at the left-hand side of the keyboard and the four arrow keys at the right-hand side of the keyboard. The events are numbered: the soft keys are events 1 to 10; the up arrow key is event number 11; the left, right, and down arrows are events number 12, 13, and 14.

To use an event trap in BASIC you must (1) tell the computer what to do if the event occurs, and (2) turn the trap on. To tell the computer what to do when one of these keys is pressed, you use the ON KEY statement. The ON KEY statement consists of the words ON KEY, the number of the event you want to trap enclosed in parentheses, the word GOSUB, and the statement number of the subroutine to perform when the event occurs. Statements 2190 to 2240 in Fig. 5-1 are examples:

```
2190        ON KEY(9)  GOSUB 6600
2210        ON KEY(11)  GOSUB 6100
2220        ON KEY(12)  GOSUB 6200
2230        ON KEY(13)  GOSUB 6300
2240        ON KEY(14)  GOSUB 6400
```

They tell the computer to GOSUB to statement 6600 if you press key 9 (the F9 key) and to statements 6100, 6200, 6300, or 6400 if you press keys 11, 12, 13, or 14 (the four arrow keys). *This statement is entirely unrelated to the KEY ON statement, which turns the soft key display at the bottom of the screen on. The similarity is coincidental.*

After statements 2190 to 2240, the computer knows what to do if you press one of the arrow keys or the F9 key, but it pays no attention to those operations until the program tells it to do so. Statements 2250 to 2300 in Fig. 5-1 tell the computer to pay attention:

```
2250        KEY (9)  ON
2270        KEY (11)  ON
2280        KEY (12)  ON
2290        KEY (13)  ON
2300        KEY (14)  ON
```

The KEY ON statement consists of the word KEY, the number of the key you want the computer to pay attention to in parentheses, and the word ON. (This statement is also unrelated to the KEY ON statement. Another coincidence.) Until the computer gets to the KEY ON statements, you can press the keys all you like and the computer won't do a thing. After these statements are executed, the computer will perform the GOSUBs it was told about in statements 2190 to 2240 whenever you press one of the keys. You therefore cannot get any results from the arrow keys or the F9 key until the computer is finished drawing the playing area.

You can tell the computer to stop paying attention to a key in two ways:

```
5000 KEY (12) OFF
5000 KEY (12) STOP
```

The first one tells the computer to ignore key 12. If you subsequently press key 12, nothing will happen. The second causes the computer to continue to pay attention to the key but not to do the GOSUB right away. If you press key 12 after the KEY STOP statement is executed, the computer will notice it, but it will wait until a KEY (12) ON statement is executed before it does the GOSUB. Consider these two examples:

```
5000 KEY (12) OFF        5000 KEY (12) STOP
 . . .                     . . .
 . . .                     . . .
 . . .                     . . .
5999 KEY (12) ON         5999 KEY (12) ON
```

If you press key number 12 while the computer is doing the statements between 5000 and 5999 in the left-hand example, nothing will happen, even when the program gets to statement 5999 and key 12 is turned back on. If you press key number 12 in the right-hand example, the computer will perform the GOSUB associated with key number 12 as soon as it gets to statement 5999.

Event traps entail some subtleties, which are discussed below. As you can see, the erase program STOPs event traps if you press one of the arrow keys. If you wish to know more about event traps now, skip ahead.

Speed Considerations

The Erase game must move quickly to be interesting. The areas in the program where speed is critical are the loop between statements 3000 and 4160 and the subroutines at statements 6100 through 6600. The program is reasonably fast as it stands, but if you get good at it or if you add new features to the game that require additional computing, you may need to use some of the techniques below.

1. Variables that change frequently use up a lot of computing time, some of which can be saved by using *integer variables,* with which the computer can calculate more rapidly than with the regular *single precision* variables. Integer variables differ from single precision variables in that their values must be whole numbers, not fractions, and in that their names end with a percent sign (%). The most frequently used variables in this program— GOOD.X, GOOD.Y, BAD.X, BAD.Y, ERS.X, ERS.Y, SPEED, GOOD.DIRC, BAD.DIRC, and ERS.DIRC—could be changed to integer variables by changing their names to GOOD.X%, GOOD.Y%, BAD.X%, and so forth, with consequent improvement in the speed of the game. Alternatively, since all of the variables in the game could be turned to integer variables (no fractions occur anywhere in the game), you can insert this statement

DEFINT A-Z

at the beginning of the program. This will change all of the variables to integer variables automatically, whether or not percent signs appear in their names.

2. You can put several statements on one line and separate them with colons. Since certain overhead time is used just to get to the next statement number, putting more than one statement on a line speeds up the program. This has been done at statements 3220, 3360, 3400, and 3440, and at the equivalent statements in the calculations of the new locations of the other squares. It has been avoided as much as possible, though, since this technique makes programs far harder to understand. It makes no sense to use this technique anywhere except in the loop from statement 3000 to statement 4160 and in the subroutines at statements 6100, 6200, and so on.

3. Reducing the number of remark statements speeds up the program. A certain amount of time is used whenever the computer executes a remark. Hence, for example, you can speed up the program slightly by changing the ON KEY statements to GOSUB to the first executable statement in the subroutines and not to the remark at the beginning of the subroutine. This technique also obfuscates the program's operation and should be avoided whenever possible.

Subtleties of Event Traps

Event traps can be tricky, and it pays to be cautious whenever you work with them. The problem is that event traps can occur *at any time* after you have given a KEY ON statement, and there are always times (though not always obvious) in every program when you would rather that they wouldn't occur. On the surface, it would seem to make no difference when you press the arrow keys, but one problem arises. Suppose that you omit the GOSUB to the subroutine at statement 6800 that suspends event traps for the arrow keys, and suppose you press, say, the up arrow key and the right arrow key in rapid succession. A rather good chance exists that you will press both keys before the program gets back to the top of the loop from statement 3000 to statement 4160. The up arrow key changes the value of CNTRL.DIRC to 3, but this has no immediate effect on the game. The right arrow key then changes CNTRL.DIRC to 0. When the program does get to the top of the loop, CNTRL.DIRC is equal to 0, and the program has no idea that it was ever equal to 3. The square that you are controlling moves to the right as though you had never pressed the up arrow key.

With the program as it stands, when you press the up arrow key, the program GOSUBs to the subroutine at statement 6100 and changes CNTRL.DIRC to 3. The subroutine at statement 6800 STOPs the event traps for the arrow keys. When you press the right arrow key, this event is remembered but does not affect program execution immediately. At the top of the loop, CNTRL.DIRC still equals 3, so the program moves the square you are controlling up one space. When events are subsequently turned back on, the program GOSUBs to statement 6300 to handle the pending right arrow request. The program thus remembers the right arrow keystroke until the up arrow has had a chance to have an effect.

You might try removing the calls to statement 6800 to see how aggravating the game becomes when it ignores some of your keystrokes if you press the arrow keys rapidly.

Possible Improvements

You can make several improvements to this game. They include:

1. Speed the game up by changing the variables to integer variables and by judiciously putting several statements on one line wherever possible.

2. Put the scoring mechanism inside the main loop so that the game prints a current score on the screen each time through the loop. To calculate

the score efficiently, it is easiest for the program to check how each of the three squares it draws each time through the loop affect your score. If the magenta square changes the color of a previously blank square, then your score is increased. If the white square or the erase square covers up a previously magenta square, then your score is reduced.

3. Allow yourself to control the white square in addition to the other two. What effect does this have on your optimal strategy?

4. Use a subroutine to calculate the new x and y coordinates of each of the squares. With care, you can shorten the program considerably with this technique.

5. Change the game to be more to your liking. Possibilities include making a two-player game out of it or making the object of the game to make both the blank areas and the magenta areas as large as possible or to make them equal.

5.2 "WORM"—AN EXAMPLE OF CHARACTER GRAPHICS

The program in Fig. 5-6 uses some of the special characters available with the CHR$ function to draw a worm snaking randomly around a monochrome display. This program is *not* a game, but *is* just for fun, and it is therefore included here. As shown in Fig. 5-6, the program runs on a monochrome display, but it can easily be modified to run on a color/graphics display instead.

The program moves the worm one character space across the screen each time around the main program loop. Each time through the loop, one new character is drawn at the head of the worm and one character is erased at the tail. Although the body of the worm never moves—new characters are simply added at the head and erased at the tail—the illusion of motion is quite convincing.

The worm is not allowed to cross over itself. If the program finds that its chosen location for a new segment of the worm contains a previous segment of the worm, then it stops adding segments to the head of the worm until the tail "catches up" enough to erase the segment of the worm that is in the way. After this happens, new segments are once again added to the head. Since the worm is now shorter than it was—segments were erased from the tail while the head stood still—it must grow later. At the point where the head was held up, the tail pauses to allow the worm to grow back to its normal length.

Fig. 5-6   Program to Draw the "Worm"

```
100   ' --- PROGRAM TO PUT THE WORM ON THE SCREEN
110   '
120   '
130   ' --- INITIALIZE THE WORM TO BE AT POINT T(10,40)
140   '
150        WORMLENGTH = 25
160        CLS
170        WORM.MOVING = 1
180        DIM WORM.XY(100,2)
190        FOR X = 1 TO WORMLENGTH
200           LET WORM.XY(X,2) = 10
210           LET WORM.XY(X,1) = 40
220           LOCATE WORM.XY(X,2),WORM.XY(X,1)
230           PRINT CHR$(205)
240        NEXT X
250   '
260   ' --- INITIALIZE NEXT SQUARE;  NEXTX AND NEXTY ARE
270   ' --- COORDINATES OF THE NEXT SQUARE THE WORM WILL ENTER
280        NEXTX = 41
290        NEXTY = 10
300        OLD.DIRC = 0
310        PTR = WORMLENGTH
320   '
330   ' --- LOOP TO MOVE WORM AROUND THE SCREEN
340           DIRC.IS.OK = 1
350           CHANGE.DIRECTION = RND(1)
360           IF  CHANGE.DIRECTION < .25  THEN LET DIRC.IS.OK = 0
370   '
380   ' ---    FIND DIRECTION TO MOVE THIS TIME
390   ' ---      DIRC = 1    WORM IS MOVING UPWARDS
400   '                 2    WORM IS MOVING TO THE LEFT
410   '                 3    WORM IS MOVING DOWNWARDS
420   '                 4    WORM IS MOVING TO THE RIGHT
430   '
440           IF  DIRC = 1 AND NEXTY = 1   THEN
                    LET DIRC.IS.OK = 0
450           IF  DIRC = 2 AND NEXTX = 1   THEN
                    LET DIRC.IS.OK = 0
460           IF  DIRC = 3 AND NEXTY = 24 THEN
                    LET DIRC.IS.OK = 0
470           IF  DIRC = 4 AND NEXTX = 79 THEN
                    LET DIRC.IS.OK = 0
480   '
490           IF  DIRC.IS.OK = 1  GOTO 550
500   '
510           DIRC = INT(4*RND(1) + 1)
520           IF  DIRC = OLD.DIRC + 2  GOTO 510
525           IF  DIRC + 2 = OLD.DIRC  GOTO 510
530           DIRC.IS.OK = 1
540        GOTO 380
```

continued on p. 171

continued from p. 170

```
550   '
560             IF  (DIRC + OLD.DIRC) MOD 2 <> 0 GOTO 620
570   ' ---       WORM HAS NOT CHANGED DIRCTIONS; DRAW VERTICAL
580   '           OR HORIZONTAL STRAIGHT LINE
590               IF DIRC MOD 2 = 0 THEN WORMCHAR$ = CHR$(205)
600               IF DIRC MOD 2 <> 0 THEN WORMCHAR$ = CHR$(186)
610               GOTO 700
620   ' ---    ---
630   ' ---       WORM HAS GONE AROUND A CORNER; SELECT THE
640   '           APPROPRIATE CORNER CHARACTER
650               IF   DIRC = 2 OR OLD.DIRC = 4   THEN TEMP = 187
                       ELSE TEMP = 201
660               IF   DIRC = 1 OR OLD.DIRC = 3   THEN
                       TEMP = TEMP + 1
670               IF   TEMP = 202   THEN LET TEMP = 200
680               WORMCHAR$ = CHR$(TEMP)
690   '
700   '
710   ' ---     PRINT WORMCHAR$ AT NEW LOCATION OF HEAD OF WORM
720             LOCATE NEXTY,NEXTX
730             IF   SCREEN(NEXTY,NEXTX) <> 32   THEN
                       LET WORM.MOVING = 0
740             IF   WORM.MOVING = 1   THEN PRINT WORMCHAR$;
750   '
760   ' ---     ERASE TAIL OF WORM
770             LET NEXT.PTR = PTR + 1
780             IF NEXT.PTR > WORMLENGTH   THEN LET NEXT.PTR = 1
790             LOCATE WORM.XY(NEXT.PTR,2) , WORM.XY(NEXT.PTR,1)
800             PRINT " ";
810   '
820   ' ---     ADVANCE THE ARRAY
830             PTR = PTR + 1
840             IF   PTR > WORMLENGTH   THEN PTR = 1
850             LET WORM.XY(PTR,1) = NEXTX
860             LET WORM.XY(PTR,2) = NEXTY
870             IF   WORM.MOVING = 0   GOTO 940
880                 IF   DIRC = 1   THEN LET NEXTY = NEXTY - 1
890                 IF   DIRC = 2   THEN LET NEXTX = NEXTX - 1
900                 IF   DIRC = 3   THEN LET NEXTY = NEXTY + 1
910                 IF   DIRC = 4   THEN LET NEXTX = NEXTX + 1
920                 OLD.DIRC = DIRC
940             WORM.MOVING = 1
950         GOTO 330
```

Moving the Worm

The variables NEXT.X and NEXT.Y keep track of the next screen location
(in terms of character spaces for the LOCATE statement) into which the worm
will move; the variable OLD.DIRC stores the direction that the worm last
moved; the variable DIRC stores the direction that the worm will move next.

The values of DIRC and OLD.DIRC represent directions as follows:

Value of DIRC or OLD.DIRC	Direction of Travel
1	Upward
2	To the Left
3	Downward
4	To the Right

From statement 330 to statement 540, the program picks a direction for the worm to move. The variable DIRC.IS.OK keeps track of whether it is reasonable for the worm to continue moving in the same direction as before or if the program has found a reason to change directions. The reasons to change are that it is time to make a random change (statements 350 and 360) and that the worm is about to run into the edge of the screen (statements 440 to 470). If necessary, a new direction is chosen by statement 510. Statements 520 and 525 check that the worm has not doubled back on itself.

When the program gets to statement 560, it must figure out which of the double-line characters used to display the worm should be drawn. Statement 560 determines if the worm is progressing in a straight line or if it has gone around a corner. If the worm is moving in a straight line, then statements 590 and 600 decide whether that line is horizontal or vertical and store either character number 205 or character number 186 in the variable WORM-CHAR$. If the worm has gone around a corner, then statements 650 to 680 store the suitable corner character is WORMCHAR$. See Fig. 5-7 for a list of the special characters used to draw the worm.

Statements 720 to 740 draw the new segment of the worm at the location NEXT.X, NEXT.Y. Statements 770 to 790 erase the tail end of the worm. How the computer knows the location of the tail end of the worm is discussed below.

Next, the value of one of the two variables NEXT.X and NEXT.Y is incremented or decremented by statements 880 to 930 to indicate the location for the next segment to be added to the head of the worm. Then the value of OLD.DIRC is set to indicate the same direction as does the value of DIRC.

The variable WORM.MOVING keeps track of whether the head of the worm is moving: it equals 1 when the head of the worm is moving and 0 when the head of the worm is waiting for the tail to get out of its way. Statement 730 determines whether a segment of the worm is already at the screen location represented by NEXT.X and NEXT.Y. If that screen location is not blank, then it must contain one of the double-line characters that represent a segment of the worm, so WORM.MOVING is set to 0. At statement 870, the program decides whether to move the head of the worm by changing one of the values NEXT.X and NEXT.Y.

Fig. 5-7   Characters Used in "Worm"

The following characters are used in the "Worm" program.

Character Number	Appearance
186	‖
187	⌐
188	⌐
200	⌐
201	⌐
205	=

Finding the Tail of the Worm—A Circular Buffer

In order to erase the tail of the worm, the program must keep track of the locations at which segments of the worm are drawn. It uses the array WORM.XY for this purpose: whenever it draws a character representing a segment of the worm, the x and y coordinates of the screen location of the new segment are stored in WORM.XY.

Two *pointers* indicate special entries of interest in the array WORM.XY. The first one, the variable PTR, indicates where in the array the program should write the coordinates of the head of the worm. Each time around the main loop, PTR is incremented, and NEXT.X and NEXT.Y are stored in the array. The second pointer, the variable NEXT.PTR, always stays one step ahead of PTR. This place in the array turns out always to contain the location of the tail of the worm, the location that was the head of the worm 25 segments ago. PTR and NEXT.PTR move from the first entry in the array to the twenty-fifth, and then jump back to the beginning again so that the array is used over and over again as the program runs. This arrangement is called a *circular buffer*. See Fig. 5-8.

Fig. 5-8   How the Array WORM.XY Is Used

The figure below shows how the array WORM.XY is used. If the program has been running for a while, PTR might be, for example, 22 at statement 830. Statements 850 and 860 store the coordinates of the new head of the WORM in WORM.XY(22,1) and WORM.XY(22,2). The coordinates for the new head of the worm are calculated and stored in NEXT.X and NEXT.Y by statements 880 to 910. Then the program loops back to statement 330, at which point the condition of the array and the pointers is as shown below.

When the program gets to statement 770, it sets NEXT.PTR to 23, which is the location in the array that contains the coordinates of the worm segment drawn 25 segments ago. The character at this location is erased from the screen.

At statement 830, PTR is incremented to 23, and the coordinates of the segment just erased are overwritten by the new values of NEXT.X and NEXT.Y. The following time around the loop at statement 770, NEXT.PTR will be 24 and the next most recent character will be erased.

Note that whenever one of the pointers gets beyond the length of the worm, 25, it gets set back to the beginning of the array.

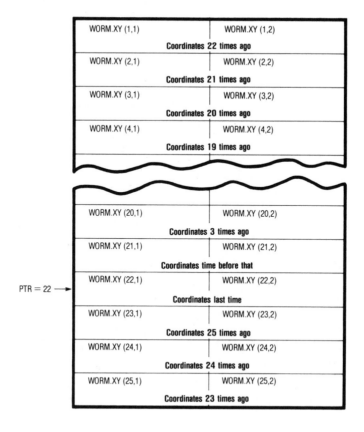

NOTES

All of the code prior to statement 330 is initialization code.

The variable WORMLENGTH can be changed to anything from 1 to 100 and the length of the worm will change accordingly.

5.3 THE IBM SAMPLE GAME "DONKEY"

In the relatively simple-minded game of "Donkey," one of the IBM sample programs, you control an automobile driving down a two-lane road. Periodically, a donkey appears standing in one of the lanes of the road, and you must change lanes (by pressing the space bar on the keyboard) to avoid hitting the donkey. If you dodge donkeys long enough, you win and earn a point. If you run into a donkey, then both automobile and donkey explode, and the donkeys earn a point. (Why the donkeys earn a point when one is run down by a speeding automobile is not explained.) Your activity during the course of the game consists of pressing the space bar to change lanes to avoid donkeys.

A much rewritten version of the "Donkey" program appears in Fig. 5-9. This program works as does the IBM sample program, but this version has been extensively modified for readability. In Fig. 5-10 is an outline of the algorithm of the program. The significant variables and explanations of their uses appear in Fig. 5-11. Since this program contains no concepts that we have not already discussed, our commentary will be brief.

Several things might puzzle you about this program if you study it:

1. The car is seldom moved on the screen. The program creates the illusion that you are driving down the road simply by moving the dashed line on the road. The car itself stands still, except that it moves very slowly up the screen as the game progresses.

2. The dashed line is drawn only once on the screen. After that, it is changed when a PUT statement with the XOR action puts the array DASHED.LINE% on top of the existing dashed line. The array DASHED.LINE% is set up so as to change the parts of the dashed line that were dark to light and vice versa. The illusion that you are driving up the screen (as opposed to down it) occurs because the donkeys standing in the road move down the screen.

3. Although the program directions on the screen tell you to press the space bar to change lanes, you can actually press almost any key for this purpose.

Fig. 5-9 The Program to Play "Donkey"

```
1000 ' --- THIS PROGRAM PLAYS THE GAME OF DONKEY
1010 '
1020 '
1030 ' --- INITIALIZE ALL VARIABLES
1040 '
1410        COLOR O
1420        DEFINT A-Y
1440        SCREEN 1,0 : COLOR 8,1 : CLS : KEY OFF
1445 '
1460        DIM DNK.LEFT%(150),DNK.RIGHT%(150),
                CAR.LEFT%(200),CAR.RIGHT%(200)
1470        DIM DNK%(300)
1480        GOSUB 1940
1490        GOSUB 1780
1500        CLS
1510        DIM DASHED.LINE%(300)
1518        DASHED.LINE%(0)=2
1519        DASHED.LINE%(1)=193
1520        FOR I=2 TO 300
1521            DASHED.LINE%(I)=-16384+192
1522        NEXT I
1540 '
1545 '
1546 ' --- LOOP TO PLAY THE GAME AS MANY TIMES AS YOU WANT
1550            CAR.X=110
1551            CLS
1560 '
1570 '
1580 '     --- DRAW THE SCREEN FOR THE GAME
1590            LINE (0,0)-(305,199),,B
1600            LINE (6,6)-(97,195),1,BF
1610            LINE (183,6)-(305,195),1,BF
1620            LOCATE 3,5:PRINT "Donkey"
1630            LOCATE 3,29:PRINT "Driver"
1631            LOCATE 19,25:PRINT"Press Space  ";
1632            LOCATE 20,25:PRINT"Bar to switch";
1633            LOCATE 21,25:PRINT"lanes        ";
1635            LOCATE 23,25:PRINT"Press ESC    ";
1636            LOCATE 24,25:PRINT"to exit      ";
1640            FOR Y=4 TO 199 STEP 20
1645                LINE (140,Y) - (140,Y+10)
1646            NEXT Y
1650            CAR.Y=105 : CAR.X=105
1660            LINE (100,0)-(100,199) : LINE(180,0)-(180,199)
1661 '
1662 '
```

continued on p. 177

continued from p. 176

```
1665 '          --- LOOP TO MOVE THE CAR, THE DONKEY, ETC.
1670                LOCATE 5,6:PRINT SCORE.DONKEY
1671                LOCATE 5,31 : PRINT SCORE.DRIVER
1675 '
1680                LET CAR.Y=CAR.Y-4
1684 '
1685                IF  CAR.Y < 60  THEN  GOSUB 2230 ' DRIVER WINS
1686                IF  CAR.Y < 60  THEN  1774
1687 '
1690                PUT (CAR.X,CAR.Y),CAR%,PRESET
1700                LET DONKEY.X = 105+42*INT(RND*2)
1710                FOR DONKEY.Y=(RND*-4)*8 TO 124 STEP 6
1720                   SOUND 20000,1
1731                   A$ = INKEY$
1732                   IF A$ = CHR$(27)  THEN  22000  ' ESCAPE KEY
1733                   POKE 106,0
1734                   IF LEN(A$) = 0  THEN  1739     ' LANE CHANGE
1735                      LINE(CAR.X,CAR.Y)-(CAR.X+28,CAR.Y+44),0,BF
1736                      LET CAR.X = 252 - CAR.X
1737                      PUT (CAR.X,CAR.Y),CAR%,PRESET
1738                      SOUND 200,1
1739 '                 ---
1740                   IF  DONKEY.Y=>3  THEN
                             PUT (DONKEY.X,DONKEY.Y),DNK%,PSET
1744 '
1745 '             TEST FOR COLLISION
1750                   IF  CAR.X=DONKEY.X AND DONKEY.Y+25>=CAR.Y
                             THEN  GOSUB 2060
1751                   IF  CAR.X=DONKEY.X AND DONKEY.Y+25>=CAR.Y
                             THEN  1774
1752 '
1755 '             MOVE DASHED LINE
1760                   IF DONKEY.Y AND 3  THEN
                             PUT (140,6),DASHED.LINE%
1771                NEXT DONKEY.Y
1772                LINE (DONKEY.X,124) - (DONKEY.X+32,149),0,BF
1773             GOTO 1670
1774          GOTO 1540
1775 '
1776 '
1778 '
1779 '
1780 '       SUBROUTINE TO DRAW THE RACE CAR AND STORE IT IN CAR%
1781         CLS
1790         DRAW "S8 C3"
1800         DRAW "BM12,1 R3 M+1,3 D2 R1 ND2 U1 R2 D4 L2 U1 L1"
1810         DRAW "D7 R1 ND2 U2 R3 D6 L3 U2 L1 D3 M-1,1 L3"
1820         DRAW "M-1,-1 U3 L1 D2 L3 U6 R3 D2 ND2 R1 U7 L1 D1 L2"
1830         DRAW "U4 R2 D1 ND2 R1 U2"
1840         DRAW "M+1,-3"
1850         DRAW "BD10 D2 R3 U2 M-1,-1 L1 M-1,1"
1860         DRAW "BD3 D1 R1 U1 L1 BR2 R1 D1 L1 U1"
1870         DRAW "BD2 BL2 D1 R1 U1 L1 BR2 R1 D1 L1 U1"
1880         DRAW "BD2 BL2 D1 R1 U1 L1 BR2 R1 D1 L1 U1"
1890         LINE(0,0)-(40,60),,B
1900         PAINT (1,1)
1910         DIM CAR%(900)
1920         GET(1,1)-(29,45),CAR%
1930         RETURN
```

continued on p. 178

continued from p. 177

```
1935 '
1936 '
1940 '     SUBROUTINE TO DRAW THE DONKEY AND STORE IT IN DNK%
1941       CLS
1950       DRAW "S8"
1960       DRAW "BM14,18"
1970       DRAW "M+2,-4 R8 M+1,-1 U1 M+1,+1 M+2,-1"
1980       DRAW "M-1,1 M+1,3 M-1,1 M-1,-2 M-1,2"
1990       DRAW "D3 L1 U3 M-1,1 D2 L1 U2 L3 D2 L1 U2 M-1,-1"
2000       DRAW "D3 L1 U5 M-2,3 U1"
2010       PAINT (21,14),3
2020       PRESET (37,10):PRESET (40,10)
2030       PRESET (37,11):PRESET (40,11)
2040       GET (13,0)-(45,25),DNK%
2050       RETURN
2054 '
2055 '
2056 ' --- DRIVER HAS HIT THE DONKEY.  EXPLODE.
2060       SCORE.DONKEY = SCORE.DONKEY + 1
2061       LOCATE 14,6 : PRINT "BOOM"
2070       GET (DONKEY.X,DONKEY.Y)-(DONKEY.X+16,DONKEY.Y+25) ,
              DNK.LEFT%
2090       GET (DONKEY.X+17,DONKEY.Y)-(DONKEY.X+31,DONKEY.Y+25) ,
              DNK.RIGHT%
2091       LET DONKEY.LEFT.X = DONKEY.X
2092       LET DONKEY.RIGHT.X = DONKEY.X + 17
2093       LET DONKEY.EXP.Y = DONKEY.Y
2100       GET (CAR.X,CAR.Y)-(CAR.X+14,CAR.Y+44) , CAR.LEFT%
2110       GET (CAR.X+15,CAR.Y)-(CAR.X+28,CAR.Y+44) , CAR.RIGHT%
2121       LET CAR.LEFT.X = CAR.X
2122       LET CAR.RIGHT.X = CAR.X + 15
2123       LET CAR.EXP.Y = CAR.Y
2130       FOR P=6 TO 0 STEP -1
2140          PUT (CAR.LEFT.X,CAR.EXP.Y) , CAR.LEFT%
2141          PUT (CAR.RIGHT.X,CAR.EXP.Y) , CAR.RIGHT%
2149          PUT (DONKEY.LEFT.X,DONKEY.EXP.Y) , DNK.LEFT%
2150          PUT (DONKEY.RIGHT.X,DONKEY.EXP.Y) , DNK.RIGHT%
2151          LET Z = 1/ (2^P)
2152          LET Z1 = 1 - Z
2161          LET CAR.LEFT.X = CAR.X * Z1
2162          LET CAR.RIGHT.X = CAR.RIGHT.X +
                 (291 - CAR.RIGHT.X) * Z
2163          LET CAR.EXP.Y = CAR.EXP.Y + (155 - CAR.EXP.Y) * Z
2171          LET DONKEY.LEFT.X = DONKEY.X * Z1
2172          LET DONKEY.RIGHT.X = DONKEY.RIGHT.X +
                 (294 - DONKEY.RIGHT.X) * Z
2173          LET DONKEY.EXP.Y = DONKEY.Y * Z1
2180          PUT (CAR.LEFT.X,CAR.EXP.Y) , CAR.LEFT%
2181          PUT (CAR.RIGHT.X,CAR.EXP.Y) , CAR.RIGHT%
2190          PUT (DONKEY.LEFT.X,DONKEY.EXP.Y) , DNK.LEFT%
2191          PUT (DONKEY.RIGHT.X,DONKEY.EXP.Y) , DNK.RIGHT%
2200          SOUND 37+RND*200,4
2205       NEXT P
2210       FOR DELAY = 1 TO 2000 : NEXT DELAY
2220       CLS
2222       RETURN
```

continued on p. 179

continued from p. 178

```
2225  '
2226  ' --- TIME IS OUT AND DONKEY HAS LOST
2230        SCORE.DRIVER = SCORE.DRIVER + 1
2231        LOCATE 7,25 : PRINT "Donkey loses!"
2240        FOR DELAY = 1 TO 1000 : NEXT DELAY
2250        CLS
2251        RETURN
2260  '
2270  '
```

Fig. 5-10   Pseudo-Code for Donkey Program

Program Activity	Statements
INITIALIZE ALL VARIABLES	1030–1522
Subroutine at 1780 gets picture of the car	
into the array CAR%	
Subroutine at 1940 gets picture of the donkey	
into the array DNK%	
LOOP TO PLAY GAME REPEATEDLY	1546–1774
SET UP SCREEN FOR THE GAME	1580–1660
LOOP TO MOVE CAR UP THE SCREEN	1665–1773
MOVE CAR UP THE SCREEN	1680
CHECK TO SEE IF DRIVER HAS WON	1685–1686
Subroutine at 2226 restarts game after	
driver wins	
LOOP TO MOVE DONKEY DOWN THE SCREEN	1710–1771
CHECK IF DRIVER WANTS TO STOP PLAYING	1731–1732
CHECK IF DRIVER WANTS TO CHANGE	
LANES	1734
CHANGE LANES	1735–1738
CHECK FOR COLLISION	1750–1751
Subroutine at 2056 creates the	
explosion	
END OF LOOP	
END OF LOOP	
END OF LOOP	

Fig. 5-11   Variables Used in "Donkey"

The program in Fig. 5-9 uses the variables shown here. The names of the variables have been changed from the original IBM sample program.

DNK%—stores a picture of a donkey. The variable is initialized with a GET statement in the subroutine at statement 1940 and is drawn on the screen by the PUT statement at 1740.

CAR%—stores a picture of the car. It is initialized with a GET statement in the subroutine at statement 1780 and is used at statement 1690, when the car is moved up the screen, and at statement 1737, when the driver changes lanes.

DASHED.LINE%—stores a picture of the dashed line down the center of the road. It is initialized at statements 1518 to 1521 by storing in the elements of the array the values that they would get if you actually drew a dashed line on the screen and used a GET statement. The dashed line is drawn at statement 1760.

CAR.X—stores the x coordinate of the car. It can be either 105 or 147, depending on which lane the car is in. CAR.X is initialized at statement 1650; it is changed at statement 1736 if the driver changes lanes. Statement 1750 uses CAR.X to check if there is a collision, and the subroutine at statement 2056 uses it to help create the explosion after a collision.

CAR.Y—stores the y coordinate of the car. It is initialized at statement 1650. It is changed at 1680 as the game progresses; it is used to check if the driver has won at statements 1685 and 1686; statement 1750 uses CAR.Y to check if there has been a collision; the subroutine at statement 2056 uses it to help create the explosion.

DONKEY.X—stores the x coordinate of the donkey currently on the screen. It is selected randomly at statement 1700 to be either 105 or 147, depending on which lane the donkey is in.

DONKEY.Y—stores the y coordinate of the donkey. DONKEY.Y is the index variable of the FOR-NEXT loop from statement 1710 to statement 1771, and it is used at statement 1740 to decide whether the donkey is on the screen, at statements 1750 and 1751 to decide if a collision has occurred, and in the subroutine at statement 2056 to help create the explosion.

SCORE.DONKEY—stores the number of times there has been a collision and the donkey has "won." This score is printed at statement 1670, and it is incremented in the subroutine at statement 2056 whenever a collision occurs.

SCORE.DRIVER—stores the number of times the driver evaded the donkey long enough to win. This variable is printed on the screen at statement 1671 and is incremented in the subroutine at statement 2226.

DNK.LEFT%—stores a picture of the left half of a donkey. This is used in the explosion subroutine at statement 2056.

DNK.RIGHT%, CAR.LEFT%, and CAR.RIGHT%—store pictures of pieces of the donkey and the car in the explosion subroutine at statement 2056.

DONKEY.LEFT.X and DONKEY.RIGHT.X—store the x coordinates of the left and right halves of the donkey during the explosion.

DONKEY.EXP.Y—stores the y coordinate of both pieces of the donkey during the explosion.

CAR.LEFT.X and CAR.RIGHT.X—store the x coordinates of the left and right halves of the car during the explosion.

CAR.EXP.Y—stores the y coordinate of both pieces of the car during the explosion.

5.4 THE IBM SAMPLE PROGRAM "SPACE"

The program in Fig. 5-12 is a rewritten version of the IBM sample program "Space." It differs from the IBM version of this program in the usual ways. Since it uses only concepts we have discussed, it is left to you to figure out how it works. It is not particularly complex, as you will see.

Fig. 5-12   IBM Sample Program "Space"

```
1000 ' --- IBM SAMPLE PROGRAM "SPACE"
1010 '
1020 '
1400       KEY OFF
1410       DEFINT I-N : DIM SAUCER(800)
1420       SCREEN 1,0 : COLOR 8,0
1426 '
1427 '
1428 ' --- DRAW THE FLYING SAUCER AND GET IT INTO AN ARRAY
1430       CLS
1431       CIRCLE (160,100),30,1,,,.45
1432       PAINT (160,100),1,1
1433       DRAW "BM160,100 E30 BM160,100 H30"
1434       LINE (130,100)-(190,100),2
1435       GET (130,70)-(190,130) , SAUCER
1436 '
1437 '
1438 ' --- DRAW THE SCREEN BACKGROUND
1440       LINE (0,0)-(100,199),0,BF
1441       LINE (101,0)-(200,199),2,BF
1442       LINE (201,0)-(300,199),3,BF
1450       LOCATE 23,2 : PRINT "Press ESC ";
1460       LOCATE 24,2 : PRINT "to exit";
1465 '
1466 '
1467 ' --- MOVE THE FLYING SAUCER AROUND THE SCREEN
1470          FOR J = 2 TO 6
1471             FOR SCALE = 1 TO 2
1472                PLAY "MB L64 T255 O=J; C C# D D# E F F#
                              G G# A A# B"
1473             NEXT SCALE
1480             X.SAUCER = RND*259
1481             Y.SAUCER = RND*138
1482             PUT (X.SAUCER,Y.SAUCER) , SAUCER , XOR
1483             FOR DELAY = 1 TO 30
1484             NEXT DELAY
1485             PUT (X.SAUCER,Y.SAUCER) , SAUCER , XOR
1486          NEXT J
1490          LET A$ = INKEY$ : IF  A$=CHR$(27)   THEN 3000
1500       GOTO 1470
3000       END
```

6 Business Applications and Graphing

Making sense out of large tables of numbers is difficult. Most people can grasp a graphics presentation of the same data far more easily. Making graphs from a table of numbers by hand, however, is a chore. Since many computer programs crank out large tables, it makes sense to extend these programs to produce the graphs as well. Three commonly used types of graphs are (1) the pie chart, in which numbers are represented by segments of a circle; (2) the bar chart, in which numbers are represented by the heights of vertical bars; and (3) the scatter chart, in which numbers are represented by dots on a graph.

The three sections of this chapter explain programs that draw these three kinds of charts. In addition to illustrating how to draw the charts, however, the three programs also serve as examples of solutions to various problems germane to many other graphics programs. Section 6.1, which discusses pie charts, explains the mathematics of drawing circles and sectors and the calculations used to make text and graphics appear on the screen at the same location. The program on bar graphs, Section 6.2, illustrates the rudiments of an interactive graphics editor, a program through which the user can make changes to pictures already on the screen. Section 6.3 on scatter charts also discusses in more depth the problems of making a graph fit on the screen.

6.1 PIE CHARTS

The Sample Program "Piechart"

A rewritten version of the IBM sample program "Piechart" is shown in Fig. 6-1. This program draws pie charts identical to those drawn by the IBM version of the program but is lacking the title screen and the other usual things. Run the IBM sample program to see what it does. We will not describe its function here except as necessary for the discussion of how specific parts of the program work.

As the remark statements in Fig. 6-1 point out, the subroutine starting at statement 1450 asks you for the information the computer needs in order to draw the chart. The FOR-NEXT loop from statement 1515 to statement 1525 "normalizes" the input, a process whose purpose is discussed below. The statements from 1550 to 1560 print the title on the chart and draw a box around it. The FOR-NEXT loop from 1570 to 1670 draws the pie chart itself, text and all. Starting at statement 1673 the program finds out if you want to draw another chart: if you do, the program repeats the entire process; if you do not, the program ends.

Fig. 6-1   IBM Sample "Piechart" Program (Rewritten)

```
1200 ' --- IBM PIECHART SAMPLE, REWRITTEN
1210 '
1220 '
1230 '
1300       DIM R(100),A$(100)
1400       CLS
1420       SCREEN 1,0
1430       COLOR 8,0
1442 '
1443 '
1444 ' --- GET INPUT CONCERNING CHART FROM THE USER
1450       INPUT "title of chart" ; TITLE$
1460       INPUT "how many items in chart" ; ITEMS
1470       LET SUM = 0
1480       FOR I = 1 TO ITEMS
1490          INPUT "Numeric value, Name" ; R(I),A$(I)
1500          LET SUM = SUM + R(I)
1510       NEXT I
1511 '
1512 ' --- "NORMALIZE" THE INPUT, THAT IS, MAKE IT SUM TO 1.
1515       FOR I = 1 TO ITEMS
1520          LET R(I) = R(I) / SUM
1525       NEXT I
1526 '
1527 '
```

continued on p. 184

continued from p. 183

```
1528 ' --- DRAW THE CHART
1529 ' --- FIRST THE TITLE
1540       CLS
1545       TITLE.START = 20 -  LEN(TITLE$)/2
1550       LOCATE 2,TITLE.START : PRINT TITLE$
1555       LET TITLE.LEFT = 8 *  (19.5 - LEN(TITLE$)/2) - 8
1556       LET TITLE.RIGHT = 8 * (19.5 + LEN(TITLE$)/2)
1560       LINE (TITLE.LEFT,7)-(TITLE.RIGHT,16),3,B
1561 '
1564       LET STOP.ANGLE = 0
1565       LET SHORT.RADIUS = 44
1566       LET LONG.RADIUS = 50
1567       LET DISTANCE = LONG.RADIUS - SHORT.RADIUS
1568 '
1569 ' --- NOW THE CHART ITSELF
1570       FOR SEGMENT = 1 TO ITEMS
1580          LET START.ANGLE = STOP.ANGLE
1581          LET STOP.ANGLE = STOP.ANGLE  +
                    R(SEGMENT) * 2*3.1415926#
1590          LET AVERAGE.ANGLE = (START.ANGLE + STOP.ANGLE) / 2
1600          LET CENTER.X = 160  +  COS(AVERAGE.ANGLE) *
                    DISTANCE
1610          LET CENTER.Y = 100  -  SIN(AVERAGE.ANGLE) *
                    DISTANCE
1620          CIRCLE (CENTER.X,CENTER.Y),SHORT.RADIUS,1,
                    -START.ANGLE-.001,-STOP.ANGLE , 5/6
1628          LET FILL.X = CENTER.X  +
                    COS(AVERAGE.ANGLE) * .8*SHORT.RADIUS
1629          LET FILL.Y = CENTER.Y  -
                    SIN(AVERAGE.ANGLE) * .8*SHORT.RADIUS
1630          PAINT (FILL.X,FILL.Y),SEGMENT MOD 4,1
1635          LET CENTER.X = CENTER.X  +
                    COS(AVERAGE.ANGLE) * (16+SHORT.RADIUS)
1640          LET LEFT.X = CENTER.X  -  4 * LEN(A$(SEGMENT))
1645          LET LEFT.Y = CENTER.Y -
                    SIN(AVERAGE.ANGLE) * (SHORT.RADIUS + 16)
1646          LET TEXT.START.X = LEFT.X \ 8  + 1
1647          LET TEXT.START.Y = LEFT.Y \ 8  + 1
1650          LOCATE  TEXT.START.Y,TEXT.START.X :
                    PRINT A$(SEGMENT);
1655          LET TEXT.LEFT.X = 8 * (TEXT.START.X - 1)
1656          LET TEXT.RIGHT.X = TEXT.LEFT.X + 8 *
                    LEN(A$(SEGMENT))
1660          LINE (TEXT.LEFT.X,8*TEXT.START.Y) -
                    (TEXT.RIGHT.X,8*TEXT.START.Y),1
1670       NEXT SEGMENT
1671 '
1672 '
1673 ' --- DOES THE USER WANT ANOTHER CHART?
1675 ' --- LOOP TO GET 'Y' OR 'N' FOR AN ANSWER
1680          LOCATE 23,1
1700          PRINT"Another Chart? (Y or N)";
1710          A$=INKEY$:IF A$="" THEN 1710
1730          IF A$="N" OR A$="n" THEN CLS : END
1740          IF A$="Y" OR A$="y" THEN 1400
1750       GOTO 1675
```

Sample Pie Chart Drawn by Program

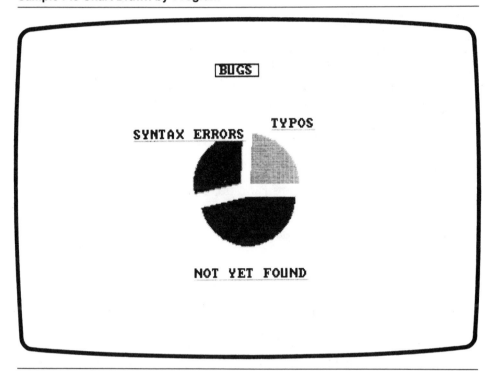

NORMALIZING THE DATA

Note that the actual numbers you give do not determine the sizes of the segments in a pie chart; the ratios among the numbers is the determining factor. If, for example, you want a pie chart with three segments, and input 1, 2, and 3 for the three values, the resulting pie chart is identical to the one that results if you type 1,000, 2,000, and 3,000. In both cases, the second segment will be twice the size of the first, and the third will be three times the size of the first.

The size of a segment within a pie chart is determined by the size of its angle. Since the segments in a pie chart exactly use up one circle, the sum of the segment angles must be 360 degrees. As we discussed in Section 3.6, 360 degrees is the same as 2 pi radians. Obviously, if the program were to get either 1, 2, and 3 or 1,000, 2,000, and 3,000 as input, it could not draw segments with angles of 1, 2, and 3 degrees, or with 1,000, 2,000, and 3,000 degrees. Angles of 1, 2, and 3 degrees would take up only a scant part of a circle (perhaps it could be called a "sliver chart"), and angles of 1,000, 2,000, and 3,000 degrees would use up many circles. Neither do segments of 1, 2, and 3 radians or 1,000, 2,000, and 3,000 radians fill up just one circle. The program must do some algebra to figure out how big the various segment angles must be for their sizes to bear the relationship to one another demanded by the input but at the same time sum up to just one whole circle.

The first step in the process is taken at statement 1500, where the program keeps a running total of the input numbers. In the FOR-NEXT loop starting at statement 1515, the computer divides each of the input numbers by that total. If the input numbers are 1, 2, and 3, then their sum is 6, and the result of dividing each of them by 6 is:

1/6   2/6   3/6

These three numbers add up to 1. Similarly, if you input 1,000, 2,000, and 3,000, then the sum of the inputs is 6,000, and the loop at statement 1515 stores this data in the array R:

1,000/6,000   2,000/6,000   3,000/6,000

These numbers are the same as:

1/6   2/6   3/6

which add up to 1, as before. Whatever you input, the numbers in the array R will add up to 1 after the loop at statement 1515 is executed.

At statement 1581, the computer calculates the angle for each of the segments in the graph by multiplying the number stored in the array R by 2 times pi. The result of this is that the angles of the segments always add up to 2 times pi, the size of the circle.

Normalization is a useful technique whenever you write a program that gets input data and must display it in a predetermined space. In the discussion above, the allowable space was the 2 pi radians in a circle. In drawing other charts, the limitation might be 320, the number of pixels across the screen, or it might be the number of dots across the printer line or maybe the number of text lines on the screen. In any of these cases, the technique is to divide each input by the sum of the inputs to obtain a series of numbers that add up to 1, which can then be multiplied by the appropriate factor to produce a graph that fits in the assigned space.

DRAWING THE PIE CHART

Unlike some pie charts, which consist simply of a circle divided into segments, the program here draws an "exploded" pie chart, in which each segment is drawn slightly away from the center of the circle so that there are gaps among them. See Fig. 6-2. To do this, the program draws each segment as part of a circle whose center is slightly offset from the actual center of the graph.

Fig. 6-2   Geometric Interpretation of Variables Used to Draw Pie Chart

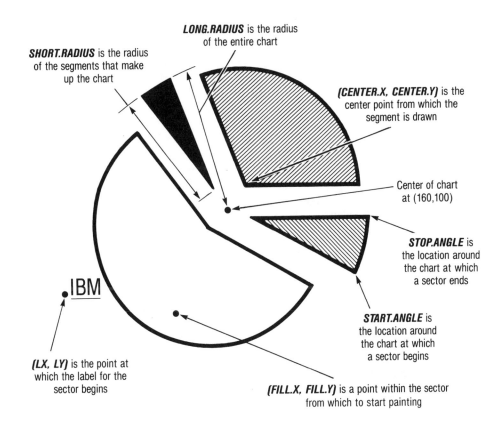

LONG.RADIUS is the radius
of the entire chart

SHORT.RADIUS is the radius
of the segments that make
up the chart

(CENTER.X, CENTER.Y) is the
center point from which the
segment is drawn

Center of chart
at (160,100)

STOP.ANGLE is
the location around
the chart at which
a sector ends

START.ANGLE is
the location around
the chart at which
a sector begins

IBM

(LX, LY) is the point at
which the label for the
sector begins

(FILL.X, FILL.Y) is a point within the sector
from which to start painting

The following discussion of how to draw the pie chart involves some formulas that include trigonometric functions. Although you do not need to know trigonometry to follow the discussion, since it is all explained here, readers who have not studied trigonometry may want to investigate the program in Fig. 6-3 before continuing. The program in Fig. 6-3 is the same as the one in Fig. 6-1 with the following changes: (1) it does not label the segments; (2) it draws a regular pie chart rather than an exploded one; (3) it does not PAINT the segments. It involves no trigonometry, and you should be able to understand it on the basis of what we have discussed so far. Readers who have studied trigonometry may find the following discussion somewhat elementary.

Fig. 6-3   Simplified Program to Draw a Pie Chart

```
1200  ' --- IBM PIECHART SAMPLE, REWRITTEN
1210  '
1220  '
1230  '
1300       DIM R(100)
1400       CLS
1420       SCREEN 1,0
1430       COLOR 8,0
1442  '
1443  '
1444  ' --- GET INPUT CONCERNING CHART FROM THE USER
1450       INPUT "title of chart" ; TITLE$
1460       INPUT "how many items in chart" ; ITEMS
1470       LET SUM = 0
1480       FOR I = 1 TO ITEMS
1490          INPUT "Numeric value" ; R(I)
1500          LET SUM = SUM + R(I)
1510       NEXT I
1511  '
1512  ' --- "NORMALIZE" THE INPUT, THAT IS, MAKE IT SUM TO 1.
1515       FOR I = 1 TO ITEMS
1520          LET R(I) = R(I) / SUM
1525       NEXT I
1526  '
1527  '
1528  ' --- DRAW THE CHART
1529  ' --- FIRST THE TITLE
1540       CLS
1545       TITLE.START = 20 -  LEN(TITLE$)/2
1550       LOCATE 2,TITLE.START : PRINT TITLE$
1555       LET TITLE.LEFT = 8 *  (19.5 - LEN(TITLE$)/2) - 8
1556       LET TITLE.RIGHT = 8 * (19.5 + LEN(TITLE$)/2)
1560       LINE (TITLE.LEFT,7)-(TITLE.RIGHT,16),3,B
1561  '
1564       LET STOP.ANGLE = 0
1566       LET RADIUS = 80
1568  '
1569  ' --- NOW THE CHART ITSELF
1570       FOR SECTOR = 1 TO ITEMS
1580          LET START.ANGLE = STOP.ANGLE
1581          LET STOP.ANGLE = STOP.ANGLE  +
                   R(SECTOR) * 2*3.1415926#
1590          LET AVERAGE.ANGLE = (START.ANGLE + STOP.ANGLE) / 2
1620          CIRCLE (160,100),RADIUS,1,
                   -START.ANGLE-.001,-STOP.ANGLE , 5/6
1670       NEXT SECTOR
1671  '
1672  '
1673  ' --- DOES THE USER WANT ANOTHER CHART?
1675  ' --- LOOP TO GET 'Y' OR 'N' FOR AN ANSWER
1680          LOCATE 23,1
1700          PRINT"Another Chart? (Y or N)";
1710          A$=INKEY$:IF A$="" THEN 1710
1730          IF A$="N" OR A$="n" THEN CLS : END
1740          IF A$="Y" OR A$="y" THEN 1400
1750       GOTO 1675
```

Sample of Pie Chart Drawn by Above Program

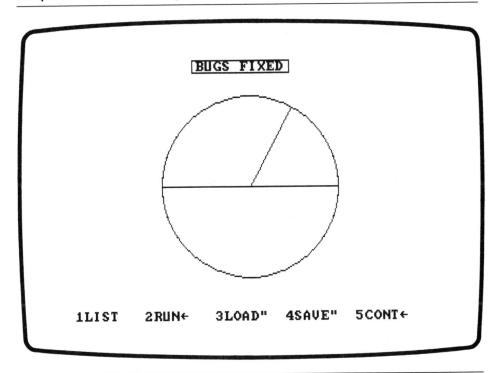

To find the center of a circle of which a segment in the exploded pie chart is a part, the program calculates first the START.ANGLE and STOP.ANGLE that the segment is to have, based on the input numbers as normalized by the program. The AVERAGE.ANGLE is then calculated at statement 1590 and used later as the direction in which the segment center should be offset from the graph center. How angles determine direction was discussed in Section 3.6. The distance that the center should be offset from the center of the graph was arbitrarily determined by whoever wrote this program to be

LONG.RADIUS − SHORT.RADIUS

This always turns out to be 6.

If you start at a point whose coordinates are

(START.X , START.Y)

and move a certain DISTANCE in the direction of the angle given by ANGLE, then the formulas for the coordinates NEW. X and NEW.Y of the point you will arrive at are

NEW.X = START.X + COS(ANGLE)*DISTANCE
NEW.Y = START.Y + SIN(ANGLE)*DISTANCE

In these formulas, COS and SIN are *trigonometric functions* that (among other things) make this formula work. Those who have had trigonometry may recognize these formulas. The SIN and COS functions are BASIC functions that the computer can calculate. In Fig. 6-1 statements 1600 and 1610 calculate CENTER.X and CENTER.Y with these formulas, where START.X and START.Y are replaced by 160 and 100, respectively. The point (160,100) is the center of the screen and the center of the graph. DISTANCE is replaced by

LONG.RADIUS − SHORT. RADIUS

and ANGLE is replaced by

AVERAGE.ANGLE

See Fig. 6-4.
   Once a center for the segment has been found, it is drawn from that center, using the CIRCLE statement in 1620. Consult Fig. 6-2 to determine why the circle has a radius equal to SHORT.RADIUS. Notice that the two angles given to the CIRCLE statement are both negative, causing the program to draw not only the arc of the circle, but also the lines connecting that arc to the center of the segment. This creates a closed area that can be subsequently filled with the PAINT statement.
   Statements 1628 and 1629 calculate the location of the point

(FILL.X,FILL.Y)

which is the point used in statement 1630 to PAINT the segment. The formula used to calculate this point from the center of the segment is the same one that was used to calculate the center of the segment from the center of the graph.

Fig. 6-4   Calculating the Center of a Segment to Use for an "Exploded" Pie Chart

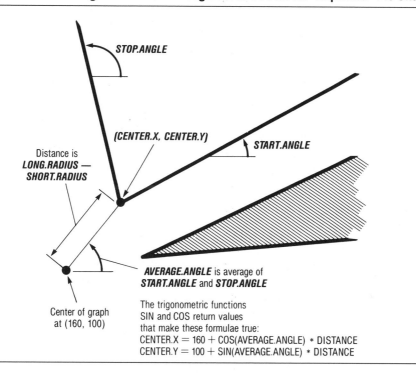

STOP.ANGLE

(CENTER.X, CENTER.Y)

START.ANGLE

Distance is
LONG.RADIUS —
SHORT.RADIUS

AVERAGE.ANGLE is average of
START.ANGLE and STOP.ANGLE

Center of graph
at (160, 100)

The trigonometric functions
SIN and COS return values
that make these formulae true:
CENTER.X = 160 + COS(AVERAGE.ANGLE) * DISTANCE
CENTER.Y = 100 + SIN(AVERAGE.ANGLE) * DISTANCE

GETTING TEXT IN THE RIGHT PLACE

The "Piechart" program labels each segment of the chart and prints a title for the chart at the top of the screen. The segment labels are underlined, and the chart title is surrounded by a box. In each case, text and graphics must be aligned, as discussed in Section 4.4.

Statement 1550 centers the title for the chart on the second row of the screen. The LEN function returns the number of letters in the title. By dividing this number by two and subtracting from 20 (since the screen is 40 letters wide, column 20 is the center), the computer finds the location the first letter of the title must have for the title to be centered. The computer then draws the box around the title with the LINE statement at 1560. Since the text is on text line 2 of the screen, 8 and 16 are possible y coordinates for corners of a box that surrounds that text. The x coordinates must be found using the length of the title. (Incidentally, the formula for the size of the box isn't quite right, although it is the one in the IBM sample program. The formula sometimes leaves a little blank space in the box to the right or left of the title. Can you fix it?)

A location for each segment label on the chart is found by the statements starting at statement 1635. In statements 1635 and 1645, the program finds a location for the center of the segment label using the same formulas it used to find the centers of the segments themselves and using SHORT.RADIUS + 16 as the offset from the center of the graph. It stores the results of this calculation, the graphics coordinates for the center of the segment label, in the variables CENTER.X and LEFT.Y. Statement 1640 uses the length of the title to find the x coordinate of the left end of the label, which it stores in LEFT. X. The y coordinate of the left end is, of course, the same as the y coordinate of the center, since the lettering is horizontal. In order to find the text coordinates for the LOCATE statement at 1650, these two variables must be divided by 8, and 1 must be added to each. Review Section 4.4 if this doesn't make sense to you.

POSSIBLE ENHANCEMENTS TO THIS PROGRAM

There are two ways to enhance this program and make it more useful:

1. You can add the capability to save pie charts. To do this, a subroutine in the program must ask you for a file name in which to save a chart and then write the values of TITLE$ and ITEMS and the contents of the arrays R and A$ into the file. A second routine should be able to ask you for a file name, read the values of these variables out of the file, and then jump down to the statements starting at 1569, where the pie chart is drawn, thereby drawing the chart whose information was stored in the file. It would probably be wise to restructure the program somewhat so that the part of the existing program that actually draws the chart becomes a subroutine.

2. You can modify the program in such a way that it will allow you to make changes to a chart you have just drawn. After the computer draws a chart, it should ask you if you wish to make changes. If you do, you should be allowed to make changes to the values of the segments on the chart. (Just how to do this requires more detailed specification. This is left to you.)

6.2 BAR GRAPHS

The program in Fig. 6-5 is a *bar graph editor,* a program that displays a bar graph on the screen and allows you to modify it as you wish. When it starts, the program first displays a bar graph with six bars, each with six blocks of color. See Fig. 6-6. You can then give various commands to modify the bar graph. Color Plate 6 shows a bar graph created with this program.

Fig. 6-5   Bar Chart Editing Program

```
1000 ' --- THIS PROGRAM ALLOWS THE USER TO EDIT A BAR GRAPH
1010 '
1020 '
1030 '
1040 '       THE FUNCTIONS IN THIS PROGRAM INCLUDE
1050 '          MAKE A BLOCK OF COLOR TALLER OR SHORTER
1060 '          PUT TITLES ON THE BARS
1070 '          SAVE THE BAR CHART IN A FILE
1080 '          GET A BAR CHART OUT OF A FILE
1090 '
1100 '       OTHER POSSIBLE FUNCTIONS THAT COULD BE IMPLEMENTED
1110 '          CHANGE THE NUMBER OF BLOCKS OF COLOR
1120 '          PRINT THE BAR CHART
1130 '          ADD A BAR TO THE CHART
1140 '          ELIMINATE A BAR FROM THE CHART
1150 '
1160 '
1170 '
1180 '       THE MAIN DATA STRUCTURE IS THE ARRAY BARS
1190 '          BARS(1,N) IS THE X-COORDINATE OF THE NTH BAR
1200 '          BARS(2,N) IS THE Y-COORDINATE OF THE FIRST
1210 '                    COLOR BLOCK ON THE NTH BAR
1220 '          BARS(3,N) IS THE Y-COORDINATE OF THE SECOND
1230 '                    COLOR BLOCK ON THE NTH BAR
1240 '          . . .
1250 '          BARS(7,N) IS THE Y-COORDINATE OF THE TOP
1255 '                    BLOCK ON THE NTH BAR
1260 '          BARS(8,N) IS THE Y-COORDINATE OF THE TOP
                          OF THE BAR
1270 '
1280 '
1290 '
1300 '       THE MAIN SUBROUTINES ARE
1310 '          2000   INITIALIZATION
1320 '          3000   USER COMMAND PARSING
1330 '          4000   DRAW ONE BAR
1340 '          5000   ERASE ONE BAR
1350 '          6000   REDRAW THE WHOLE CHART
1360 '          7000   PERFORM USER FUNCTIONS
1370 '          8000   PUT DATA IN A FILE AND RETRIEVE IT
1380 '          9000   CHANGE TO GRAPHIC SCREEN
1390 '
1400 '
1410 '
2000 ' --- INITIALIZATION
2010       DIM BARS(8,6)
2020       DIM PICTURE.BUFFER%(164)
2030       FOR BAR = 1 TO 6
2040          BARS(1,BAR) = 40 + BAR*40
2050          FOR BLOCK = 2 TO 8
2060             BARS(BLOCK,BAR) = 20* (BLOCK - 2)
2070          NEXT BLOCK
2080       NEXT BAR
```

continued on p. 194

continued from p. 193

```
2090 '
2100          PROMPT.ARROW$ = "C3 R15 H3 BD6 E3"
2110 '
2120          ERASE.ARROW$ = "C0 R15 H3 BD6 E3"
2130 '
2135          NUMBER.OF.BARS = 6
2140          PROMPT.BAR = 1
2150          PROMPT.BLOCK = 1
2160          PROMPT.X = 38
2170          PROMPT.Y = 150
2180 '
2190          BAR.WIDTH = 20
2200          ON KEY(11) GOSUB 3300
2210          ON KEY(12) GOSUB 3400
2220          ON KEY(13) GOSUB 3500
2230          ON KEY(14) GOSUB 3600
2240          KEY (11) ON
2250          KEY (12) ON
2260          KEY (13) ON
2270          KEY (14) ON
2280 '
2290          KEY OFF
2300          GOSUB 9000
2310          GOSUB 6000
2320          GOSUB 3800
2330 '
2340 '
2350 '
3000 ' --- USER COMMAND PARSING AND EXECUTION
3010 '      THE FOUR ARROW KEYS ARE HANDLED BY INTERRUPTS AND THE
3020 '          FOUR SUBROUTINES AT 3300, 3400, 3500, AND 3600
3030 '      THE KEYS THE USER CAN TYPE ON THE KEYBOARD ARE:
3040 '          T                PUT TEXT ON THE GRAPH
3050 '          S                SAVE THE GRAPH IN A FILE
3055 '          G                GET A GRAPH OUT OF A FILE
3056 '          +, -, AND =   CHANGE THE HEIGHT OF A BLOCK OF COLOR
3060 '
3070 '
3080 '
3090 ' --- LOOP TO GET INPUT FROM THE USER
3100          LET USER.KEY$ = INKEY$
3110          IF USER.KEY$ = ""   GOTO 3100
3120          IF USER.KEY$ = "S" THEN GOSUB 8000
3130          IF USER.KEY$ = "T" THEN GOSUB 7500
3140          IF USER.KEY$ = "G" THEN GOSUB 8500
3150          IF USER.KEY$ = "+"   THEN GOSUB 7000
3160          IF USER.KEY$ = "="   THEN GOSUB 7000
3170          IF USER.KEY$ = "-"   THEN GOSUB 7000
3180      GOTO 3090
3190 '
3200 '
3210 '
3300 ' --- HANDLE UP ARROW
3310          PROMPT.BLOCK = PROMPT.BLOCK + 1
3320          IF  PROMPT.BLOCK > 6  THEN  LET PROMPT.BLOCK = 6
3330          GOSUB 3800
3340          RETURN
```

continued on p. 195

continued from p. 194

```
3350 '
3400 ' --- HANDLE LEFT ARROW
3410      PROMPT.BAR = PROMPT.BAR - 1
3420      IF  PROMPT.BAR < 1  THEN  LET PROMPT.BAR = 1
3430      GOSUB 3800
3440      RETURN
3450 '
3500 ' --- HANDLE RIGHT ARROW
3510      PROMPT.BAR = PROMPT.BAR + 1
3520      IF  PROMPT.BAR > NUMBER.OF.BARS  THEN
                 LET PROMPT.BAR = NUMBER.OF.BARS
3530      GOSUB 3800
3540      RETURN
3550 '
3600 ' --- HANDLE DOWN ARROW
3610      PROMPT.BLOCK = PROMPT.BLOCK - 1
3620      IF  PROMPT.BLOCK < 1  THEN LET PROMPT.BLOCK = 1
3630      GOSUB 3800
3640      RETURN
3650 '
3660 '
3670 '
3800 ' --- ERASE OLD PROMPT AND PUT NEW PROMPT UP
3810      PSET (PROMPT.X,PROMPT.Y) , 0
3820      DRAW  ERASE.ARROW$
3830      LET PROMPT.X = BARS(1,PROMPT.BAR) - 17
3840      LET Y1 = BARS(PROMPT.BLOCK + 1 , PROMPT.BAR)
3850      LET Y2 = BARS(PROMPT.BLOCK + 2 , PROMPT.BAR)
3860      LET PROMPT.Y = 160  -  (Y1 + Y2) / 2
3870      PSET (PROMPT.X,PROMPT.Y)
3880      DRAW  PROMPT.ARROW$
3890      BLOCK.HEIGHT = Y2 - Y1
3900      LOCATE 23,5
3910      PRINT "HEIGHT: " ; BLOCK.HEIGHT ; TAB(23) ;
                 "TOP: " ; Y2 ; "       "
3920      RETURN
3930 '
3940 '
3950 '
4000 ' --- THIS SUBROUTINE DRAWS ONE BAR ON THE SCREEN
4010 '       THE BAR IS PASSED IN THE VARIABLE BAR.PARAMETER
4020 '
4030 '
4040      FOR BLOCK = 1 TO 6
4050         BLOCK.COLOR = BLOCK MOD 3   + 1
4060         LOW.X = BARS(1,BAR.PARAMETER)
4070         HIGH.X = LOW.X + BAR.WIDTH
4080         LOW.Y = 160 - BARS(BLOCK+1 , BAR.PARAMETER)
4090         HIGH.Y = 160 - BARS(BLOCK+2 , BAR.PARAMETER)
4100         LINE(LOW.X,LOW.Y) - (HIGH.X,HIGH.Y) ,
                 BLOCK.COLOR , BF
4110      NEXT BLOCK
4120 '
4130      RETURN
```

continued on p. 196

continued from p. 195

```
5000 ' --- THIS SUBROUTINE ERASES ONE BAR FROM THE SCREEN
5010 '     THE BAR TO ERASE IS IN THE VARIABLE BAR.PARAMETER
5020 '
5030       LOW.X = BARS(1,BAR.PARAMETER)
5040       HIGH.X = LOW.X + BAR.WIDTH
5050       LOW.Y = 160 - BARS(2 , BAR.PARAMETER)
5060       HIGH.Y = 160 - BARS(8,BAR.PARAMETER)
5070       LINE (LOW.X,LOW.Y) - (HIGH.X,HIGH.Y) , 0 , BF
5080 '
5090       RETURN
5100 '
5110 '
6000 ' --- THIS SUBROUTINE DRAWS THE ENTIRE BAR CHART BY CALLING
6010 '     THE SUBROUTINE TO DRAW A SINGLE BAR MULTIPLE TIMES
6020 '
6030       FOR BAR = 1 TO NUMBER.OF.BARS
6040           BAR.PARAMETER = BAR
6050           GOSUB 4000
6060       NEXT BAR
6070 '
6080       RETURN
6090 '
6100 '
7000 ' --- THIS ROUTINE MAKES A BLOCK TALLER BY, SHORTER BY, OR
7010 '     EQUAL TO A USER INPUT AMOUNT.  THE PARAMETERS
7020 '     PROMPT.BLOCK AND PROMPT.BAR TELL IT WHICH TO CHANGE.
7030 '
7040 ' --- GET THE AMOUNT
7050       LOCATE 23,5
7060       PRINT SPACE$(33)
7070       LOCATE 23,5
7080       INPUT "AMOUNT:" , VALUE.INPUT$
7090       VALUE.INPUT = VAL(VALUE.INPUT$)
7100       OLD.SIZE = BARS(PROMPT.BLOCK+2 , PROMPT.BAR) -
                  BARS(PROMPT.BLOCK+1,PROMPT.BAR)
7110       IF  USER.KEY$ = "="  THEN LET NEW.SIZE = VALUE.INPUT
7120       IF  USER.KEY$ = "+"  THEN LET NEW.SIZE = OLD.SIZE +
                  VALUE.INPUT
7130       IF  USER.KEY$ = "-"  THEN LET NEW.SIZE = OLD.SIZE -
                  VALUE.INPUT
7140       IF  NEW.SIZE < 0  THEN LET NEW.SIZE = 0
7150       IF  NEW.SIZE > 200  THEN LET NEW.SIZE = 200
7160 '
7170 ' --- CHANGE THE ARRAY
7180       BAR.PARAMETER = PROMPT.BAR
7190       GOSUB 5000
7200       BLOCK.SIZE.CHANGE = NEW.SIZE - OLD.SIZE
7210       FOR I = PROMPT.BLOCK + 2 TO 8
7220          BARS(I,PROMPT.BAR) = BARS(I,PROMPT.BAR) +
                  BLOCK.SIZE.CHANGE
7230       NEXT I
7240 '
7250       GOSUB 4000
7260       GOSUB 3800
7270       RETURN
```

continued on p. 197

continued from p. 196

```
7280 '
7290 '
7300 '
7500 ' --- THIS ROUTINE PUTS TEXT ON THE SCREEN
7510 '
7520 '      ERASE THE GRAPHICS ARROW
7530        PSET (PROMPT.X , PROMPT.Y) , 0
7540        DRAW  ERASE.ARROW$
7550 '
7560 '      PUT ALPHA CURSOR ON SCREEN
7570        LOCATE 1,1,1,1,7
7580 '
7590        KEY (11) OFF
7600        KEY (12) OFF
7610        KEY (13) OFF
7620        KEY (14) OFF
7630 '
7640        LINE INPUT ; DUMMY$
7650 '
7660        KEY (11) ON
7670        KEY (12) ON
7680        KEY (13) ON
7690        KEY (14) ON
7700 '
7710 '      REMOVE ALPHA CURSOR
7720        LOCATE ,,0
7730 '
7740 '      RESTORE GRAPHIC CURSOR
7750        PSET (PROMPT.X , PROMPT.Y) , 3
7760        DRAW  PROMPT.ARROW$
7770 '
7780        RETURN
7790 '
7800 '
7810 '
8000 ' --- THIS ROUTINE SAVES THE BAR GRAPH IN A FILE
8010 '
8020 ' --- GET THE FILE OPEN
8030        LOCATE 23,5
8040        PRINT SPACE$(33)
8050        INPUT ; "FILE NAME: " , F.NAME$
8060        ON ERROR GOTO 8310
8070        OPEN F.NAME$ FOR OUTPUT AS #1
8080        ON ERROR GOTO 0
8090 '
8100 ' --- WRITE BARS ARRAY INTO FILE
8110        FOR I = 1 TO 8
8120           FOR J = 1 TO 6
8130              WRITE #1,BARS(I,J)
8140           NEXT J
8150        NEXT I
```

continued on p. 198

continued from p. 197

```
8160  '
8170  ' --- PUT PICTURE IN FILE
8180        FOR Y = O TO 198 STEP 2
8190           GET  (O,Y) - (319,Y+1) , PICTURE.BUFFER%
8200           FOR I = O TO 164
8210              WRITE #1 , PICTURE.BUFFER%(I)
8220           NEXT I
8230        NEXT Y
8240  '
8250        CLOSE #1
8260  '
8270        RETURN
8280  '
8290  '
8300  '
8310  ' --- HANDLE FILE ERROR
8320  '
8330        LOCATE 23,5
8340        PRINT SPACE$(33)
8350        LOCATE 23,5
8360        PRINT "COULDN'T OPEN FILE; SAVE ABORTED"
8370        RESUME 8270
8380  '
8390  '
8400  '
8500  ' --- THIS ROUTINE GET A BAR GRAPH FROM A FILE
8510  '
8520  ' --- GET THE FILE OPEN
8530        LOCATE 23,5
8540        PRINT SPACE$(33)
8550        INPUT ; "FILE NAME: " , F.NAME$
8560        ON ERROR GOTO 8860
8570        OPEN F.NAME$ FOR INPUT AS #1
8580        ON ERROR GOTO 0
8590  '
8600  ' --- READ BARS ARRAY FROM FILE
8610        FOR I = 1 TO 8
8620           FOR J = 1 TO 6
8630              INPUT #1,BARS(I,J)
8640           NEXT J
8650        NEXT I
8660  '
8670  ' --- GET PICTURE FROM FILE
8680        FOR Y = O TO 198 STEP 2
8690           FOR I = O TO 164
8700              INPUT #1 , PICTURE.BUFFER%(I)
8710           NEXT I
8720           PUT  (O,Y)  , PICTURE.BUFFER% , PSET
8730        NEXT Y
8740  '
8750        CLOSE #1
8760  '
8770        GOSUB 6000
8780        GOSUB 3800
8790  '
8800  '
8810  '
8820        RETURN
```

continued on p. 199

continued from p. 198

```
8830 '
8840 '
8850 '
8860 ' --- HANDLE FILE ERROR
8870 '
8880      LOCATE 23,5
8890      PRINT SPACE$(33)
8900      LOCATE 23,5
8910      PRINT "COULDN'T OPEN FILE; GET ABORTED"
8920      RESUME 8770
8930 '
8940 '
9000      DEF SEG = 0
9010      POKE &H410, (PEEK(&H410) AND &HCF) OR &H10
9020      SCREEN 1,0,0,0
9030      SCREEN 0
9040      SCREEN 1,0,0,0
9050      WIDTH 40
9060      LOCATE ,,1,6,7
9070      RETURN
```

Sample Bar Chart Produced by Above Program

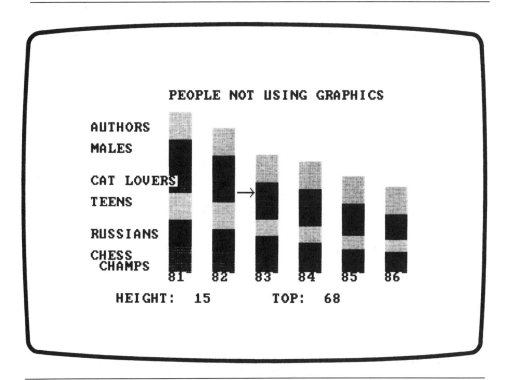

Fig. 6-6   Bar Chart Initially Displayed by Bar Chart Editor

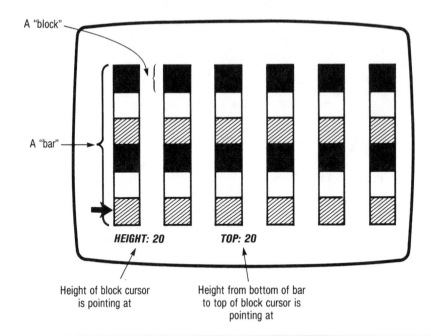

The program displays a *graphics cursor,* a small right-pointing arrow that indicates one of the blocks of color in one of the bars. You can move the cursor from one position to the next color block above, below, to the right, or to the left with the four arrow keys at the right-hand side of the keyboard. To change the graph, you move the cursor to the block you wish to change and then indicate the change you wish to make. These are the possible changes: (1) to specify a new size for the block by pressing the equal sign (=) key and then entering the new height that the block is to be; (2) to specify an increase in the height of the block by pressing the plus sign (+) key and then specifying the increase; and (3) to specify a decrease in the height of the block by pressing the minus sign (−) key and then giving the amount by which the height of the block is to be decreased. The system will erase the bar and redraw it with the block at its new size.

To add text or labels to the graph, you press the "T" key, and the program replaces the arrow with the regular block cursor. You can now move this block cursor around the screen with the four arrow keys, and you can enter text anywhere on the screen by moving the cursor to the suitable location and typing the text in. When you are done entering text, you press the enter key, and the computer will replace the block cursor with the graphics cursor.

You can save your bar graph in a file by pressing the "S" key and giving the computer the name of the file in which it should save the graph. You can retrieve ("get") a saved graph by pressing the "G" key and giving the computer the name of a file in which it saved the graph.

This program uses the DRAW statement to maintain the graphics cursor on the screen, the LINE statement to draw the bars, and the GET and PUT statements to save the entire bar graph in a file.

An Internal Representation of Graphics Data

In programs we have discussed so far in this book, the screen itself has been the only data storage medium for pictures. The programs drew the pictures on the screen and then more or less forgot what they had drawn; they kept no internal representation of the data presented on the screen. The program examples in Chapter 3 and Chapter 4 are not particularly useful because they have little idea about the picture on the screen and don't have the data organized in any useful fashion. In Section 5.1, the only way the Erase game program can score the game is to retrieve the data from the screen, a somewhat slow and clumsy process.

In order to program the bar chart editor effectively, the programmer must save the data internally in addition to drawing the graph on the screen. If the user asks to increase the height of one of the color blocks by three pixels, for example, the program must know the current height of the block in order to calculate the new height, and it must know the heights of the other blocks in the same bar in order to redraw the bar. To move the graphics cursor from bar to bar, the program must know where the bars are and where the blocks are within the bars. Finding out these facts by using the POINT function to search the screen for pixels with the right color is complicated to program, slow in execution, and entirely unnecessary. The dots on the screen are not a compact, easily accessible method of storing the information in a bar graph.

The program stores the bar graph data in the two-dimensional array BARS. Whenever you request to change the height of one of the blocks, the program treats it not as a request to change the display on the screen but as a request to change one of the array elements. The display on the screen is an afterthought from the program's point of view: it happens because subroutines within the program use the array to re-create the graphics display after the array has been changed.

The array BARS is dimensioned in statement 2010:

```
2010 DIM BARS(8,6)
```

It contains data as shown in this table:

BARS(1,1)	contains the x coordinate of the left side of the first bar
BARS(2,1)	contains the height of the bottom of the first block of color in the first bar
BARS(3,1)	contains the height of the top of the first block (which is the bottom of the second block) in the first bar
BARS(4,1)	contains the height of the top of the second block (which is the bottom of the third block) in the first bar
. . .	
. . .	
BARS(7,1)	contains the height of the top of the fifth block (which is the bottom of the sixth block) in the first bar
BARS(8,1)	contains the height of the top of the sixth block
BARS(1,2) through BARS(8,2)	contain the same information about the second bar
BARS(1,3) through BARS(8,3)	contain the same information about the third bar
. . .	
. . .	
BARS(1,6) through BARS(8,6)	contain the same information about the sixth bar

This array can handle up to six bars of color, each with up to six blocks of color in it.

Each of the x coordinates of the left-hand edges of the bars is stored as a number of pixels from the left-hand side of the screen. The heights of the blocks are represented as *pixels from the bottom of the bar*. If, for example, the first bar had four blocks of color, whose heights were 10, 7, 8, and 11, respectively, then

BARS(2,1) would be	0 (the bottom of the first bar)
BARS(3,1)	10 (the top of the first bar)
BARS(4,1)	17 (the top of the second bar)
BARS(5,1)	25 (the top of the third bar)
BARS(6,1)	36 (the top of the fourth bar)

The advantage of this method of storing the numbers is that it is intuitive, since we tend to think of numbers getting larger as things move upward. In order to display the bar graph on the screen, the program must go to the trouble of calculating y coordinates, which is a nuisance, but it is generally preferable to store the data in this intuitive manner and let a subroutine deal with converting the data to screen coordinates.

Getting Data from the Array to the Screen

The principal subroutine for copying the data from the array to the screen is found at statement 4000, which draws one bar of the bar graph using the data in the BARS array. For each block in the bar, the subroutine first picks a color at statement 4050, the result of which is to draw the first three blocks with colors 1, 2, and 3, respectively, and the fourth, fifth, and sixth blocks again with colors 1, 2, and 3, respectively. At statement 4060 the subroutine fetches the left-hand edge of the bar from the BARS array and stores it in LOW.X. At statement 4070 it calculates HIGH.X, the right-hand edge of the bar, from LOW.X and the width of the bars, stored in the variable BARS.WIDTH. BARS.WIDTH is initialized in the code following statement 2000. The subroutine then calculates a LOW.Y and HIGH.Y for the block and uses the LINE statement with the box fill option to draw it. This subroutine is called to draw one bar whenever you change any of the blocks within that bar, and it is called by the subroutine at statement 6000 to draw the entire bar chart when the program is first started.

The subroutine at statement 5000 erases one bar from the chart. It finds LOW.X and HIGH.X in the same way as the subroutine at statement 4000; but instead of finding a LOW.Y and a HIGH.Y for each block of color, this subroutine finds the very bottom of the lowest block and the top of the highest, and it uses just one LINE statement with the box fill option to erase the entire bar. The subroutine at statement 5000 is called whenever you change any block in the bar.

The Graphics Cursor

The right-pointing arrow tells you and the program which block of color is to be changed. Whenever you press one of the arrow keys to move this graphics cursor, and whenever you make a change to the bar graph, the system erases the old arrow, calculates where on the screen a new arrow should be placed, and draws it there. The subroutine that maintains the graphics cursor is at statement 3800. It assumes that the values of these variables are set before it is called:

PROMPT.BAR—tells the subroutine which bar should be pointed to by the new cursor.

PROMPT.BLOCK—tells this subroutine what block (from 1 to 6) should be pointed to by the new cursor.

PROMPT.X—tells the subroutine the x coordinate of the old cursor so that the subroutine can erase it. The subroutine later calculates the x coordinate of the new cursor and stores it in PROMPT.X so that the next time it is called, it will know where the cursor is in order to be able to erase it.

PROMPT.Y—gives the subroutine the y coordinate of the old cursor, which this subroutine also updates.

PROMPT.ARROW$—is a string that, when fed to the DRAW statement, draws a white arrow pointing to the right. This variable is set when the program initializes and never changes.

ERASE.ARROW$—is a string that, when fed to the DRAW statement, draws a black arrow pointing to the right, thereby erasing an arrow drawn with PROMPT.ARROW$. This variable is set when the program initializes and never changes.

The subroutine at statement 3800 first erases the old cursor by using the PSET statement to establish a screen location at (PROMPT.X,PROMPT.Y) and then using the DRAW statement to draw ERASE.ARROW$. If there was no prompt previously—as when the program first starts, for example—then this has no effect. The subroutine calculates a new PROMPT.X (just to the left of the left-hand edge of the bar) and PROMPT.Y (the average of the top and bottom of the block). It then uses the PSET statement to establish this as a new location and uses the DRAW statement to draw PROMPT.ARROW$ on the screen at that location. It also prints the height of the selected block and the total height of the block from the bottom of the bar.

Making Changes

Whenever you request to change one of the blocks by pressing the plus, equal, or minus key, the program calls the subroutine at statement 7000.

That subroutine first inputs an amount from you and does the arithmetic to figure out what the new height for the changed block will be. It then erases the bar that you want to change by calling the subroutine at statement 5000, changes the BARS array to reflect your request, calls the subroutine at statement 4000 to redraw the changed bar, and calls the subroutine at statement 3800 to re-center your cursor on the modified block.

Adding Text

When you request to put in text by pressing the T key, the program calls the subroutine at statement 7500. This routine first erases the graphics cursor and disables the trap functions of the arrow keys. It then performs a LINE INPUT statement. This statement puts the IBM Personal Computer's regular text cursor on the screen. You can move this cursor to any location on the screen with the four arrow keys (the computer does this without special programming) and can enter text anywhere on the screen. When you press the enter key, the LINE INPUT statement ends. The computer then removes the alpha cursor (this is also automatic), and the subroutine restores the graphics cursor. The advantage of the LINE INPUT statement over a regular INPUT statement in this application is that the LINE INPUT statement is not confused by commas and quotes in your input and will not give error messages concerning that input. The data read by the LINE INPUT statement is ignored. Unlike the data concerning the size of the bar chart itself, this program treats text as something that appears on the screen and is otherwise to be ignored. It treats text in the way that other programs we have discussed treat graphics.

Command Parsing

The program uses the four arrow keys to move the graphics cursor from block to block. The four event trap subroutines are found at statements 3300, 3400, 3500, and 3600, and each of them changes either PROMPT.BLOCK or PROMPT.BAR and then calls the subroutine at statement 3800 to move the graphics cursor. The way that the arrow keys call these subroutines was discussed in Section 5.1.

The program uses the INKEY$ variable to get one letter from the keyboard as soon as you press any key (and even before you press the ENTER key). The special variable INKEY$ is always set by BASIC to the first letter that you have typed. Instead of stopping to get a command from you in the input subroutine at statement 3000, which would disable the arrow keys, the program goes into a loop in which it tests the value of the INKEY$ variable. As long as that variable is equal to " ", you have not yet pressed any key (other than an arrow key) and the program goes back to wait for you to do so. When you press one of the keys, the program tests INKEY$ to see which you have pressed and decides which subroutine to execute.

Saving the Bar Graph in a File

If you wished to save only the graph in a file and did not care about the associated text, then the program could store just the BARS array, which contains enough information to reconstruct the graph later. The subroutine to save the data could consist of just the two nested FOR-NEXT loops in statements 8110 to 8150. Similarly, the subroutine to retrieve the data from a file could consist of just the statements from 8610 to 8650. This, in fact, is one of the principal advantages of using the BARS array to store the bar chart rather than relying on the screen itself for data storage: the BARS array is an extremely compact storage method for this data.

To save the text, however, the program must store the entire screen image in addition to the BARS array. The problem is that the program keeps no record of the text you put on the screen, and the only way to find out about it is to get the data back from the screen, pixel by pixel. The FOR-NEXT loop from 8180 to 8230 does this. The GET statement at statement 8190 stores a horizontal strip of the screen in the array PICTURE.BUFFER%, and this array is subsequently written to the file. When you ask to read your file, the statements from lines 8680 to 8730 reverse the process by reading the array back out of the file and using a PUT statement to redraw the screen. If there was text on the screen originally, then it will be found (as a series of white pixels) and stored in the file for later recovery.

Storing BARS in the file takes very little time and very little file space, since the array is not very large. Storing the entire screen, however, is a slow process, and it creates a very large file. This reflects the fact that the method chosen for storing the bar chart itself is good, whereas the method for dealing with text is not.

Possible Improvements

This is not the end-all program for editing and storing bar charts. Although its editing facilities are good as far as they go, a few important capabilities have been left out, and some features of the program are clumsy. Here are several suggestions for improvement to this program:

1. It could allow you to add bars to or delete bars from the graph. The program has been written with this improvement in mind. When you request to add or delete a bar, the program need only modify the variables NUMBER.OF.BARS and BAR.WIDTH, which control the number of bars and their widths, and the elements BARS(1,1), BARS(1,2), and so on, which tell the x coordinates on the screen at which bars are to be drawn. It will then have to call the subroutines that erase the old bars, draw the new bars, and place the prompt at a new location.

2. It could allow you to change the colors of your graph. Obviously, you can only change the background color or the palette, but the difficult programming problem is to allow the user to make these changes without having to look up the possibilities in the IBM manual.

3. It could allow the user to output his bar chart to a printer. With the subroutine in Chapter 7, you can print whatever is on the screen on the printer, but this subroutine must be plugged into the program.

4. It could handle text differently, so that the text that you input is stored in an array rather than just on the screen. A string array with twenty-four elements, one for each line of the screen, is one possible way to store the text. On the one hand, this will simplify the function of saving the data in a file, because the program will be able to save just the BARS array and the new text array and can skip the process of reading the data back from the screen. On the other hand, the subroutine at statement 7500 must be made considerably smarter to capture your input and store it in the appropriate locations in the appropriate elements of the array.

6.3 SCATTER CHARTS

Examine the data in Fig. 6-7, which purportedly show what brand of computer each of a large group of small computer purchasers bought, how much each one paid, and each owner's level of satisfaction on a scale from 1 to 100. From the table it is almost impossible to discern which computers (at which prices) give the most satisfaction to their owners. (This data did not come from a fancy questionnaire; it was actually created with the random number generator of an IBM Personal Computer and a small program we shall discuss later, and it therefore reflects absolutely nothing about the small computer–buying public. Fortunately, our discussion concerns only the mechanics of the graphing, not the significance of the data.)

Fig. 6-7   Data about Personal Computer Satisfaction

This table shows which of three brands of small computer a person bought, how much he paid for it, and how satisfied he is with it on a scale of 0 to 100.

Cost ($)	Satisfaction	Brand	Cost ($)	Satisfaction	Brand	Cost ($)	Satisfaction	Brand
3368.97	67	1	3781.41	82	1	1892.50	5	2
3568.90	61	1	3852.25	83	1	2279.16	7	2
3594.28	70	1	3499.83	65	1	1774.09	90	2
3965.56	64	1	3597.12	52	1	1861.41	86	2
2588.92	21	1	3605.99	48	1	1727.05	96	2
2615.68	9	1	3686.52	77	1	2050.94	92	2
3051.63	32	1	3556.44	72	1	1642.97	18	2
4116.44	73	1	1904.34	93	2	1131.55	26	2
3353.01	46	1	1965.14	19	2	1702.63	15	2
4486.87	96	1	2660.24	19	2	2121.19	86	2
3035.53	25	1	1821.27	28	2	1834.34	16	2
3667.89	78	1	2095.04	90	2	1808.34	15	2
3313.56	51	1	2392.50	88	2	3068.00	10	2
3022.30	40	1	1629.99	94	2	1794.85	95	2
3573.33	49	1	2139.29	86	2	2833.05	30	2
2834.76	24	1	1616.63	47	2	1634.51	27	2
3872.93	72	1	1818.66	29	2	2732.96	99	2
3811.82	58	1	3012.95	12	2	2082.74	8	2
3442.36	49	1	2716.97	88	2	2151.38	98	2
3581.89	63	1	1978.07	97	2	2323.26	93	2
4183.46	76	1	2022.53	2	2	2625.52	93	2
3195.27	32	1	1315.78	88	2	2588.99	86	2
4169.97	71	1	2258.39	29	2	2037.55	35	2
3624.12	54	1	2564.73	100	2	2413.72	53	2
4147.50	85	1	2629.49	16	2	1432.11	96	2
4262.50	89	1	1611.63	34	2	1271.13	31	2
3033.51	32	1	1358.49	39	2	1776.41	87	2
3426.31	59	1	2354.05	97	2	1726.99	49	2
3417.38	46	1	1692.86	4	2	2070.05	96	2
3853.35	67	1	2137.71	93	2	1100.41	8	2
4060.32	87	1	2325.03	42	2	2700.85	42	3
3203.28	38	1	2134.49	95	2	3044.98	52	3
3395.45	69	1	1787.51	29	2	3595.25	53	3
3557.66	60	1	1510.83	29	2	2889.90	63	3
4027.74	79	1	1476.03	86	2	3291.07	40	3
3919.90	85	1	1354.81	86	2	3483.46	33	3
3234.06	41	1	2001.83	40	2	2746.55	47	3
3715.28	82	1	1886.12	91	2	3376.01	51	3
4463.12	71	1	1425.07	91	2	2859.36	61	3
3290.99	44	1	2584.94	32	2	3336.24	44	3

continued on p. 209

continued from p. 208

2835.54	32	1	2313.62	88	2	2729.31	50	3
3416.06	69	1	2330.85	91	2	2861.21	49	3
3643.80	79	1	2451.56	85	2	2844.35	68	3
2921.57	63	3	3100.98	74	3	2735.25	51	3
3588.29	48	3	3261.18	53	3	3428.65	45	3
3527.85	64	3	2912.35	56	3	2706.88	44	3
3492.59	49	3	2905.41	57	3	2701.83	65	3
2724.52	55	3	3593.16	47	3	2710.37	54	3
3329.39	52	3	3011.54	50	3	2997.93	58	3
3027.93	48	3	2889.05	49	3	3158.58	51	3
2748.33	44	3	2842.53	46	3	2974.65	48	3
2785.32	46	3	3106.72	47	3	2850.05	63	3
2718.74	48	3	3361.20	66	3	2772.17	47	3
2794.66	45	3	3496.67	54	3	2999.16	66	3
2867.44	54	3	3286.19	52	3	2762.49	54	3
3383.53	60	3	3478.31	51	3	3222.46	37	3
3342.17	65	3	2780.32	47	3	2740.91	39	3
2731.75	34	3	3593.02	56	3	3200.11	50	3
2719.76	30	3	2931.47	34	3	2722.28	50	3
3341.49	85	3	2851.69	65	3	3231.63	42	3
2997.63	64	3	2958.91	62	3	2978.69	45	3
2709.25	30	3	2920.52	60	3	3575.19	38	3
3471.46	42	3	2710.69	28	3	3365.42	41	3
2730.24	37	3	3557.83	41	3	2878.69	61	3
3380.04	64	3	2952.89	32	3	2801.30	44	3
3301.03	55	3	2763.05	41	3	2822.79	55	3
2767.49	47	3	3271.22	67	3	2700.57	50	3
3513.61	66	3	2706.45	38	3	3543.88	54	3
3349.10	59	3	3198.17	46	3	3160.78	36	3
3572.46	31	3	2838.45	50	3	2757.27	49	3
3241.20	59	3	2733.77	26	3	2944.45	52	3
2771.19	31	3	2776.56	58	3	2847.21	64	3

Examine the graph in Fig. 6-8, a representation of the same data, in which each dot represents one customer. The horizontal position of the dot represents the price that the corresponding customer paid, its vertical position represents the buyer's satisfaction level, and its shape represents the brand the consumer bought. Just a glance at this graph tells you that the brand 2 computer is the cheapest but that its owners fall into two groups: those who are very satisfied, and those who aren't. Brand 1 is the most expensive, and of those who bought it, those who paid the most are the happiest with their purchases. Brand 3 carries an intermediate price tag, and its owners are moderately satisfied, whatever they paid. The prices paid for brand 2 computers vary the most, from about $1,200 to $1,500. A $3,000 model of brand 3 must sell very well, since many customers paid about that much. This sort of graph is called a *scatter chart*.

Fig. 6-8   Scatter Chart of Personal Computer Satisfaction Data

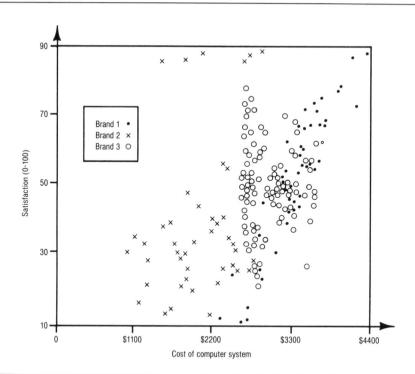

Examine the program in Fig. 6-9. As you have no doubt guessed, it drew the graph in Color Plate 7, which is the computer-drawn equivalent of Fig. 6-8. In fact, it is a general program for drawing scatter charts: it reads the data to graph from a file whose name the user gives and graphs it, scaling the data according to input given by the user.

Fig. 6-9   Program to Create Scatter Chart from any Data

```
1000 ' --- THIS PROGRAM HANDLES A SCATTER CHART
1010 '
1020 '
1030 '
1050      KEY OFF
1060 '
1070 '
1080 '
```

continued on p. 211

continued from p. 210

```
2000 ' --- THIS IS THE MAIN ROUTINE
2010      GOSUB 4000
2015      PRINT "TYPE THE MINIMUM AND MAXIMUM X VALUES
                    TO SHOW ON THE GRAPH"
2016      PRINT "AND THE MINIMUM AND MAXIMUM Y VALUES,
                    SEPARATED BY COMMAS."
2020      INPUT MIN.X,MAX.X,MIN.Y,MAX.Y
2030      GOSUB 21100
2040      SCREEN 1,0
2050      SCREEN 1,0
2060      GOSUB 5000
2070      GOSUB 6000
2080      LOCATE 22,1
2090      GOSUB 22100
2100      GOTO 2020
2110 '
2120 '
2130 '
4000 ' --- DIMENSION THE ARRAYS
4010      DIM POINTS(3,500)
4020 '
4030 '
4040 ' --- INITIALIZE THE ARRAY
4050 '
4060 ' --- GET NAME OF FILE
4070      INPUT "NAME OF FILE FROM WHICH TO READ DATA:" ,
              NAME.OF.FILE$
4080 '
4090          TEMP = RND
4100          ON ERROR GOTO 4170
4110 '
4120          OPEN NAME.OF.FILE$ FOR INPUT AS #1
4130          ON ERROR GOTO 0
4140          GOTO 4230
4150 '
4160 '
4170 ' --- COULD NOT FIND FILE NAME
4180      PRINT "COULD NOT OPEN FILE " ; NAME.OF.FILE$
4190      PRINT "TRY AGAIN."
4200      RESUME 4070
4210 '
4220 '
4230 ' --- READ DATA FROM THE FILE
4240 '
4250      ON ERROR GOTO 4360
4260      LET POINT.COUNT = 0
4270 '
4280 ' --- LOOP TO READ EACH POINT FROM THE FILE
4290          INPUT #1,X,Y,PTCOLOR
4300          LET POINT.COUNT = POINT.COUNT + 1
4310          LET POINTS(1,POINT.COUNT) = X
4320          LET POINTS(2,POINT.COUNT) = Y
4330          LET POINTS(3,POINT.COUNT) = PTCOLOR
4340      GOTO 4280
```

continued on p. 212

continued from p. 211

```
4350 '
4360 ' --- HAVE READ ALL THE DATA FROM THE FILE
4370        RESUME 4390
4380        ON ERROR GOTO 0
4390        CLOSE #1
4400        RETURN
4410 '
4420 '
5000 ' --- SUBROUTINE TO DRAW APPROPRIATE AXES ON THE SCREEN
5010 '
5020        RANGE.X = MAX.X - MIN.X
5030        RANGE.Y = MAX.Y - MIN.Y
5040        STEP.X = RANGE.X / 5
5050        STEP.Y = RANGE.Y / 5
5060        X.PRINT = MIN.X
5070        Y.PRINT = MIN.Y
5080        LINE (40,0) - (320,160) , 3 , B
5090        FOR TICK = 1 TO 5
5100            TICK.Y = 160 - 32 * (TICK-1)
5110            TICK.X = 40  + 56 * (TICK-1)
5120            LINE (32,TICK.Y) - (40,TICK.Y) , 3
5130            LINE (TICK.X,160) - (TICK.X,168) , 3
5140        NEXT TICK
5150 '
5160 ' --- LABEL THE AXES
5170        FOR ROW = 20 TO 4 STEP -4
5180            LOCATE ROW,2
5190            PRINT USING "####" ; Y.PRINT
5200            LET Y.PRINT = Y.PRINT + STEP.Y
5210        NEXT ROW
5220 '
5230        FOR COLUMN = 2 TO 30 STEP 7
5240            LOCATE   22  , COLUMN
5250            PRINT   USING "####" ; X.PRINT
5260            LET X.PRINT = X.PRINT + STEP.X
5270        NEXT COLUMN
5280 '
5290 '
5300        RETURN
5310 '
5320 '
5330 '
6000 ' --- SUBROUTINE TO DRAW THE GRAPH ON THE SCREEN
6010        RANGE.X = MAX.X - MIN.X
6020        RANGE.Y = MAX.Y - MIN.Y
6030        SCALE.X = 280 / RANGE.X
6040        SCALE.Y = 160 / RANGE.Y
6050 '
```

continued on p. 213

continued from p. 212

```
6060            FOR I = 1 TO POINT.COUNT
6070               STEP.X = POINTS(1,I) - MIN.X
6080               POINT.X = STEP.X * SCALE.X     + 40
6090               STEP.Y = POINTS(2,I) - MIN.Y
6100               POINT.Y = 200   - STEP.Y * SCALE.Y    - 40
6110               POINT.COLOR = POINTS(3,I)
6120               IF   POINT.X < 40     GOTO 6170
6130               IF   POINT.Y < O     GOTO 6170
6140               IF   POINT.X > 320   GOTO 6170
6150               IF   POINT.Y > 160   GOTO 6170
6160                  PSET (POINT.X,POINT.Y) , POINT.COLOR
6170               '
6180            NEXT I
6190            RETURN
6200 '
21000 ' -- SUBROUTINE TO CHANGE TO GRAPHIC SCREEN
21010 '
21100            DEF SEG = 0
21110            POKE &H410, (PEEK(&H410) AND &HCF) OR &H10
21120            SCREEN 1,0,0,0
21130            SCREEN 0
21140            WIDTH 40
21150            LOCATE ,,1,6,7
21160            RETURN
21170 '
21180 '
21190 '
22000 ' -- SUBROUTINE TO CHANGE BACK TO ALPHA SCREEN
22010 '
22100            DEF SEG = 0
22110            POKE &H410, (PEEK(&H410) OR &H30)
22120            SCREEN 0
22130            WIDTH 40
22140            WIDTH 80
22150            LOCATE ,,1,12,13
22160            RETURN
```

Review of BASIC Serial Data Files

Unlike the programs in Sections 6.1 and 6.2, in which you input data and the program immediately draws the graph, the program here expects its data already to have been input and to reside in a file. We shall start, therefore, with a short discussion of *serial files* on the IBM Personal Computer in BASIC. You can skip this section if you already understand serial files.

The scatter chart program can't read data out of a data file until you create a data file and put data into it. Therefore, let's first discuss the programs in Fig. 6-10 and Fig. 6-11, which do just that. The program in Fig. 6-10 gets (presumably legitimate) input from you and builds a data file that can be used by the scatter chart program. The program in Fig. 6-11 generated the random data shown in Fig. 6-7.

Fig. 6-10   Program to Write User Data into a File

```
1000 ' --- PROGRAM TO LOAD DATA FILES FOR SCATTER CHARTS
1010 '
1020 '
1030 '
1040 ' --- GET THE NAME OF THE FILE FROM THE USER AND OPEN IT
1050        PRINT "GIVE THE FILE NAME IN WHICH YOU WISH
                   THE DATA SAVED:"
1060        INPUT ":" , NAME.OF.FILE$
1070 '
1080 ' --- DETERMINE IF THE USER IS ADDING TO AN OLD FILE
1090        INPUT "ARE YOU ADDING TO AN OLD FILE (Y/N)" ;
                   RESPONSE$
1100           IF RESPONSE$ = "Y"  OR  RESPONSE$ = "y"  THEN 1130
1110           IF RESPONSE$ = "N"  OR  RESPONSE$ = "n"  THEN 1130
1120        GOTO 1090
1130 '
1140 ' --- OPEN THE FILE
1150        IF RESPONSE$ = "Y"  OR  RESPONSE$ = "y"  THEN  1200
1160           ON ERROR GOTO 1300
1170           OPEN NAME.OF.FILE$ FOR OUTPUT AS #1
1180           GOTO 1500
1200 '        ---
1210           ON ERROR GOTO 1300
1220           OPEN NAME.OF.FILE$ FOR APPEND AS #1
1230           GOTO 1500
1240 '
1250 '
1300 ' --- DEAL WITH AN ERROR WHEN OPENING THE FILE
1310        PRINT "COULD NOT OPEN FILE WITH NAME " ; NAME.OF.FILE$
1320        PRINT "RUN THE PROGRAM AGAIN TO TRY AGAIN.
1330 '
1340 '
1350 '
1500 ' --- GET DATA ITEMS AND PRINT THEM OUT INTO THE FILE
1505        ON ERROR GOTO 0
1510        PRINT "AFTER EACH COLON PRINTED BY THE COMPUTER,
                   ENTER A DATA TRIPLE"
1520        PRINT "YOU WANT STORED IN THE FILE.
                   A DATA TRIPLE IS ENTERED AS "
1530        PRINT "THREE NUMBERS SEPRATED BY COMMAS,
                   FOLLOWED BY THE ENTER KEY."
1540        PRINT
1550        PRINT "TO STOP ENTERING DATA, ENTER 0,0,0 AS YOUR DATA
1560 '
1570 '        ---
1580           INPUT ":" , X , Y , HUE
1585           IF  X = 0  AND  Y = 0  AND  HUE = 0  THEN  1800
1590 '
1600           WRITE #1 , X , Y , HUE
```

continued on p. 215

continued from p. 214

```
1610  '
1620          GOTO 1570
1800  ' --- USER GAVE 0,0,0 AS DATA.  SEE IF HE WANTS TO STOP
1810  ' --- OR IF THIS IS REAL DATA
1890          INPUT "IS THIS DATA OR DO YOU WISH TO QUIT?  (D/Q)" ,
                  RESPONSE$
1900          IF RESPONSE$ = "Q"  OR  RESPONSE$ = "q"  THEN  END
1910          IF RESPONSE$ = "D"  OR  RESPONSE$ = "d"  THEN 1600
1920          GOTO 1890
```

Fig. 6-11   Program to Generate Random Data about User Satisfaction

This program generated the random data shown in Fig. 6-7 and Fig. 6-8. It wrote that data into the file for the subsequent uses of the graphing program in Fig. 6-9.

```
4000  ' --- PROGRAM TO GENERATE RANDOM DATA
4020  '
4030  '
4040  ' --- INITIALIZE
4050          LET TEMP$ = TIME$
4060          SECONDS = VAL(RIGHT$(TEMP$,2))
4070          RANDOMIZE SECONDS
4071  '
4075          OPEN "SCATTER.DTA" FOR OUTPUT AS #1
4076  '
4080          FOR I = 1 TO 50
4085              COST = 2000 + 1000*RND + 1000*RND + 1000*RND
4100              SATISFACTION = 20 + SIN((COST-3000)/1000) * 50  +
                      RND * 30
4110              BRAND = 1
4115              WRITE #1,COST,SATISFACTION,BRAND
4120          NEXT I
4130  '
4140          FOR I = 1 TO 66
4150              COST = 500 + 750*RND + 750*RND + 750*RND + 750*RND
4160              SATISFACTION = RND
4170              IF  SATISFACTION > .5  THEN
                      LET SATISFACTION = 70 + 30*SATISFACTION
4180              IF  SATISFACTION < .5  THEN
                      LET SATISFACTION =
                          -10 + 40*(1-SATISFACTION)^2 + 30 * RND
4190              LET BRAND = 2
4200              WRITE #1,COST,SATISFACTION,BRAND
4210          NEXT I
4220  '
4230          FOR I = 1 TO 100
4240              COST = 2700 + 1000*(RND^2)
4250              SATISFACTION = 10 + 20*RND + 20 * RND +
                      20*RND + 20*RND
4260              BRAND = 3
4265              WRITE #1,COST,SATISFACTION,BRAND
4270          NEXT I
4280  '
4290          END
```

The OPEN statement tells the computer four things about a file:

1. That you intend to use it. Until your program executes an OPEN statement, the computer won't let you write data into a file or read data out of it.

2. The name of the file. The rules for naming files are shown in Fig. 6-12.

Fig. 6-12 Rules for Naming Files

The rules for naming files are as follows:

1. The file name is divided into two parts: the *main name* and the *extension*. The main name is one to eight characters long; the extension is one to three characters long, or it may be omitted.

2. If there is an extension on the file name, then there is a period between the main name and the extension.

3. If you are one of those lucky people who have more than one diskette drive, you can tell the computer which of the two drives you mean by preceding the main name with the name of the drive you want, either A: or B:. If you do not specify which of the two drives you want, the computer will pick drive A (unless you have changed the default drive).

4. You may use the letters A to Z, the digits 0 to 9, and any of the following characters as part of your file names: $, &, #, @, !, %, ', (,), −, <, >, [,], _, \, ^, ~, ¦, and '. You may use no other characters.

5. You can have only one file with a given name on a diskette. However, if you take out one diskette and insert a different one, you can name a file on the second diskette the same as a file on the first one. If you do this, be sure you have some way to tell which file you want later.

Illegal File Names:

XYZ123RTXAABSC	*main name too long*
SYZSF.1234	*extension too long*
S2345123XXY.123	*main name too long*
AB+CD.EFG	*plus sign not legal in file names*
ABC.DEF.GHI	*only one extension allowed*
.MN	*no main name*

Legal File Names:

123XYZ.WWW	
MN##><.@@)	
ABCDEFG	
A.B	
A:XYZ	
B:XYZ	*(a different file, since it is on a different diskette)*

continued on p. 217

continued from p. 216

Reasonable File Names:

TAX1982
PACMAN.BAS
CUSTOMER.81
1983. CHK
FEBP&L.82
MARP&L.82
RESULTS.TMP
PHONE.NUM
WINE.15
MENU.TUE

---

3. An arbitrary number, which the program will use to refer to the file. Although the file has a name, it is always referred to by a number in the body of a BASIC program. The OPEN statement associates the number with the file.

4. Whether you intend to read data from or write data into the file. A serial file can be used for only one of these functions at a time, and the OPEN statement tells the computer which you intend to do. If you are writing into a file that already has data in it, the OPEN statement also tells the computer whether the new data should be added to the data already in the file or whether the old data should be erased.

Here is an example of an OPEN statement:

4075 OPEN "SCATTER.DTA" FOR OUTPUT AS #1

"SCATTER.DTA" is the name of the data file, OUTPUT is what the program intends to do, and #1 is the number the program will use to refer to the file. Instead of OUTPUT, you can put INPUT or APPEND, which have the meanings you might guess they have. Note that the file name must be in quotes (unless you give it as a string variable, as discussed below). Other examples of the OPEN statement are:

100 OPEN "DATAFILE" FOR APPEND AS #2

This tells the computer that you wish to use a file named DATAFILE, that you intend to refer to it as file number 2, and that you intend to put new data in that file. You can put a string variable in for the file name as is done in Fig. 6-9:

4070 INPUT NAME.OF.FILE$
4120 OPEN NAME.OF.FILE$ FOR INPUT AS #1

This tells the system that you intend to read data from the file whose name is typed in statement 4070. The file number can also be a variable:

130 INPUT FILE.NUMBER
140 OPEN "FILEX" FOR INPUT AS #FILE.NUMBER

You can probably figure this out. You cannot use a variable in the OPEN statement to tell the computer what you intend to do with the file.

If you open a file for APPEND, then data written to the file will be added to the end of the file, which will be expanded for the new data. The old data, if any, will stay in place. If you open a file for OUTPUT, then new data written to the file will take the place of whatever data was in the file before.

When you open a file for OUTPUT or APPEND, the system looks for a file with the given name. If it finds one, the program uses it. If it doesn't, the program creates a new file with that name and then uses it. When you open a file for INPUT, the computer expects to find a file with data in it. If the computer finds no file with the name given, you get an error.

The WRITE # Statement

Once you have opened a file for OUTPUT or APPEND, you can write data to it with the WRITE # statement. The WRITE # statement works like the PRINT statement except that (1) you have to tell the computer the number corresponding to the file where you wish it to write the data, (2) the WRITE # statement ignores semicolons and commas between data items, and, of course, (3) the WRITE # puts the data in a file instead of on your screen. Here is an example of a WRITE # statement:

10 WRITE #1, COST, SATISFACTION, BRAND

This writes the values of numeric variables COST, SATISFACTION, and BRAND in whatever file was opened as #1.

Here is a simple program:

```
10  OPEN "EXAMPLE" FOR APPEND  AS #1
20  WRITE #1, "HAPPY" , "BIRTHDAY"
30  FOR I = 1 TO 10
40     WRITE #1 ; I ; 2*I
50  NEXT I
60  END
```

It creates a file called EXAMPLE and puts the following data into it:

HAPPY   BIRTHDAY   1   2   2   4   3   6   4   8   5   10
                            6   12   7   14   8   16   9   18   10   20

Note that starting a new WRITE # statement does not start a new line in the file. Also note that commas and semicolons make no difference in how the data are written.

The programs in Fig. 6-10 and Fig. 6-11 write values to the files in threes:

X   Y   COLOR   X   Y   COLOR   X   Y   COLOR   X   Y
COLOR   X   Y   COLOR   X   Y   COLOR   X   Y   COLOR
X   Y . . .

or equivalently

COST   SATISFACTION   BRAND   COST   SATISFACTION
BRAND   COST   SATISFACTION   BRAND   COST
SATISFACTION   BRAND . . .

The INPUT # Statement

Data files are useless unless you know how to get data out of them. You can use the OPEN statement to tell the computer that you wish to input data from a file. The INPUT # statement then works like the regular INPUT statement except that instead of waiting for you to type input on the keyboard, it looks for its data in the file. The INPUT # statement reads the data back out of the file in the same order as it was put in with WRITE # statements. Take, for example, the file EXAMPLE that we built with the program fragment above:

HAPPY   BIRTHDAY   1   2   2   4   3   6   4   8   5   10
                            6   12   7   14   8   16   9   18   10   20

This can be read back with the following program fragment:

```
10   OPEN "EXAMPLE"   FOR INPUT   AS #2
20   INPUT P$ , Q$
30   FOR I = 1 TO 4
40      INPUT #2, A, B, C, D, E
50      PRINT  A, B, C, D, E
60   NEXT I
70   END
```

P$ will equal HAPPY, and O$ will equal BIRTHDAY. The printout will be:

```
 1     2     2     4     3
 6     4     8     5    10
 6    12     7    14     8
16     9    18    10    20
```

EXAMPLE is file #1 in one program and #2 in the other, but that doesn't bother the computer, nor does the fact that the number of variables in the WRITE # statements in one program doesn't match the number of variables in the INPUT # statements in the other. To the computer, the file is a series of values (rather like a DATA statement), and to set a variable in an INPUT # statement it just reads the next value from the file. The computer does need to know when a string value can be expected to pop out of the file, and it must have a string variable in its INPUT # statement in which to store it.

In the program in Fig. 6-9, this statement:

4290 INPUT #1,X,Y,PTCOLOR

reads the data that are written by either of the two programs in Fig. 6-10 and Fig. 6-11.

Scaling the Data

As we mentioned in the previous section, it is a good idea to store data in a form that relates to the real world and to convert that data later so that they fit on the graphics screen. The data stored in the file read by the scatter chart program consist of an x coordinate, a y coordinate, and a color, which in the case of the sample data represent the price the user paid, the user's degree of satisfaction, and the brand purchased. One problem arises: the x coordinates in the file may not run from 0 to 320 and the y coordinates may not run from 0 to 200, the legal screen coordinates. In the sample data, for instance, the prices that the customers paid vary from $500 to $5,000 and the satisfaction levels vary from 0 to 100. Both must be scaled to fit on the screen.

We are saddled with two sets of coordinates: the "real-world" coordinates in the input data, and the "screen" coordinates with which the graph will be drawn. The following process solves the problem of converting the input real-word coordinates to screen coordinates.

The technique for fitting things on the screen is outlined below and illustrated in Fig. 6-13. Follow along in the figure while reading these three steps:

1. Subtract the value of the minimum real-world x coordinate that you wish to show on the screen from the real-world x coordinate of each point and subtract the value of the minimum real-world y coordinate that you wish to show on the screen from the real-world y coordinate of each point.

2. Calculate the range of the real-world x coordinates to be graphed by subtracting the smallest real-world x coordinate of points to show on the screen from the largest; calculate the range of real-world y coordinates similarly by subtracting the smallest real-world y coordinate of points to show on the screen from the largest. Calculate the allowable ranges of screen x and y coordinates. Take all the coordinates that resulted from step 1 and multiply them by the ratios of these ranges of coordinates.

3. If the graph on the screen does not begin at the left-hand edge, where the x coordinate is 0, then add the minimum screen x coordinate you intend to use on the screen to the x coordinates you got in step 2. Since the y coordinates on the screen number from the top whereas real-world y coordinates number from the bottom, you must calculate the screen y coordinate by subtracting the y coordinates you got in step 2 from the largest y coordinate you intend to use on the screen.

The code that performs these steps in the scatter chart program is contained in the subroutine at statement 6000. That subroutine first calculates RANGE.X, RANGE.Y, SCALE.X, and SCALE.Y in preparation for step 2, using the minimum and maximum values given in statement 2020. (If the program finds a point in the file whose x or y coordinate is ouside the range you give, then that point is not drawn.) If you input

0,5600,10,90

at statement 2020, then the legal range for real-world x coordinates runs from 0 to 5600 and the legal range for real-world y coordinates runs from 10 to 90. RANGE.X is 5600, and RANGE.Y is 80 (90 − 10). The x coordinates on the screen run from 40 to 320 for a range of 280. Therefore, SCALE.X is

280 / 5600

or

1 / 20

The y coordinates on the screen run from 0 to 160 for a range of 160.

Therefore, SCALE.Y is

   160 / 80

which is

   2

Step 1 of this process occurs in statements 6070 and 6090. Steps 2 and 3 are carried out by statements 6080 and 6100.

The statements from lines 6120 to 6150 determine if a point is off the graph and prevent it from being drawn if it is.

Fig. 6-13   Scaling Coordinates to Fit on the Screen

Suppose that in the real data you are using, the x coordinates run from 0 to 5,600 and the y coordinates run from 10 to 90. Suppose also that you are using the part of the screen running from x = 40 to x = 320 and from y = 0 to y = 160. Your real world might look like this:

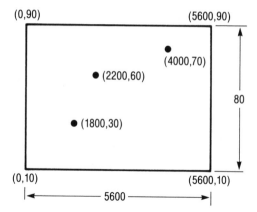

Your screen might look like this:

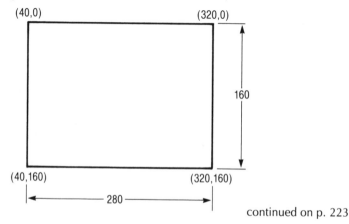

continued on p. 223

continued from p. 222

Step 1 of the transformation process described in the text indicates that we should subtract 10 from each of the y coordinates:

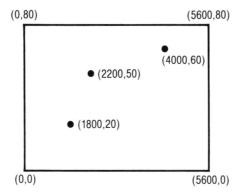

Step 2 requires that we multiply the x coordinates by 0.05 (which is 280/5,600) and multiply the y coordinates by 2 (40/20):

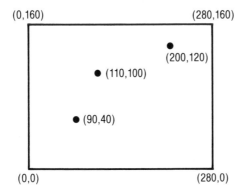

Step 3 requires that we add 40 to each x coordinate (the x coordinate of the lower left-hand corner of the screen) and subtract each y coordinate from 160:

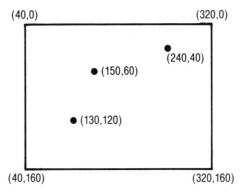

These new coordinates fit nicely in the available screen space.

Miscellaneous Observations

The subroutine at statement 5000 draws the outline of the graph on the screen, adds five tick marks on each axis (as shown in Fig. 6-14), and prints values associated with the tick marks. It would be difficult to change the number of tick marks, since the program must align the labels with the tick marks by aligning text and graphics. Since text can be inserted only at locations whose graphics coordinates are multiples of eight, the program must be careful about where it puts tick marks. It could not arbitrarily insert, say, seven tick marks and still be able to align the text with them.

Possible improvements that could be made to this program include:

1. The program could allow the user to select how the third coordinates coming from the file determine the colors of the corresponding points. For example, you might allow the third number to be anything and then let the user tell the computer what ranges represent what colors.

2. The user should have some way of ending the program. Currently, only holding down the control key and pressing the break key does this.

3. The program should print titles for the x and y axes. This is easy for the x axis, since the program need only print the x axis title along the bottom of the screen. The label for the y axis, however, is harder, since the program must print it letter by letter down the left-hand edge of the screen.

Fig. 6-14   Screen Coordinates of Graph Drawn by Scatter Chart Program

The screen coordinates shown here are the ones used by the scatter chart program.

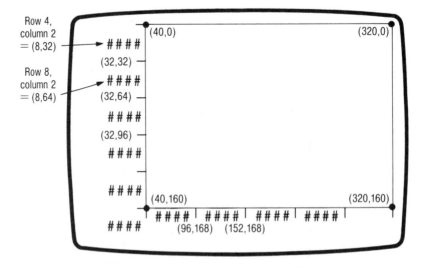

7 | Graphics on Dot Matrix Printers

To use the information in this chapter, you must have a *dot matrix printer* capable of doing graphics—preferably the IBM Personal Computer Graphics Printer or the Epson MX-80—and not a *character printer*. Dot matrix printers form letters by printing patterns of dots; character printers print whole letters at one blow. A close squint at a sample printout from your printer will reveal to you whether or not the printed letters are made up of patterns of tiny dots. A close squint at the manual will reveal whether or not your printer has been designed for graphics. If you have the IBM Personal Computer Graphics Printer or the Epson MX-80, you will be able to use the programs in this chapter as they stand. (The IBM Personal Computer Graphics Printer is built for IBM by Epson; it and the Epson MX-80 are substantially identical.) If you have a different sort of dot matrix printer, you can follow the concepts discussed in this chapter, but since dot matrix printers do graphics in different ways, you'll probably have to do some reprogramming to make the examples work. If you have a character printer, the discussion in this chapter won't apply. You can read on and decide whether to purchase a dot matrix printer. If you have an IBM Personal Computer (nongraphics) Printer, IBM will exchange the few necessary electronic parts to make it into a graphics printer for a relatively reasonable charge.

7.1 FUNDAMENTALS OF DOT MATRIX PRINTERS

Dot matrix printers print patterns of dots. The print head contains a vertical column of pins—the IBM Personal Computer Graphics Printer has nine of them—each of which prints a dot on the paper when it is fired. The print head moves across the print line in steps much smaller than the width of a letter. At each step, the printer can command the various pins to fire. The printer contains a small electronic memory that tells it what pins to fire at what steps in order to form the various letters. To print a letter, the print head steps to the left-most edge of the letter, and various pins fire; the print head then steps a fraction to the right, and other pins fire; the process continues with the print head stepping to the right and various pins firing until the letter is complete. See Fig. 7-1.

Fig. 7-1   How a Dot Matrix Printer Prints the Letter K

To print the letter K, a dot matrix printer moves its print head to the left-hand edge of the letter:

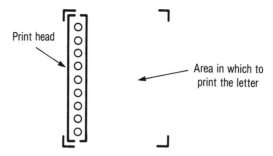

Most pins fire, forming the vertical stem of the K:

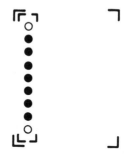

The print head steps to the right:

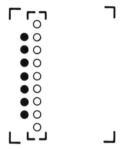

continued on p. 227

continued from p. 226

One dot fires, starting the two arms of the K, and the print head steps to the right:

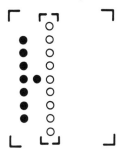

Two dots fire, and the print head steps again:

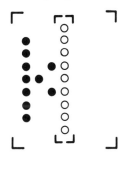

Eventually . . .

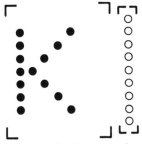

Most dot matrix printers print dots much closer together than shown in this figure in order to print smoother letters.

Whenever it is printing, the computer sends the printer a stream of numbers between 1 and 255. When the printer is in what we shall call *character mode*, in which it behaves "normally" and prints letters, digits, punctuation, and so on, the computer does not control the individual pins in the print head. Instead, the numbers that the computer sends are the *ASCII codes* of the letters to print. Each of the letters A to Z, each of the digits 0 to 9, and many punctuation and other symbols have been assigned ASCII codes, numbers between 1 and 255, in a more or less standard way in the computer industry. A table of the assignments of the ASCII code numbers can be found in the appendix of the IBM BASIC manual. In character mode, when the printer receives an ASCII code, it raids its memory for the dot pattern that forms the letter assigned that ASCII code and then fires the appropriate pins at the appropriate times to form that pattern. Since the ASCII code for the letter K is 75, for example, sending the number 75 to the printer causes it to print a pattern of dots that looks like a K.

To allow any pattern of dots to be printed, *graphics mode* turns control of the individual pins in the print head over to the computer. The computer still sends the printer numbers between 1 and 255, but the printer, instead of interpreting these numbers as ASCII codes and printing the corresponding letters, treats them as instructions about which pins to fire at each horizontal step of the print head.

Graphics Mode on the IBM Graphics Printer

When you turn it on, the IBM Personal Computer Graphics Printer is in character mode. A special sequence of ASCII codes from the computer is used to tell it to change to graphics mode. This sequence is an *escape* symbol followed by a K or an L and two more characters that encode the number of graphics mode instructions the computer will send the printer. You must figure out the number of instructions in advance, because no set of codes tells the printer to go back into character mode. The printer treats everything sent to it as a graphics mode instruction until it receives the number of graphics mode instructions it was told to expect; then it goes back to character mode on its own.

The ASCII code of the *escape* symbol is 27, and the ASCII codes of K and L are 75 and 76. When the printer receives a 27 followed by either a 75 or 76, it does not print anything; it simply shifts into graphics mode. The difference between using a K and using an L is discussed below. The third character is the remainder you get when you divide the number of graphics mode instructions you wish to send by 256. The fourth character is the quotient you get from the same division. Here are a few examples:

If you wish to send 33 graphics mode instructions to the printer, then the following statement must appear in your program just before you send the graphics instructions to the printer:

147 LPRINT CHR$(27) ; "L" ; CHR$(33) ; CHR$(0) ;

The CHR$ function sends to the printer the number sent to it. We will use it extensively for printer graphics. Therefore, the result of this instruction is to send the printer these four numbers:

27　75　33　0

If you wish to send 700 characters of graphics data to the printer, you divide 700 by 256, which gives 2 with a remainder of 188. You therefore use this statement:

178 LPRINT CHR$(27) ; "L" ; CHR$(188) ; CHR$(2) ;

KEEPING BASIC OUT OF YOUR WAY

Note the semicolons on the ends of the above two statements. These *must* be there, because otherwise BASIC thinks you are now done printing on the current print line. If you let BASIC think this, it will tell the printer to go to the next line by sending the ASCII codes for "carriage return" and "line feed." The printer, however, now in graphics mode instead of character mode, treats these two ASCII codes as graphics mode instructions instead of doing a carriage return and advancing the paper. This prints some dots you probably don't want. Furthermore, the two ASCII codes count as your first two graphics mode instructions, since the printer doesn't care that BASIC sent them on its own without permission, and this will mess up your count of graphics mode instructions.

Since BASIC knows nothing about printer graphics mode, it has one more perverse habit. After eighty "characters" are "printed" on one line, BASIC assumes that the printer has come to the end of the line, so it helpfully shovels the ASCII codes for a carriage return and a line feed into the stream of numbers being sent to the printer to get you to the next line. This means that after eighty of your graphics mode instructions, BASIC will insert two of its own, yielding the same attendant problems we discussed above. Since you are likely to want to send more than eighty graphics mode instructions at a time—eighty graphics mode instructions do not come close to filling an entire line—you will want to turn this helpful feature of BASIC off. Here is the statement to do this:

103 WIDTH "LPT1:" , 255

After this statement, BASIC never sends a carriage return and line feed to the printer just because it thinks that you have run out of space on the line. (It will still send them, though, if you are so injudicious as to end an LPRINT statement without a semicolon.)

K AND L: MEDIUM AND HIGH RESOLUTION GRAPHICS MODE

The printer moves its print head horizontally either 1/60 inch or 1/120 inch between graphics mode instructions. If you use a K when you enter graphics mode, the printer will move the print head 1/60 inch after each graphics command, a state of affairs that we shall call *medium resolution graphics*. If you use an L instead, the printer moves the print head 1/120 inch after each graphics command; we shall call this *high resolution graphics*. The dots are 1/72 inch apart vertically in either mode. In high resolution graphics you must print twice as many dots as in medium resolution graphics, but you can print much clearer pictures, with smoother curves, blacker black areas, and so on.

CONTROLLING THE PRINT HEAD PINS IN GRAPHICS MODE

Eight pins on the print head can be used in graphics mode. (The print head has nine, but the ninth one is used only in character mode.) They are numbered from the top of the print head to the bottom, as follows:

* 128
* 64
* 32
* 16
* 8
* 4
* 2
* 1

The graphics mode instruction to fire a single pin is the number of that pin. For example, to fire just the bottom pin, you could use this statement:

417 LPRINT CHR$(1) ;

To fire the next to the top pin, you could use this statement:

776 LPRINT CHR$(64) ;

Examine the program in Fig. 7-2, which prints a horizontal line across the page. Statement 140 suppresses the carriage return and line feed that BASIC normally sends after eighty characters. Statement 160 tells the printer to expect three hundred graphics mode instructions and to print in high resolution graphics. The loop from statement 170 to 190 sends the number 1 to the printer 300 times. Each time, the printer fires the bottom pin and moves the print head 1/120 inch to the right. When the program is over, the printer reverts to character mode, since it will have received the expected 300 graphics mode instructions.

The program in Fig. 7-3 is similar, except that it prints forty each of the various pins on the print head. The output from the program is shown in Fig. 7-4.

Fig. 7-2 Program to Print a Horizontal Line

```
100 ' --- PROGRAM TO PRINT LINE 300 DOTS LONG
110 '
120 '
130 ' --- SET UP PRINTER
140     WIDTH "LPT1:",255
150 '
160     LPRINT  CHR$(27) ; "L" ; CHR$(44) ; CHR$(1) ;
170     FOR DOT = 1 TO 300
180        LPRINT CHR$(1);
190     NEXT DOT
200     LPRINT
210     END
```

Fig. 7-3 Program to Print Stair Steps

```
100 ' --- PROGRAM TO PRINT STAIR STEPS
110 '
120 '
130 ' --- SET UP OUTPUT CHARACTER ARRAY
140     OUTPUT.CHARACTER(1) = 1
150     OUTPUT.CHARACTER(2) = 2
160     OUTPUT.CHARACTER(3) = 4
170     OUTPUT.CHARACTER(4) = 8
180     OUTPUT.CHARACTER(5) = 16
190     OUTPUT.CHARACTER(6) = 32
200     OUTPUT.CHARACTER(7) = 64
210     OUTPUT.CHARACTER(8) = 128
220 '
230 '
240 ' --- SET UP PRINTER
250     WIDTH "LPT1:",255
260 '
270     LPRINT  CHR$(27) ; "L" ; CHR$(64) ; CHR$(1) ;
280     FOR HEIGHT = 1 TO 8
290        FOR DOT = 1 TO 40
300           LPRINT CHR$(OUTPUT.CHARACTER(HEIGHT));
310        NEXT DOT
320     NEXT HEIGHT
330     LPRINT
340     END
```

Fig. 7-4   Output from Stair Step Program

To fire two or more of the pins in the print head simultaneously, send the printer the sum of the numbers of the pins that you wish to fire. For example, to fire the top and bottom pins simultaneously, you send 128 + 1, or 129. To fire all the pins, you send 128 + 64 + 32 + 16 + 8 + 4 + 2 + 1, which is 255. To fire no pins, you send a 0; the printer prints no dots, but it does move its print head one step to the right. Readers familiar with base 2 arithmetic will note that the number that the computer sends to the printer is a binary representation of the pattern of pins to be fired.

Fig. 7-5   Firing More Than One Pin at a Time

```
100 ' --- PROGRAM TO PRINT MORE STAIR STEPS
110 '
120 '
130 ' --- SET UP OUTPUT CHARACTER ARRAY
140        OUTPUT.CHARACTER(1)  = 1
150        OUTPUT.CHARACTER(2)  = 3
160        OUTPUT.CHARACTER(3)  = 7
170        OUTPUT.CHARACTER(4)  = 15
180        OUTPUT.CHARACTER(5)  = 31
190        OUTPUT.CHARACTER(6)  = 63
200        OUTPUT.CHARACTER(7)  = 127
210        OUTPUT.CHARACTER(8)  = 255
220 '
230 '
240 ' --- SET UP PRINTER
250        WIDTH "LPT1:",255
260 '
270        LPRINT  CHR$(27) ; "L" ; CHR$(64) ; CHR$(1) ;
280        FOR HEIGHT = 1 TO 8
290           FOR DOT = 1 TO 40
300              LPRINT CHR$(OUTPUT.CHARACTER(HEIGHT));
310           NEXT DOT
320        NEXT HEIGHT
330        LPRINT
340        END
```

Fig. 7-6   Output from More Stair Step Program

The program in Fig. 7-5 prints the set of stair steps shown in Fig. 7-6. The computer first sends the printer forty 1's, which causes it to print forty times with just the bottom pin, as it did in the previous programs. Then the computer sends forty 3's. Since 3 is 2 + 1, the bottom two pins now fire. When the computer next sends out 7's, which is 4 + 2 + 1, the printer fires the three bottom pins, and so on. At the end of the program, when the computer is sending 255's to the printer, the printer is firing all of its pins at every print position. This is noisy, by the way, which is normal. The picture is twice as wide as that printed by the program in Fig. 7-3 because this program uses medium resolution graphics printing. If it used high resolution graphics printing, the picture would be half as wide but twice as black as it is now.

Vertical Spacing: Program to Draw a Rectangle

Consider a program to print a rectangle 2 inches wide by 1 inch tall. Printing something 2 inches wide presents no problem: in high resolution graphics printing, with 120 dots per horizontal inch, a line 2 inches long takes 240 dots, and in medium resolution graphics, with 60 dots per inch, it takes 120 dots. Similarly, since there are 72 dots to the inch vertically, it takes 72 dots to make a 1-inch vertical line. Making the rectangle 1 inch tall, however, introduces a new problem. Although the outputs of our example programs so far have been restricted to one printer line, a rectangle 1 inch tall cannot be squeezed onto one printer line. Therefore, we must learn how to control vertical spacing.

In character mode, the printer prints six lines to the inch; each time the printer moves from one line to the next, the paper advances 1/6 inch. Since the letters themselves are only about 1/8 inch tall, this leaves a space between each pair of consecutive lines on the page. This space is suitable in character mode, where it makes the text easier to read, but it is anathema in graphics mode, where you don't want gaps in your pictures. The eight dots on the print head used for graphics are 1/72 inch from one another. Each line printed in graphics mode is therefore 8/72 inch high. To get a continuous picture, the printer must therefore advance the paper 8/72 inch from one line to the next rather than 1/6 (12/72) inch. You achieve this by giving a sequence of numbers to the printer that tells it how far to advance the paper between lines. The sequence of numbers is a 27 (the ASCII code for "escape") followed by a 65 (the ASCII code for the letter A) followed by the number of 72nds of an inch to advance. The statement to set the printer to space 8/72 inch after each line is therefore:

442 LPRINT CHR$(27) ; "A" ; CHR$(8) ;

Your program must execute this statement while still in character mode before it embarks on any graphics mode printing.

Figure 7-7 shows schematically how the program in Fig. 7-8 draws a rectangle. On the first line, the first graphics command must print the bottom four dots on the print head, making up the start of the left-hand side of the

Fig. 7-7   Plan for Drawing a 1-by-2-Inch Rectangle

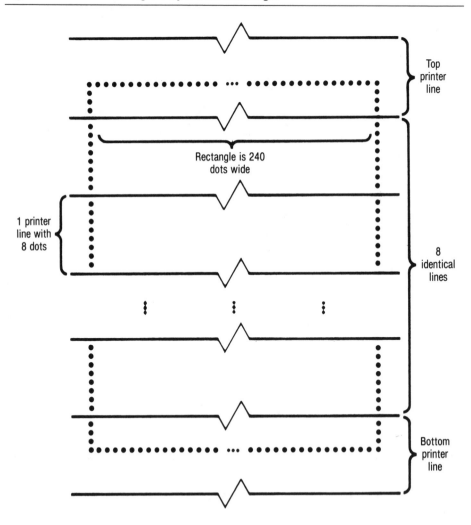

rectangle. Only the fourth dot prints at the next 238 graphics positions, forming the horizontal top of the rectangle. At the last print position, the bottom four dots print once again to start the right-hand side of the rectangle. On each of the next eight printer lines, the first graphics instruction must print all eight dots to continue forming the left-hand side of the rectangle, the next 238 instructions must print no dots, and the final instruction must print all eight dots to continue the right-hand side of the rectangle. On the last printer line, the first graphics instruction must print the top four dots to finish the left-hand side of the rectangle, after which must follow 238 instructions with just the dot fourth from the top to form the horizontal bottom of the rectangle, and then finally an instruction with the top four dots to finish the right-hand side of the rectangle.

In the program in Fig. 7-8, line 150 sets the space between printer lines to 8/72 inch, as we discussed. Since 15 is 8 + 4 + 2 + 1, statement 200 starts by printing the bottom four dots at the first character position on the line. The STRING$ function then sends 238 eights to the printer. At the end of statement 200, a second 15 is sent. The loop from 230 to 260 prints eight identical printer lines, each of which has eight dots at each end and 238 spaces of blank in between. Statement 300 draws the bottom of the rectangle and the bottoms of the left- and right-hand sides. Notice that the LPRINT

Fig. 7-8   Program to Draw a Rectangle

```
100 ' --- PROGRAM TO PRINT RECTANGLE
110 '
120 '
130 ' --- SET UP PRINTER
140       WIDTH "LPT1:",255
150       LPRINT  CHR$(27) ; "A" ; CHR$(8) ;
160 '
170 '
180 ' --- PRINT TOP OF RECTANGLE
190       LPRINT  CHR$(27) ; "L" ; CHR$(240) ; CHR$(0) ;
200       LPRINT  CHR$(15) ; STRING$(238,8) ; CHR$(15)
210 '
220 ' --- PRINT THE SIDES OF THE RECTANGLE
230       FOR P.LINE = 1 TO 8
240          LPRINT  CHR$(27) ; "L" ; CHR$(240) ; CHR$(0) ;
250          LPRINT  CHR$(255) ; STRING$(238,0) ; CHR$(255)
260       NEXT P.LINE
270 '
280 ' --- PRINT THE BOTTOM OF THE RECTANGLE
290       LPRINT  CHR$(27) ; "L" CHR$(240) ; CHR$(0) ;
300       LPRINT  CHR$(240) ; STRING$(238,16) ; CHR$(240)
310 '
320       END
```

statements at 200, 250, and 300 do not end with semicolons. When these statements are over, the printer is in character mode, since these statements send the 240 graphics instructions that statements 190, 240, and 290 promised the printer. Therefore, the printer responds to the carriage return and line feed sent by BASIC by advancing the paper 8/72 inch to the next line. You must always let the printer return to character mode to get from one printer line to the next.

Double-Width Text

Two sequences of commands can be sent to the printer when it is in character mode to control the use of *double-width text*. After the first of these,

        345 LPRINT CHR$(27) ; "W" ; CHR$(1) ;

the printer prints all text with letters that are twice as wide as normal. To turn this feature back off, use this statement:

        356 LPRINT CHR$(27) ; "W" ; CHR$(0) ;

The printer also has features to print compressed text, subscripts, super-scripts, underlined characters, and other things too numerous to cover in detail here. All these features are controlled with statements similar to the above.

Text and Graphics Combined

You can combine text and graphics on the same printer line just by moving back and forth between character mode and graphics mode. The only problem you must solve is to get the text and the graphics to line up. The number of graphics positions taken up by each letter depends on whether you are using medium resolution graphics printing or high resolution graphics printing, and the size of letters you are using, as summarized in this table:

	Low Resolution	High Resolution
Regular Letters	6 dots/letter	12
Double Width	12	24

The program in Fig. 7-9 draws a rectangle 240 dots wide in medium resolution printing and centers the words "PRINTER GRAPHICS" in it. In medium resolution graphics printing, regular letters take up six dots on the line. The phrase "PRINTER GRAPHICS" has sixteen letters (including the space between the words, which also takes up six dots on the line), so it uses a total of 16 × 6, or 96, dots. To print a graphics line 240 dots wide, 144 graphics commands must be sent to the printer in addition to the letters (240 total minus the 96 taken by the letters).

Lines 270 to 274 of the program in Fig. 7-9 print the line that includes the text. The 144 necessary graphics characters are divided into two blocks of 72 each, one to the left and one to the right of the text (thereby centering the text

Fig. 7-9   Combining Text and Graphics

```
100   ' --- PROGRAM TO PRINT RECTANGLE
110   '
120   '
130   ' --- SET UP PRINTER
140       WIDTH "LPT1:",255
150       LPRINT  CHR$(27) ; "A" ; CHR$(8) ;
160   '
170   '
180   ' --- PRINT TOP OF RECTANGLE
190       LPRINT  CHR$(27) ; "K" ; CHR$(240) ; CHR$(0) ;
200       LPRINT  CHR$(15) ; STRING$(238,8) ; CHR$(15)
210   '
220   ' --- PRINT THE SIDES OF THE RECTANGLE
230       LPRINT  CHR$(27) ; "K" ; CHR$(240) ; CHR$(0) ;
240       LPRINT  CHR$(255) ; STRING$(238,0) ; CHR$(255)
245   '
250       LPRINT  CHR$(27) ; "K" ; CHR$(240) ; CHR$(0) ;
260       LPRINT  CHR$(255) ; STRING$(238,0) ; CHR$(255)
265   '
270       LPRINT  CHR$(27) ; "K" ; CHR$(72) ; CHR$(0) ;
271       LPRINT  CHR$(255) ; STRING$(71,0) ;
272       LPRINT  "PRINTER GRAPHICS" ;
273       LPRINT  CHR$(27) ; "K" ; CHR$(72) ; CHR$(0) ;
274       LPRINT  STRING$(71,0) ; CHR$(255)
275   '
290       LPRINT  CHR$(27) ; "K" ; CHR$(240) ; CHR$(0) ;
300       LPRINT  CHR$(255) ; STRING$(238,0) ; CHR$(255)
305   '
310       LPRINT  CHR$(27) ; "K" ; CHR$(240) ; CHR$(0) ;
320       LPRINT  CHR$(255) ; STRING$(238,0) ; CHR$(255)
330   '
340   ' --- PRINT THE BOTTOM OF THE RECTANGLE
350       LPRINT  CHR$(27) ; "K" CHR$(240) ; CHR$(0) ;
360       LPRINT  CHR$(248) ; STRING$(238,8) ; CHR$(248)
370   '
380       END
```

in the rectangle). Statements 270 and 271 print the left-hand side of the rectangle plus 71 blanks. Statement 272 prints the text. Statements 273 and 274 print another 71 graphics blanks and the right-hand side of the rectangle.

A Special Bug Possible in Printer Graphics

If you write graphics printing programs, sooner or later you will accidentally write some program that tells the printer to expect a certain number of graphics instructions and then sends it a different number of graphics instructions. If more instructions are sent than were promised, the printer will get back into character mode and print the last of the graphics instructions as letters and other symbols. This causes very strange printouts but is otherwise harmless. If the printer gets fewer graphics instructions than it expected, however, it just waits forever for the rest of them. Whatever you print next the printer assumes to be more graphics instructions. Furthermore, while it is waiting, the printer will not even let you mark it off line with the ON LINE button. This is, needless to say, a little disconcerting. The easiest way to bring your printer back to life is to turn it off and then back on, which restores it to character mode.

7.2 HORIZONTAL BAR CHARTS

The program in Fig. 7-10 draws a bar chart given the information for the chart input by the user. If the user's input is as shown in Fig. 7-12, then the chart printed by this program will be like the one shown in Fig 7-11. The program gets its input from the user in the subroutine at statement 4000, which inputs or calculates each of the following variables:

TITLE$—is the name for the bar chart.
BLOCK.NAME$—contains names for the various blocks in each bar. (We will use the same bar chart terminology we used in Chapter 6; see Fig. 6-6.)
BLOCK.COUNT—is the number of valid entries in BLOCK.NAME$.
BLOCK.LENGTH—is the number of letters in the longest block name.
BAR.NAME$—contains the titles for each of the bars in the graph.
BAR.COUNT—is the number of bars the user has input.
BAR.LENGTH—is the number of letters in the longest bar name.
BAR.VALUE—contains the sizes of the blocks in each bar, measured by the number of dots they will take up.

Fig. 7-10   Program to Print Bar Charts

```
1000 ' --- PROGRAM TO PRINT BAR GRAPHS
1010 '
1020 '
1030 '
1040       GOSUB 3000      ' INITIALIZE VARIABLES
1050       GOSUB 4000      ' GET INPUT
1060       GOSUB 5000      ' PRINT CHART
1070 '
1080       END
1090 '
1100 '
1110 '
2000 ' --- SUBROUTINE TO DRAW A BAR
2010 '        BAR.LENGTH CONTAINS THE LENGTH OF THE BAR IN DOTS
2020 '        BLOCK.COLOR CONTAINS THE COLOR (1-4) OF THE BAR
2030 '
2040       LET DOTS.256 = BAR.LENGTH \ 256
2050       LET DOTS.MOD.256 = BAR.LENGTH MOD 256
2060 '
2070       LPRINT  CHR$(27) ; "L" ; CHR$(DOTS.MOD.256) ;
              CHR$(DOTS.256) ;
2080 '
2090       FOR DOT = 1 TO BAR.LENGTH
2100          PATTERN = DOT MOD 4 + 1
2110          LPRINT  CHR$(BAR.PATTERNS(BLOCK.COLOR,PATTERN)) ;
2120       NEXT DOT
2130 '
2140       RETURN
2150 '
2160 '
2170 '
3000 ' --- SUBROUTINE TO SET UP COLORS FOR BARS
3010 '
3020 ' --- COLOR 1 IS ENTIRELY BLACK DOTS
3030       BAR.PATTERNS(1,1) = 255
3040       BAR.PATTERNS(1,2) = 255
3050       BAR.PATTERNS(1,3) = 255
3060       BAR.PATTERNS(1,4) = 255
3070 '
3080 ' --- COLOR 2 IS HORIZONTAL STRIPES
3090       BAR.PATTERNS(2,1) = 85
3100       BAR.PATTERNS(2,2) = 85
3110       BAR.PATTERNS(2,3) = 85
3120       BAR.PATTERNS(2,4) = 85
3130 '
3140 ' --- COLOR 3 IS GREY
3150       BAR.PATTERNS(3,1) = 85
3160       BAR.PATTERNS(3,2) = 170
3170       BAR.PATTERNS(3,3) = 85
3180       BAR.PATTERNS(3,4) = 170
3190 '
```

continued on p. 240

continued from p. 239

```
3200 ' --- COLOR 4 IS DIAGONAL LINES
3210        BAR.PATTERNS(4,1) = 17
3220        BAR.PATTERNS(4,2) = 34
3230        BAR.PATTERNS(4,3) = 68
3240        BAR.PATTERNS(4,4) = 136
3250 '
3260 '
3270 ' --- COLOR 5 IS VERTICAL LINES
3280        BAR.PATTERNS(5,1) = 255
3290        BAR.PATTERNS(5,2) = 0
3300        BAR.PATTERNS(5,3) = 0
3310        BAR.PATTERNS(5,4) = 0
3320 '
3330 ' --- COLOR 6 IS CROSSHATCHING
3340        BAR.PATTERNS(6,1) = 17
3350        BAR.PATTERNS(6,2) = 170
3360        BAR.PATTERNS(6,3) = 68
3370        BAR.PATTERNS(6,4) = 170
3380 '
3390 ' --- COLOR 7 IS DIAGONAL LINES
3400        BAR.PATTERNS(7,1) = 136
3410        BAR.PATTERNS(7,2) = 68
3420        BAR.PATTERNS(7,3) = 34
3430        BAR.PATTERNS(7,4) = 17
3440 '
3450        RETURN
3460 '
3470 '
3480 '
4000 ' --- THIS SUBROUTINE GETS INPUT FROM THE USER
4010        INPUT "GIVE THE TITLE FOR THE GRAPH:" , TITLE$
4020 '
4030        PRINT
4040        PRINT
4050        PRINT "GIVE THE NAMES OF UP TO SEVEN VARIABLES YOU"
4060        PRINT "WISH TO GRAPH IN YOUR BAR CHART."
4070        PRINT "PRESS 'ENTER' AND NO NAME WHEN YOU HAVE
                    FINISHED."
4080        PRINT " "
4090 '
4100        BLOCK.COUNT = 0
4110        BLOCK.LENGTH = 0
4120 ' --- LOOP TO GET BLOCK NAMES
4130 '
4140           IF  BLOCK.COUNT=7  GOTO 4250
4150 '
4160           INPUT "BLOCK NAME:" , TEMP$
4170 '
4180           IF  TEMP$ = ""  GOTO 4250
4190 '
4200           BLOCK.COUNT = BLOCK.COUNT + 1
4210           BLOCK.NAME$(BLOCK.COUNT) = TEMP$
4220           TEMP = LEN(TEMP$)
4230           IF  TEMP > BLOCK.LENGTH  THEN
                    BLOCK.LENGTH = TEMP
4240        GOTO 4120
4250 '
```

continued on p. 241

continued from p. 240

```
4260        PRINT
4270        PRINT
4280        PRINT "GIVE THE NAME FOR EACH BAR AND THEN THE VALUES"
4290        PRINT "THAT EACH OF THE BLOCKS IS TO HAVE IN THAT"
4300        PRINT "BAR (IN THE ORDER YOU GAVE THE BLOCK NAMES)"
4305        PRINT "SEPARATED BY COMMAS.  YOU MAY ENTER UP TO TEN"
4310        PRINT "BARS.  PRESS 'ENTER' WITH NO ENTRY WHEN YOU"
4320        PRINT "HAVE FINISHED."
4330        PRINT " "
4340      '
4350        BAR.COUNT = 0
4360        BAR.NAME.LENGTH = 0
4370      ' --- LOOP TO GET VALUES
4380      '
4390            IF BAR.COUNT = 10   GOTO 4610
4400      '
4410            LINE INPUT "BAR INFORMATION:" , TEMP$
4420      '
4430            IF   TEMP$ = ""   GOTO 4610
4440      '
4450            BAR.COUNT = BAR.COUNT + 1
4460            COMMA = INSTR(TEMP$,",")
4470            BAR.NAME$(BAR.COUNT) = LEFT$(TEMP$,COMMA-1)
4480            TEMP = LEN(BAR.NAME$(BAR.COUNT))
4490            IF   TEMP > BAR.NAME.LENGTH   THEN
                      BAR.NAME.LENGTH = TEMP
4500            TEMP$ = MID$(TEMP$,COMMA+1)
4510      '
4520      ' ---    LOOP TO GET EACH VALUE FROM TEMP$ STRING
4530            FOR I = 1 TO BLOCK.COUNT
4540               BAR.VALUE(BAR.COUNT,I) = VAL(TEMP$)
4550               COMMA = INSTR(TEMP$,",")
4560               IF   COMMA <> 0   THEN TEMP$ = MID$(TEMP$,COMMA+1)
4570            NEXT I
4580      '
4590        GOTO 4370
4600      '
4610        RETURN
4620      '
4630      '
4640      '
5000      ' --- SUBROUTINE TO PRINT GRAPH
5010      '
5020      '
5030        LPRINT CHR$(27) ; "W" ; CHR$(1) ; TITLE$
5040        LPRINT CHR$(27) ; "W" ; CHR$(0)
5050        LPRINT
5060        LPRINT
5070      '
5080      '
```

continued on p. 242

continued from p. 241

```
5090        FOR I = 1 TO BAR.COUNT
5100            LPRINT BAR.NAME$(I) ; TAB(BAR.NAME.LENGTH + 2) ;
5110 '
5120          FOR J = 1 TO BLOCK.COUNT
5130              BAR.LENGTH = BAR.VALUE(I,J)
5140              BLOCK.COLOR = J
5150              GOSUB 2000
5160          NEXT J
5170 '
5180          LPRINT " "
5190          LPRINT " "
5200        NEXT I
5210 '
5220        LPRINT
5230        LPRINT
5240        LPRINT "LEGEND:   ----------------------------------------"
5250        LPRINT
5260 '
5270        FOR I = 1 TO BLOCK.COUNT
5280            LPRINT BLOCK.NAME$(I) ; TAB(BLOCK.LENGTH+2) ;
5290            BAR.LENGTH = 100
5300            BLOCK.COLOR = I
5310            GOSUB 2000
5320            LPRINT " "
5330            LPRINT " "
5340        NEXT I
5350 '
5360        RETURN
```

Fig. 7-11　Bar Chart Printed by Bar Chart Printing Program

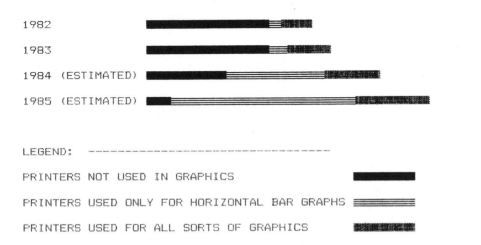

Fig. 7-12   User Input Given to Print Bar Chart in Fig. 7-11

```
RUN
GIVE THE TITLE FOR THE GRAPH:DOT MATRIX PRINTERS AND GRAPHICS


GIVE THE NAMES OF UP TO SEVEN VARIABLES YOU WISH TO
GRAPH IN YOUR BAR CHART.  PRESS 'ENTER' AND NO NAME
WHEN YOU HAVE FINISHED.

VARIABLE NAME:PRINTERS NOT USED IN GRAPHICS
VARIABLE NAME:PRINTERS USED ONLY FOR HORIZONTAL BAR GRAPHS
VARIABLE NAME:PRINTERS USED FOR ALL SORTS OF GRAPHICS
VARIABLE NAME:


GIVE THE NAME FOR EACH BAR AND THEN THE VALUES THAT EACH
OF THE VARIABLES IS TO HAVE IN THAT BAR (IN THE ORDER THAT
YOU GAVE THE VARIABLES) SEPARATED BY COMMAS.  YOU MAY ENTER
UP TO TEN BARS.  PRESS 'ENTER' WITH NO ENTRY WHEN YOU HAVE
FINISHED.

BAR INFORMATION:1982,200,20,50
BAR·INFORMATION:1983,200,30,70
BAR INFORMATION:1984 (ESTIMATED),130,160,90
BAR INFORMATION:1985 (ESTIMATED),40,300,120
```

The subroutine at statement 5000 draws the bar chart with the data from the subroutine at statement 4000. It first prints the title of the chart in double-width printing. Then it prints each of the bars in the loop from statement 5090 to 5200. At statement 5100, it prints the name of the bar it is about to print. Then it tabs to the location where the bars will start—the character position two to the right of the last character of the longest of the bar names. The loop from statement 5120 to 5150 prints each block of the bar, one at a time. The subroutine at statement 2000 draws a block whose length is given by the variable BLOCK.LENGTH using a pattern of dots selected by the variable BLOCK.COLOR. This will be explained below.

After printing all of the bars, the program prints a legend to tell the user which dot pattern represents which variable. The loop from 5270 to 5340 does this, using a scheme similar to that used to print the bars themselves: the name of the block is printed, and the printer is tabbed to the character space two beyond the last letter in the longest block name; then the subroutine at statement 2000 draws a single block 100 dots long using the appropriate dot pattern.

The subroutine at statement 2000 draws a repeating pattern of dots whose overall length is given by the variable BLOCK.LENGTH and whose color is given by the variable BLOCK.COLOR. The loop from 2090 to 2120 repeats the LPRINT statement at 2110 the number of times given by the variable BLOCK.LENGTH. The statement at 2100 gives the value of the variable PATTERN—first 1, then 2, then 3, then 4, then back to 1, and so on. In this way, the dot pattern that is printed at statement 2110 repeats:

BAR.PATTERNS (BLOCK.COLOR,1)
BAR.PATTERNS (BLOCK.COLOR,2)
BAR.PATTERNS (BLOCK.COLOR,3)
BAR.PATTERNS (BLOCK.COLOR,4)
BAR.PATTERNS (BLOCK.COLOR,1)
BAR.PATTERNS (BLOCK.COLOR,2)
BAR.PATTERNS (BLOCK.COLOR,3)
BAR.PATTERNS (BLOCK.COLOR,4)
. . .
. . .

The patterns in the array BAR.PATTERNS are initialized in the subroutine at statement 3000 to print patterns characteristic of bar charts.

7.3 COPYING FROM THE SCREEN TO THE PRINTER

The first example programs in Section 7.1 all printed pictures that fit on one printer line. The bar chart program in Section 7.2 prints each bar on a single printer line, resulting in a chart of horizontal bars rather than the more common chart of vertical bars. This is no coincidence. An intrinsic difficulty with printer graphics is that since the printer cannot back up, once the paper advances from one line to the next, the original line is gone, and anything you wanted to print on that line must already have been printed. As a consequence, the easiest programs to write are those whose data fall all on one line. The hardest programs are those that get random data—points on a scatter chart, for example—and have to figure out on which printer line each piece of data falls, sort the pieces according to which line they will be printed on, and then sort the data to be printed on each line from left to right.

You may have noticed that we also studiously avoided using complex graphics entities such as circles, ellipses, and even, for the most part, lines. This omission was also intentional. The difficulty is that whereas on the screen BASIC converts these entities into a series of pixels, no corresponding aid converts them into a series of dots for the printer. Programmers are on their own.

One technique that solves both of these problems is first to draw the picture on the graphics screen, to which you can send data in any order and which converts lines, circles, and ellipses to pixels, and then to copy the screen pixels to printer dots. The single objection to this procedure is that it limits pictures to those that fit on the screen. The printer can print pictures up to 960 dots wide by as many dots high as you can print before you run out of paper, but the screen can only display pictures 320 or 640 dots wide, depending on resolution, by 200 dots high.

One way to copy the screen is to use the IBM "print screen" program, which IBM gives away to anyone with an IBM Personal Computer Graphics Printer and DOS. As an alternative to this, you can use the program in Fig. 7-13, which also copies the screen to the printer. The IBM program has two principal advantages: (1) it is fast, and (2) you don't have to type it in before you can use it. The program in Fig. 7-13 has three advantages: (1) it prints a higher resolution picture than does the IBM program; (2) you can change it if you don't like it the way it is; and (3) it works even if you have two screens and even if you have switched back to the nongraphics screen. (The program in Fig. 7-13 printed many of the figures in this book. For the author, it also had the advantage that it was written and working before IBM released its program.)

Fig. 7-13 Program to Copy Data from Screen to Printer

```
1000 ' --- PROGRAM TO PRINT SCREEN ON PRINTER
1010 '
1020 '
1030       DEFINT A-Z
1040       DIM PATTERN(4,4,4)
1050       DIM PRNTCHAR(4)
1060       DIM PTCOLOR(4)
1070       DEF SEG=&HB800
1080 '     PATTERN (COLOR , XLOC , YLOC) IS USED TO SET UP THE
1090 '        CHARACTERS FOR THE PRINTER.
1100 '     COLOR IS THE COLOR OF THE POINT TO BE REPRESENTED
1110 '     XLOC INDICATES WHETHER THIS IS THE LEFTMOST,
1120 '        ONE OF THE CENTER TWO OR RIGHTMOST CHARACTERS
1130 '     YLOC INDICATES HOW HOW FAR ALONG THE PRINTER LINE
1140 '        THIS CHARACTER IS
1150 '
1160       FOR XLOC = 1 TO 4
1170         FOR YLOC = 1 TO 4
1180           PATTERN(0,XLOC,YLOC) = 0
1190         NEXT YLOC
1200       NEXT XLOC
```

continued on p. 246

continued from p. 245

```
1210            FOR YLOC = 1 TO 4
1220                PATTERN(3,1,YLOC) = 192
1230                PATTERN(3,2,YLOC) = 48
1240                PATTERN(3,3,YLOC) = 12
1250                PATTERN(3,4,YLOC) = 3
1260            NEXT YLOC
1270
1280            PATTERN(2,1,1) = 128
1290            PATTERN(2,1,2) = 64
1300            PATTERN(2,1,3) = 128
1310            PATTERN(2,1,4) = 64
1320            PATTERN(2,2,1) = 32
1330            PATTERN(2,2,2) = 16
1340            PATTERN(2,2,3) = 32
1350            PATTERN(2,2,4) = 16
1360            PATTERN(2,3,1) = 8
1370            PATTERN(2,3,2) = 4
1380            PATTERN(2,3,3) = 8
1390            PATTERN(2,3,4) = 4
1400            PATTERN(2,4,1) = 2
1410            PATTERN(2,4,2) = 1
1420            PATTERN(2,4,3) = 2
1430            PATTERN(2,4,4) = 1
1440
1450            PATTERN(1,1,1) = 128
1460            PATTERN(1,1,2) = 0
1470            PATTERN(1,1,3) = 64
1480            PATTERN(1,1,4) = 0
1490            PATTERN(1,2,1) = 32
1500            PATTERN(1,2,2) = 0
1510            PATTERN(1,2,3) = 16
1520            PATTERN(1,2,4) = 0
1530            PATTERN(1,3,1) = 8
1540            PATTERN(1,3,2) = 0
1550            PATTERN(1,3,3) = 4
1560            PATTERN(1,3,4) = 0
1570            PATTERN(1,4,1) = 2
1580            PATTERN(1,4,2) = 0
1590            PATTERN(1,4,3) = 1
1600            PATTERN(1,4,4) = 0
1610 '
1620 '
1630 '
1640 ' --- PRINT REGISTRATION MARKS
1645            LPRINT CHR$(27) ; "A" ; CHR$(8) ;
1650            LPRINT "+++";SPC(66);"+++"
1660            LPRINT "+   ";SPC(66);"   +"
1670            LPRINT "+   ";SPC(66);"   +"
1680 '
1690 '
1700 ' --- SET UP PRINTER
1710            WIDTH "LPT1:",255
1720            LPRINT CHR$(27) ; "A" ; CHR$(8) ;
```

continued on p. 247

continued from p. 246

```
1730  '
1740          FOR XBASE = 0 TO 316 STEP 4
1750            LPRINT SPC(3) ;
                          CHR$(27) ; "L" ; CHR$(32) ; CHR$(3) ;
1760            FOR Y = 199 TO 0 STEP -1
1770  '           --- FIRST GET COLORS OF THE FOUR POINTS
1780              LET RASTER.START.ADDR = 0
1790              IF  Y MOD 2 = 1   THEN
                          LET RASTER.START.ADDR = &H2000
1800              LET RASTER.START.ADDR =
                          RASTER.START.ADDR + 80 * INT(Y/2)
1810              LET POINT.ADDR = RASTER.START.ADDR +  XBASE/4
1820              LET SCREEN.PEEK = PEEK(POINT.ADDR)
1830              FOR INDEX = 4 TO 1 STEP -1
1840                 PTCOLOR(INDEX) = SCREEN.PEEK MOD 4
1850                 LET SCREEN.PEEK = INT(SCREEN.PEEK/4)
1860              NEXT INDEX
1870  '
1880  '           --- NOW SET UP THE FOUR CHARACTERS TO PRINT
1890              FOR INDEX = 1 TO 4
1900                 PRNTCHAR(INDEX) = 0
1910              NEXT INDEX
1920  '
1930              FOR XLOC = 1 TO 4
1940                FOR YLOC = 1 TO 4
1950                COL = PTCOLOR(XLOC)
1960                   PRNTCHAR(YLOC) =
                          PRNTCHAR(YLOC) +
                                  PATTERN(COL,XLOC,YLOC)
1970                NEXT YLOC
1980              NEXT XLOC
1990  '
2000  '           --- PRINT THE FOUR CHARACTERS
2010              FOR INDEX = 1 TO 4
2020                 LPRINT CHR$(PRNTCHAR(INDEX)) ;
2030              NEXT INDEX
2040            NEXT Y
2050            LPRINT
2060          NEXT XBASE
2070  '
2080  '
2090          LPRINT "+   ";SPC(66);"   +"
2100          LPRINT "+   ";SPC(66);"   +"
2110          LPRINT "+++";SPC(66);"+++"
2120          END  .
```

A Program to Print the Contents of the Graphics Screen

Before trying to use the program in Fig. 7-13, note one important thing about it: if you do not compile it with the BASIC compiler, it is too slow.

When compiled, this program is reasonably fast, although the IBM program is faster for two reasons: (1) it prints fewer dots than this program does, and (2) it is written in assembly language, which is faster than BASIC, and faster even than compiled BASIC. Whether or not you decide to use this program, you will find several generally useful techniques in this section.

The program in Fig. 7-13 prints the contents of the medium resolution graphics screen on the printer. It prints the picture "sideways": pixels at the bottom of the screen are printed at the left-hand edge of the paper, pixels at the right-hand edge of the screen are printed at the bottom, and so on. Each pixel is represented on the printer by a block four dots wide by two dots high. In high resolution graphics printing, the blocks are almost square, being 4/120 (about 0.0333) inch wide by 2/72 (about 0.0277) inch high. The color of the pixel determines which of four patterns of dots are printed in the block, as shown in Fig. 7-14. For each printer line, the program reads a four-pixel-wide vertical strip of the screen. The 320 pixels of the medium resolution graphics screen are therefore printed on 80 printer lines. See Fig. 7-15.

Fig. 7-14   Dot Patterns Representing the Four Colors

The four colors of pixels on the medium resolution screen are represented by four patterns of dots within a 4 × 2 grid, as shown here:

A pixel with color number:	*Is represented by:*
0	○ ○ ○ ○ ○ ○ ○ ○
1	● ○ ○ ○ ○ ○ ● ○
2	○ ● ○ ● ● ○ ● ○
3	● ● ● ● ● ● ● ●

Fig. 7-15   Translating Pixels on the Screen to Dots on the Printer

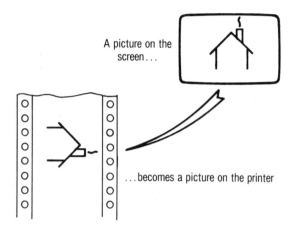

A picture on the screen...

...becomes a picture on the printer

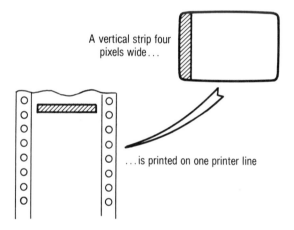

A vertical strip four pixels wide...

...is printed on one printer line

continued on p. 250

continued from p. 249

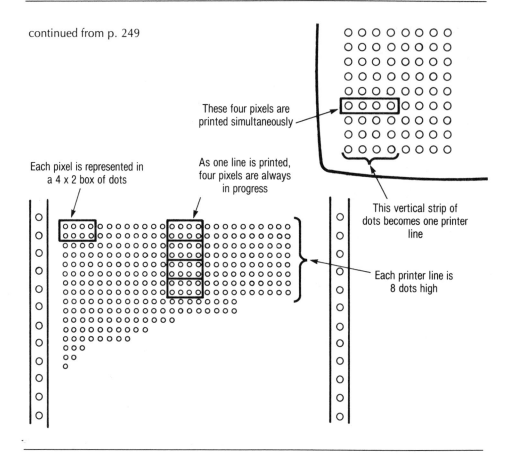

These four pixels are printed simultaneously

Each pixel is represented in a 4 x 2 box of dots

As one line is printed, four pixels are always in progress

This vertical strip of dots becomes one printer line

Each printer line is 8 dots high

HOW THE PROGRAM WORKS

Statements 1160 to 1600 build the array PATTERN, a lookup table used later in the program to print the dot patterns that represent pixel colors. Statements 1650 to 1670 print a series of plus signs to mark the upper left-hand and lower left-hand corners of the screen. Toward the end of the program, after the picture is printed, statements 2090 to 2110 mark the upper right-hand and lower right-hand corners of the screen. These marks are helpful if much of the screen is blank. Statements 1710 and 1720 set up the printer in the usual way for graphics. The nested loops from statement 1740 to 2060 assemble and send to the printer the necessary instructions to print out the contents of the graphics display. The overall structure of the program is therefore:

Statement numbers	Purpose
1160–1600	INITIALIZE PATTERN ARRAY
1640–1670	PRINT TWO CORNERS OF SCREEN
1700–1720	INITIALIZE PRINTER FOR GRAPHICS
1740	FOR X = 1 TO 316 STEP 4
1760	FOR Y = 1 TO 199
1770–1980	ASSEMBLE CHARACTERS TO PRINT AND PRINT THEM
2040	NEXT Y
2060	NEXT X
2090–2110	PRINT TWO CORNERS OF SCREEN

ASSEMBLING THE INSTRUCTIONS FOR THE PRINTER

Statements 1770 to 1860 find the colors of the four pixels that are to be printed next and store them in the array PTCOLOR, as discussed below. The program assembles patterns of dots to print that represent four pixels with these colors. The top two pins on the printer head print the pattern corresponding to the color of the first pixel; the next two pins print the pattern corresponding to the color of the second pixel; and so on. Four graphics instructions are sent to the printer for each set of pixels being printed. To review this procedure, look again at Fig. 7-15.

To assemble the dot patterns, the program uses the PATTERN array. Each element in that array contains a part of a dot pattern to be printed. The first index into the PATTERN array indicates a pixel color. Elements with a first index of 3, for example, contain information about printing pixels with color number 3. The second index indicates which pins on the print head will be used to print the pixel. Elements of the PATTERN array with this index 1 contain information about printing pixels to be printed with the two top pins on the print head. These elements contain only the numbers 0, 64, 128, and 192, which correspond to printing neither, one, the other, or both of the top two pins on the print head. Similarly, elements of the PATTERN array with a second index of 2 contain only the numbers 0, 16, 32, and 48, corresponding to printing with neither, one, the other, or both of the third and fourth pins on the print head, and elements with a second index of 3 or of 4 control the bottom two pairs of pins. The third index into the PATTERN array indicates one of the four left-to-right print positions used to represent each set of pixels. To print a pixel with color number 3 using the third and fourth print head pins, you must LPRINT the following dot patterns:

PATTERN (3,2,1)
PATTERN (3,2,2)
PATTERN (3,2,3)
PATTERN (3,2,4)

Since the program simultaneously prints four pixels, one with each of the four pin pairs on the print head, it must first add up the elements of the PATTERN array that correspond to the pixels being printed and then send the sum as the instruction to the printer. The loop from 1930 to 1970 calculates four graphics instructions for the printer; the inner loop from 1940 to 1960 adds up the four relevant elements of the PATTERN array to calculate each of the elements in the PRNTCHAR array. The elements of that array are subsequently printed in the loop from 2010 to 2030.

READING THE SCREEN MEMORY

Statements 1770 to 1860 find the colors of the pixels on the screen and store them in the array PTCOLOR. They could be replaced by four references to the POINT function:

```
1780  LET PTCOLOR(1) = POINT(XBASE,Y)
1790  LET PTCOLOR(2) = POINT(XBASE+1,Y)
1800  LET PTCOLOR(3) = POINT(XBASE+2,Y)
1810  LET PTCOLOR(4) = POINT(XBASE+3,Y)
```

If you wish, you can skip this section and replace statements 1780 to 1860 with the four statements above. The disadvantage of the POINT function is that the graphics display must be active whenever you use it. If you have both a color display and a monochrome display, and if your program changes back to the monochrome display, then you can no longer use the POINT function. Statements 1770 to 1860 find pixel colors without reference to the POINT function and can find them whether or not the graphics screen is active. They use the PEEK function to read directly from the memory where the Color/Graphics Monitor Adapter stores pixel colors. The PEEK function can tell you the contents of any piece of memory in your computer; to use it to find pixel colors, you must know where in the memory the colors of the pixels are stored and how to discover the color numbers of the pixels from the numbers that the PEEK function finds in that memory.

Memory locations in the computer are numbered with *hexadecimal numbers*. Hexadecimal numbers are a different way of expressing regular numbers, much as Roman numerals are a different way of expressing regular numbers. To read from the memory, you need know nothing about hexadecimal numbers except that the computer understands them, can convert them to regular numeric notation and back, and can do arithmetic with them. The memory in which pixel colors are stored begins at the hexadecimal number B8000 and continues from there. This statement,

1070   DEF SEG = &HB800

tells the computer that whenever we ask about the contents of a location in memory, it should add B8000 to the location we ask for. (Statement 1070 is not missing a 0. The computer appends an extra 0 on the end of any hexadecimal number you give in a DEF SEG statement. The &H tells the computer that the number that follows is expressed as a hexadecimal number.)

The colors of four pixels are stored in each memory location. The four pixels whose colors share a memory location all have the same y coordinate and have four consecutive x coordinates, the first of which is divisible by 4. For example, these four pixels share a single memory location:

(32,37)   (33,37)   (34,37)   (35,37)

The colors of pixels whose y coordinates are even are stored in locations B8000, B8001, B8002, and so on. Colors of pixels whose y coordinates are odd are stored in locations BA000, BA001, BA002, and so on. This is the formula for the location in memory of the color of a pixel with coordinates (X,Y):

POINT.ADDR = 80 * INT(Y/2) + INT(X/4)

If y is odd, you must add &H2000 to the result. In either case, the computer adds &HB8000 to the result as a consequence of statement 1070. If you want to find the color of (9,20), for example, you use this formula:

$$POINT.ADDR = 80 * INT(20/2) + INT(9/4)$$

$$= 80 * 10 + 2$$

$$= 802$$

When POINT.ADDR is 802 in statement 1820:

1820   LET SCREEN.PEEK = PEEK(POINT.ADDR)

SCREEN.PEEK will become the number stored in memory space &HB8000 + 802. As discussed above, this location stores the colors of the four pixels, which are:

(8,20)   (9,20)   (10,20)   (11,20)

One of these is the one we were interested in.

In the program in Fig. 7-13, statements 1780 and 1790 set RASTER.-START.ADDR either to 0 or to &H2000 depending on whether Y is even or odd. Statements 1800 and 1810 add the other two factors of the formula for POINT.ADDR. Statement 1820 uses the PEEK function to get a number that represents the colors of four pixels.

The colors of four pixels are lumped into one memory location using this formula:

64 ∗ color of first pixel + 16 ∗ color of second pixel + 4 ∗ color of third pixel + color of fourth pixel

The loop from statement 1830 to statement 1860 decodes the number in the memory location (found by the PEEK function and stored in the variable SCREEN.PEEK) by finding the remainder when the number is divided by 4 to get the color of the fourth pixel. It then divides the number by four and repeats the process to find the color of the third pixel, and so on.

8 Advanced Applications

8.1 GRAPHICS IN THREE DIMENSIONS

Most objects in the real world have three dimensions—length, width, and depth—rather than just the two that the computer screen has—length and width. In this section, we shall discuss techniques for squeezing three-dimensional objects onto the two-dimensional screen so as to make them appear as realistic as possible.

In general, computer graphics in three dimensions is complicated because people's perception of three dimensions is complicated. Although the images on the retinas in our eyes are two-dimensional, we construct a three-dimensional perception of the world from a variety of clues. The stereoscopic view of the world afforded us because we have two eyes helps a little. Much more useful are such clues as perspective, the apparent brighter colors of closer objects and their larger apparent sizes, and the concealment or partial concealment of distant things by closer things. Images on the IBM Personal Computer can use some of these clues. In this section, we shall discuss perspective.

Getting perspective right involves some relatively complex mathematics. To avoid a relatively complex discussion, we shall present here a series of formulas that are the results of mathematical analysis. With the formulas, you can get on with the job of programming the computer to draw realistic images of three-dimensional objects. For the benefit of the mathematically sophisticated, we shall briefly discuss the techniques by which the formulas are derived. The mathematically uninitiated may feel free to skip that discussion.

Three-Dimensional Coordinates

Readers familiar with the Cartesian coordinate system in three dimensions can skip this section.

We have described the locations of objects on the two-dimensional computer screen with two numbers: an x coordinate, which tells where the object is in the left-and-right dimension; and a y coordinate, which tells where it is in the up-and-down dimension. If one of its coordinates changes, that means an object has moved in one or another of the dimensions. In three dimensions, we will use three numbers to describe the location of an object. The additional number is the z *coordinate,* and it tells where the object is in the third dimension. You can decide arbitrarily which coordinate represents what direction; we shall interpret the three coordinates as follows. Assuming that the object whose location is to be described is in the vicinity of a table (not a table of numbers this time, but a table of the four-legged variety), then:

x coordinate: how far to the right of the left-hand edge of the table the object is
y coordinate: how far back from the front edge of the table the object is
z coordinate: how far above the table the object is.

Three-dimensional coordinates are written as three numbers separated by commas and enclosed in parentheses. The numbers are, in order, the x coordinate, the y coordinate, and the z coordinate. This, for example, is one possible three-dimensional coordinate:

(5,6,13)

This location lies five units in from the left-hand edge of the table, six units back from the front edge, and thirteen units above the table. In the sketch of the IBM Personal Computer in Fig. 8-1, the coordinates of various points have been marked. Note that points farther to the right have larger x coordinates, that points farther back on the table have larger y coordinates, and that points higher above the table have larger z coordinates.

Presenting Three-Dimensional Images on a Two-Dimensional Screen

To present a realistic two-dimensional display of a three-dimensional object, you pick a location for the viewer's eye, that is, a set of coordinates for it, and treat the computer screen as a window between the viewer's eye and the object. A light beam that starts at a particular point on the object

Fig. 8-1   Three-Dimensional Coordinate System

In this sketch of the IBM Personal Computer, various points have been marked with their coordinates in three-dimensional space. Note that points higher above the table have larger z coordinates, points farther to the right have larger x coordinates, and points farther back have larger y coordinates.

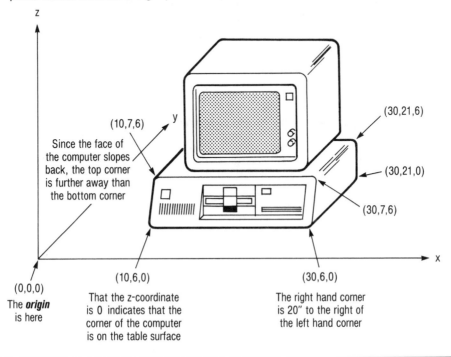

being viewed and heads for the viewer's eye passes through the window/screen on its way. Wherever that light beam comes through the window is the place on the screen at which to draw a dot to represent the point on the object. Examine Fig. 8-2. We shall now present the formulas for figuring out where the light beams pass through the window.

To make the formulas tolerably simple (and, as we shall see in a moment, "tolerably simple" is not very simple), we shall make the following assumptions about the location of the viewer's eye, the object the viewer is looking at, and the window he or she is looking through:

1. The object that the viewer is looking at is near the origin, and the viewer's eye is farther away from the origin than any part of the object he or she is looking at.

2. The viewer is looking directly back at the origin.

3. The viewer is looking through a window that is perpendicular to his or her line of sight back to the origin.

These assumptions are not particularly restrictive. You can always move an object close to the origin by adding constants to each of the three coordinates of each point in the object. The viewer must be farther from the origin than from the object for two reasons: (1) the formulas given below break down if the user's eye happens to be on part of the object; and (2) the formulas do not distinguish between things that are in front of the viewer and things that are behind; things that are behind are presented in mirror image as though they were in front; this is very confusing.

Fig. 8-2   Projecting a Three-Dimensional Image onto the Screen

This sketch shows how the IBM Personal Computer in Fig. 8-1 would be displayed on the screen. The user's eye, shown at point E in this figure, is looking through a window, which is the display screen, at the object. Light leaves the object and passes through the window on its way to the viewer's eye. The point at which the light goes through the screen is where the object should be drawn on the screen.

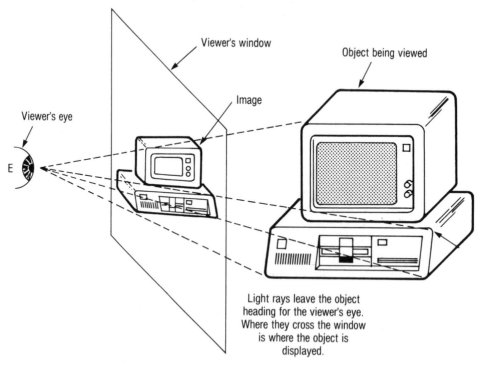

Viewer's window

Object being viewed

Image

Viewer's eye

E

Light rays leave the object
heading for the viewer's eye.
Where they cross the window
is where the object is
displayed.

The Formulas

Let us call the coordinates of the viewer's eye X.EYE, Y.EYE, and Z.EYE. Let us call the ratio between the distance from the origin to the viewer's eye to the distance from the window to the viewer's eye DISTANCE. (The only effect of changing DISTANCE is to make the image on the screen larger or smaller.) For every point on the object to be displayed, the computer must calculate the screen coordinates at which to display it. Let us call the three coordinates of one such point X.SUB, Y.SUB, and Z.SUB. Let us call the screen coordinates the computer must find to display this point on the screen X.SCREEN and Y.SCREEN.

The formulas involve five constants, SIN.THETA, COS.THETA, SIN.PHI, COS.PHI, and RHO, which can be calculated using only the coordinates of the viewer's eye. (Those with some mathematical background will recognize the names of these constants.) The formulas for these constants are:

SIN.THETA = Y.EYE / SQR(X.EYE^2 + Y.EYE^2)
COS.THETA = X.EYE / SQR(X.EYE^2 + Y.EYE^2)
RHO = SQR(X.EYE^2 + Y.EYE^2 + Z.EYE^2)
SIN.PHI = SQR(X.EYE^2 + Y.EYE^2) / RHO
COS.PHI = Z.EYE / RHO

If both X.EYE and Y.EYE are 0, then the formulas for SIN.THETA and COS.THETA will involve division by 0. If this is the case, let SIN.THETA be 1 and let COS.THETA be 0. If X.EYE, Y.EYE, and Z.EYE are all 0, then the position of the eye is at the origin, which violates assumption 1, above, and the formulas won't work.

With the above constants, we can calculate where on the screen each point on the object should be drawn with the following formulas. To make the formulas easy to write out, we first calculate three intermediate variables, X.VIEW, Y.VIEW, and Z.VIEW:

X.VIEW = −X.SUB*SIN.THETA + Y.SUB*COS.THETA
Y.VIEW = −X.SUB*COS.THETA*COS.PHI −
            Y.SUB*SIN. THETA*COS.PHI + Z.SUB*SIN.PHI
Z.VIEW = −X.SUB*COS.THETA*SIN.PHI −
            Y.SUB*SIN.THETA*SIN.PHI −
            Z.SUB*COS.PHI + RHO
X.SCREEN = X.VIEW / Z.VIEW * DISTANCE + 160
Y.SCREEN = 100 − Y.VIEW / Z. VIEW * DISTANCE

The constants 100 and 160 in the formulas for X.SCREEN and Y.SCREEN serve to center the picture in the screen.

Data Representation

The BASIC programs discussed below allow you to choose the location of the viewer's eye and then draw three-dimensional objects consisting of collections of straight lines as viewed from your chosen location. To write these programs conveniently, we must have a way to represent lists of the line endpoint coordinates. We shall do this in DATA statements using the following conventions:

1. The numbers are in the DATA statements in "groups," each consisting of four numbers. The first number is the "color" and the second, third, and fourth are the "coordinates."

2. The "coordinates" are the x, y, and z coordinates of an endpoint of one of the line segments that make up the object.

3. If the "color" is 0, then the "coordinates" represent the first endpoint of a line to be drawn. If the "color" is 1, 2, or 3, then the computer should draw a line from the "coordinates" in the previous "group" to the "coordinates" in this "group," with the color indicated by "color."

4. If the "color" is 4, it means that the object is completely drawn and that there is no more data.

To represent a line using these conventions, you must insert two "groups." The first will have "color" 0 and the coordinates of one end of the line. The second will have "color" 1, 2, or 3, the color with which the line is to be drawn, and the coordinates of the other end of the line. To represent a square, you need five "groups." The first has "color" 0 and the coordinates of one corner of the square. The second, third, and fourth have "color" set to the color with which the square is to be drawn and the coordinates of the second, third, and fourth corners of the square. The fifth has the "color" of the square and the coordinates of the first corner of the square. The first "group" tells the computer where to start drawing the square; the subsequent four "groups" tell it where to draw the four sides of the square.

The DATA statements here draw the four-sided pyramid shown in Fig. 8-3:

```
5000 ' --- DATA TO DRAW PYRAMID NEAR ORIGIN
5010         DATA 0,-1,-1,-1,   1,1,-1,-1,    1,1,1,-1
5020         DATA 1,-1,1,-1, 1,-1,-1,-1
5030 '
5040         DATA 0,-1,-1,-1,   2,0,0,2,   2,1,1,-1
5050         DATA 0,-1,1,-1,    2,0,0,2,   2,1,-1,-1
5060 '
5070         DATA 0,-.6,-1,-1,   3,0,0,2,    3,-.2,-1,-1
5080         DATA 0,.2,-1,-1,    3,0,0,2,    3,.6,-1,-1
5090 '
5100         DATA 4,0,0,0
```

DATA statements 5010 and 5020 represent a square whose corners are at

$(-1,1,-1)$ $(1,1,-1)$

$(-1,-1,-1)$ $(1,-1,-1)$

Since all four corners have z coordinate -1, this square is horizontal and one unit below the table.

DATA statements 5040 and 5050 draw lines from the four corners of the square to the peak of the pyramid at the point

$(0,0,2)$

centered above the square and three units above it.

DATA statements 5070 and 5080 draw three lines up one side of the pyramid. This is so that the user can tell one side of the pyramid from the others, since the pyramid is otherwise entirely symmetrical.

Fig. 8-3   The Pyramid Drawn by the Sample Programs

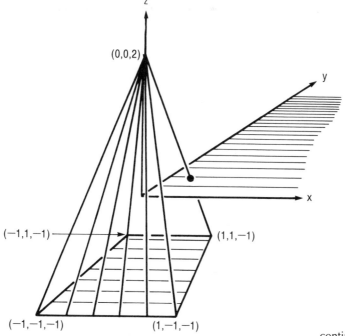

continued on p. 262

continued from p. 261

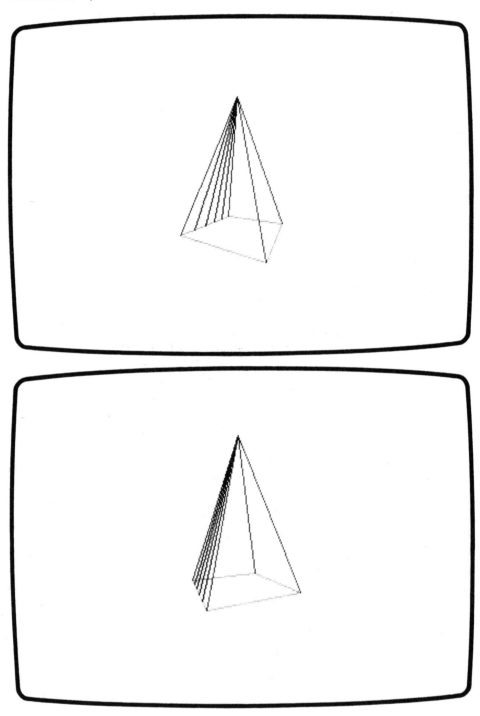

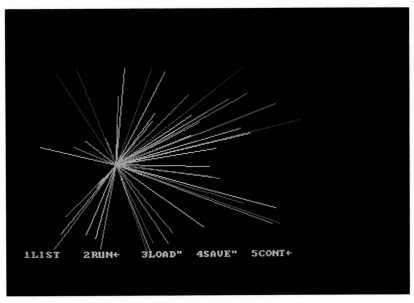

1   Output from the Starburst program in Fig. 3-8.

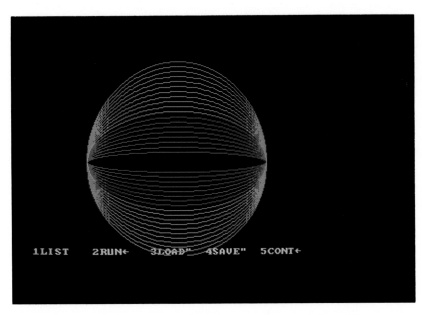

2   Appearance of the screen during execution of the Ellipse program in Fig. 3-21.

This plate shows the screen's appearance about halfway through the execution of the program .

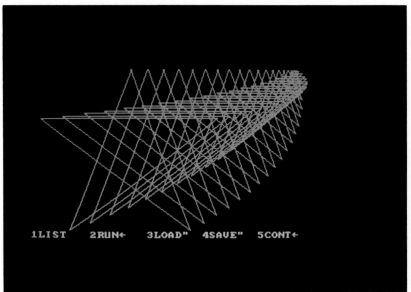

3 Screen drawn by a variant of the Shooting Star program in Fig. 3-28.

The screen produced by the program in Fig. 3-28 is the same as the one shown here except for the colors used. To get the colors shown here, the statement

```
60  COLOR  0,0
```

must be added to the program.

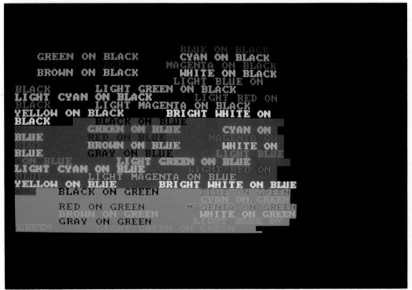

4 Screen appearance during execution of the Text Color program in Fig. 4-3.

5　Title page screen produced by the program in Fig. 4-29.

The program in Fig. 4-29 produces the screen shown here if it is run on the Color/Graphics Monitor Adapter. The same program produces a (similar) display with the Monochrome Adapter.

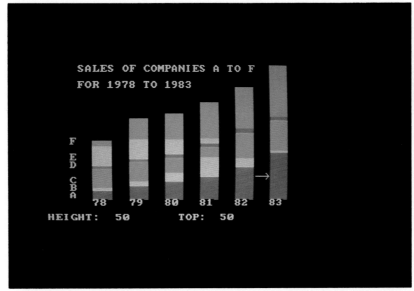

6　Possible bar chart produced by the Bar Chart Editing program in Fig. 6-5.

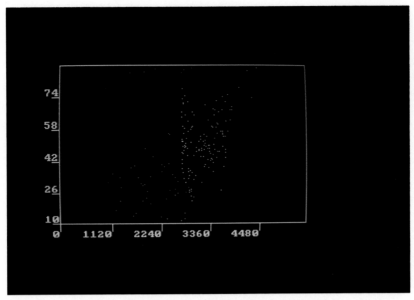

7   Scatter chart drawn by the program in Fig. 6-9.

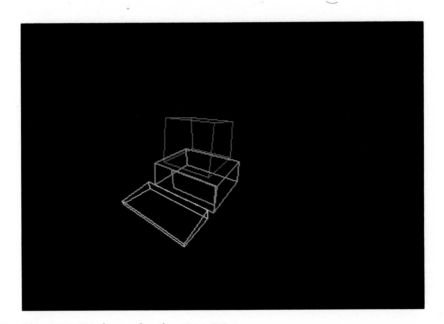

8   The IBM PC drawn by the IBM PC.

This plate shows the result if the DATA statements in Fig. 8-5 are inserted in the program in Fig. 8-8 and the picture scaled and rotated suitably.

First Example Program

The program in Fig. 8-4 uses the concepts we have discussed to display the pyramid given in the DATA statements above. Statement 2020 inputs the x, y, and z coordinates of the first location from which you wish to view the pyramid. Statement 2050 inputs amounts by which you wish to move between successive views of the pyramid. The program then gives you ten views of the pyramid. The first view is from the location input at statement 2020. The subsequent views are from locations calculated by adding to the original coordinates the amounts given to the input statement at 2050.

The loop from statement 2090 to statement 2170 draws the pyramid ten times. After it clears the screen, the program calls the subroutine at statement 4500, which calculates the constants for the formulas. The subroutine at statement 3000 then draws the pyramid by interpreting the DATA statements starting at statement 5000 according to the convention described above, putting the coordinates into X.SUB, Y.SUB, and Z.SUB, and calling the subroutine at statement 4000, which calculates screen coordinates X.SCREEN and Y.SCREEN. Then X.EYE, Y.EYE, and Z.EYE are incremented and the process is repeated.

This program will crash if your input causes the location of the viewer's eye to coincide with the origin during the course of the program. Furthermore, the display will become very peculiar if the viewer's eye goes inside the pyramid. If the viewpoint comes close enough to the pyramid that the lines making up the pyramid on the screen run off the edge of the screen, the pyramid becomes distorted. These problems could be solved by testing to make sure that the viewpoint stays an arbitrary minimal distance from the origin, perhaps five units.

The program displays the pyramid as though it were transparent. If the pyramid were not transparent, then some of the lines that make it up would be hidden and would not be drawn on the screen. Various algorithms are available for figuring out which lines are actually hidden by other parts of the object, but they are complex and beyond the scope of this book.

If you wish, you can modify this program to draw any object for which you can enter the DATA statements. An alternate set of DATA statements is shown in Fig. 8-5. This set draws the sketch of the IBM PC shown in Color Plate 8.

Fig. 8-4   Program to Draw Pyramid on the Screen

```
1000 ' --- THIS PROGRAM DISPLAYS A CUBE FROM TEN LOCATIONS
1010 ' --- IT WORKS IN RECTANGULAR COORDINATES
1020 '
2000 ' --- GET VIEW COORDINATES FROM USER AND GO FROM THERE
2010       PRINT "X, Y, AND Z OF VIEW LOCATION AND
                  DISTANCE TO VIEWING PLANE"
2020       INPUT "",X.EYE,Y.EYE,Z.EYE,DISTANCE
2030 '
2040       PRINT "INCREMENTS FOR X, Y, AND Z
2050       INPUT "",X.EYE.INC,Y.EYE.INC,Z.EYE.INC
2060 '
2070       GOSUB 21000
2080       SCREEN 1,0
2085       KEY OFF
2090       FOR I = 1 TO 10
2100          CLS
2110          RESTORE
2120          GOSUB 4500
2130          GOSUB 3000
2140          LET X.EYE = X.EYE + X.EYE.INC
2150          LET Y.EYE = Y.EYE + Y.EYE.INC
2160          LET Z.EYE = Z.EYE + Z.EYE.INC
2170       NEXT I
2180       GOSUB 22000
2190       END
2200 '
2210 '
3000 ' --- DRAW THE PICTURE IN THE DATA STATEMENTS
3010 '     ---
3020          READ FCN,X.SUB,Y.SUB,Z.SUB
3030 '
3040          IF  FCN = 4  GOTO 3120
3050 '
3060 '        --- DRAW A LINE FROM (X.OLD,Y.OLD) TO NEW LOCATION
3070          GOSUB 4000
3080          IF  FCN <> 0  THEN
                  LINE (X.OLD,Y.OLD)-(X.SCREEN,Y.SCREEN),FCN
3090          X.OLD = X.SCREEN
3100          Y.OLD = Y.SCREEN
3110       GOTO 3000
3120       RETURN
3130 '
3140 '
4000 ' --- TRANSFORM FROM 3D TO SCREEN COORDINATES
4010 '
4020 ' --- TRANSFORM TO USER-VIEW COORDINATES
4030       LET X.VIEW = -X.SUB*SIN.THETA + Y.SUB*COS.THETA
4040       LET Y.VIEW = -X.SUB*COS.THETA*COS.PHI -
                  Y.SUB*SIN.THETA*COS.PHI + Z.SUB*SIN.PHI
4050       LET Z.VIEW = -X.SUB*COS.THETA*SIN.PHI -
                  Y.SUB*SIN.THETA*SIN.PHI - Z.SUB*COS.PHI + RHO
```

continued on p. 265

continued from p. 264

```
4060  '
4070  ' --- GET SCREEN COORDINATES FROM USER-VIEW COORDINATES
4080       LET X.SCREEN = X.VIEW / Z.VIEW * DISTANCE
4090       LET Y.SCREEN = Y.VIEW / Z.VIEW * DISTANCE
4100       LET X.SCREEN = X.SCREEN + 160
4110       LET Y.SCREEN = 100 - Y.SCREEN
4120  '
4130       RETURN
4140  '
4150  '
4500  ' --- INITIALIZE FUNCTIONS FOR TRANSFORMATIONS
4510       XY.HYPOTENUSE = SQR(X.EYE^2 + Y.EYE^2)
4520       LET SIN.THETA = 1
4530       IF XY.HYPOTENUSE <> 0   THEN
                  LET SIN.THETA = Y.EYE / XY.HYPOTENUSE
4540       LET COS.THETA = 0
4550       IF XY.HYPOTENUSE <> 0   THEN
                  LET COS.THETA = X.EYE / XY.HYPOTENUSE
4560       RHO = SQR(X.EYE^2 + Y.EYE^2 + Z.EYE^2)
4570       LET SIN.PHI = XY.HYPOTENUSE / RHO
4580       LET COS.PHI = Z.EYE / RHO
4590       RETURN
4600  '
4610  '
5000  ' --- DATA TO DRAW PYRAMID NEAR ORIGIN
5010       DATA 0,-1,-1,-1,  1,1,-1,-1,   1,1,1,-1
5020       DATA 1,-1,1,-1,  1,-1,-1,-1
5030  '
5040       DATA 0,-1,-1,-1,  2,0,0,2,  2,1,1,-1
5050       DATA 0,-1,1,-1,   2,0,0,2,  2,1,-1,-1
5060  '
5070       DATA 0,-.6,-1,-1,  3,0,0,2,   3,-.2,-1,-1
5080       DATA 0,.2,-1,-1,   3,0,0,2,   3,.6,-1,-1
5090  '
5100       DATA 4,0,0,0
5110  '
5120  '
5130  '
21000      DEF SEG = 0
21010      POKE &H410, (PEEK(&H410) AND &HCF) OR &H10
21020      SCREEN 1,0,0,0
21030      SCREEN 0
21040      WIDTH 40
21050      LOCATE ,,1,6,7
21060      RETURN
22000      DEF SEG = 0
22010      POKE &H410, (PEEK(&H410) OR &H30)
22020      SCREEN 0
22030      WIDTH 40
22040      WIDTH 80
22050      LOCATE ,,1,12,13
```

Fig. 8-5   DATA Statements to Draw IBM PC

The following DATA statements can be inserted into the programs in this section to cause them to draw a view of the IBM Personal Computer instead of a pyramid.

```
5000 ' --- IBM PERSONAL COMPUTER
5010 '
5020 ' --- COMPUTER UNIT
5030      DATA 0,-10,-10,-6,   1,10,-10,-6,   1,10,-9,0
5040      DATA 1,-10,-9,0,   1,-10,-10,-6
5050 '
5060      DATA 0,-10,5,-6,    1,10,5,-6,     1,10,5,0
5070      DATA 1,-10,5,0,     1,-10,5,-6
5080 '
5090      DATA 0,-10,-10,-6,  1,-10,5,-6
5100      DATA 0,10,-10,-6,   1,10,5,-6
5110      DATA 0,10,-9,0,     1,10,5,0
5120      DATA 0,-10,-9,0,    1,-10,5,0
5130 '
5140 '
5150 ' --- SCREEN
5160      DATA 0,-7.25,-8,.5,  2,7.25,-8,.5,   2,7.25,-6,11
5170      DATA 2,-7.25,-6,11,  2,-7.25,-8,.5
5180 '
5190      DATA 0,-7.25,5,.5,   2,7.25,5,.5,    2,7.25,5,10
5200      DATA 2,-7.25,5,10,   2,-7.25,5,.5
5210 '
5220      DATA 0,-7.25,-8,.5,  2,-7.25,5,.5
5230      DATA 0,7.25,-8,.5,   2,7.25,5,.5
5240      DATA 0,7.25,-6,11,   2,7.25,5,10
5250      DATA 0,-7.25,-6,11,  2,-7.25,5,10
5260 '
5270 ' --- DISK DRIVES
5280      DATA 0,-3.75,-8.5,-5.4,   1,9.4,-8.5,-5.4,
                  1,9.4,-8.5,-.6
5290      DATA 1,-3.75,-8.5,-.6, 1,-3.75,-8.5,-5.4
5300 '
5310 ' --- KEYBOARD
5320      DATA 0,-9.5,-12,-6,    3,-9.5,-19.5,-6,
                  3,9.5,-19.5,-6
5330      DATA 3,9.5,-12,-6,     3,-9.5,-12,-6
5340 '
5350      DATA 0,-9.5,-12,-4,    3,-9.5,-19.5,-5.25,
                  3,9.5,-19.5,-5.25
5360      DATA 3,9.5,-12,-4,     3,-9.5,-12,-4
5370 '
5380      DATA 0,-9.5,-12,-6,    3,-9.5,-12,-4
5390      DATA 0,-9.5,-19.5,-6, 3,-9.5,-19.5,-5.25
5400      DATA 0,9.5,-19.5,-6,   3,9.5,-19.5,-5.25
5410      DATA 0,9.5,-12,-6,     3,9.5,-12,-4
5420 '
5430      DATA 4,0,0,0
```

IBM PC Drawn by DATA Statements

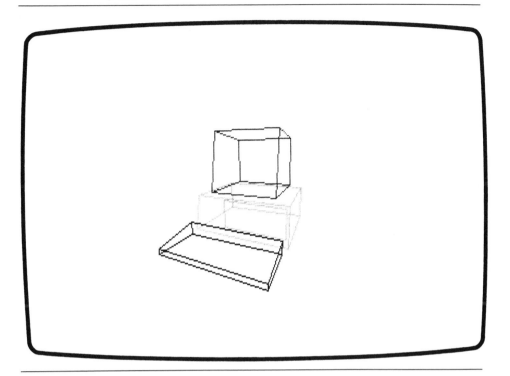

Polar Coordinates

What follows assumes some familiarity with trigonometry. Readers unfamiliar with this subject may wish to stop reading at this point and do some programming.

So far, we have represented the viewer's location with a coordinate system similar to the system we used for describing two-dimensional objects. It is, however, more convenient to specify the location of the viewer's eye in terms of *spherical coordinates*. Spherical coordinates describe a point by specifying how far from the origin it lies and in what direction. The distance is usually referred to by the Greek letter *rho*. The direction is given in terms of two angles. One, usually named by the Greek letter *theta,* is the angle between the x axis and the shadow in the horizontal plane of a line drawn from the origin to the point. The other, usually named by the Greek letter *phi,* is the angle between the line drawn from the origin to the point and a line that extends straight up from the origin. See Fig. 8-6. Theta represents a point's direction around the horizon and phi represents its height above the horizon.

Although the formulas for converting three-dimensional coordinates into screen coordinates are identical to those we used before, using spherical coordinates for the viewer's location makes the formulas for the constants discussed above somewhat simpler, because the trigonometric functions sine and cosine do some of the work:

SIN.THETA is the sine of the angle theta.
COS.THETA is the cosine of the angle theta.
SIN.PHI is the sine of the angle phi.
COS.PHI is the cosine of the angle phi.

(If you check the previous set of formulas on page 259, you will see that they, in fact, calculate the sines and cosines of theta and phi.)

Fig. 8-6   Polar Coordinates

The point P can be specified by its distance from the origin ("rho") and the two angles ("phi" and "theta") shown here.

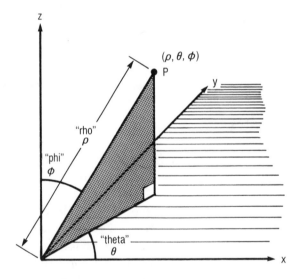

The program in Fig. 8-7 differs from the one in Fig. 8-4 in only two ways: (1) it asks you to input the coordinates of the viewer in terms of rho, theta, and phi, and (2) the subroutine at statement 4500 calculates the constants with the SIN and COS functions in BASIC. Note that since the SIN and COS functions in BASIC expect angles in radians, the input angles must be in radians. If you want the program to input angles expressed in degrees, then it must convert each input angle from degrees to radians by multiplying it by 3.14159 (pi) and dividing by 180.

Fig. 8-7   Program to Draw Pyramid Using Polar Coordinates

```
1000 ' --- THIS PROGRAM DISPLAYS A PYRAMID FROM TEN LOCATIONS
1010 ' --- IT WORKS IN POLAR COORDINATES
1020 '
2000 ' --- GET VIEW COORDINATES FROM USER AND GO FROM THERE
2010       PRINT "INPUT THETA, PHI, RHO, AND DISTANCE"
2020       INPUT "",THETA,PHI,RHO,DISTANCE
2030 '
2040       PRINT "INCREMENTS FOR THETA ,PHI, AND RHO
2050       INPUT "",THETA.INC,PHI.INC,RHO.INC
2060 '
2070       GOSUB 21000
2080       SCREEN 1,0
2085       KEY OFF
2090       FOR I = 1 TO 10
2100          CLS
2110          RESTORE
2120          GOSUB 4500
2130          GOSUB 2220
2140          LET THETA = THETA + THETA.INC
2150          LET PHI = PHI + PHI.INC
2160          LET RHO = RHO + RHO.INC
2170       NEXT I
2180       GOSUB 22000
2190       END
2200 '
2210 '
2220 ' --- DRAW THE PICTURE IN THE DATA STATEMENTS
2230 '      ---
2240          READ FCN,X.SUB,Y.SUB,Z.SUB
2250 '
2260          IF  FCN = 4  GOTO 2340
2270 '
2280 '        --- DRAW A LINE FROM (X.OLD,Y.OLD) TO NEW LOCATION
2290          GOSUB 4000
2300          IF  FCN <> 0  THEN
                     LINE (X.OLD,Y.OLD)-(X.SCREEN,Y.SCREEN),FCN
2310          X.OLD = X.SCREEN
2320          Y.OLD = Y.SCREEN
2330       GOTO 2220
2340       RETURN
2350 '
2360 '
4000 ' --- TRANSFORM FROM 3D TO SCREEN COORDINATES
4010 '
4020 ' --- TRANSFORM TO USER-VIEW COORDINATES
4030       LET X.VIEW = -X.SUB*SIN.THETA + Y.SUB*COS.THETA
4040       LET Y.VIEW = -X.SUB*COS.THETA*COS.PHI -
                 Y.SUB*SIN.THETA*COS.PHI + Z.SUB*SIN.PHI
4050       LET Z.VIEW = -X.SUB*COS.THETA*SIN.PHI -
                 Y.SUB*SIN.THETA*SIN.PHI - Z.SUB*COS.PHI + RHO
4060 '
```

continued on p. 270

continued from p. 269

```
4070 ' --- GET SCREEN COORDINATES FROM USER-VIEW COORDINATES
4080      LET X.SCREEN = X.VIEW / Z.VIEW * DISTANCE
4090      LET Y.SCREEN = Y.VIEW / Z.VIEW * DISTANCE
4100      LET X.SCREEN = X.SCREEN + 160
4110      LET Y.SCREEN = 100 - Y.SCREEN
4120 '
4130      RETURN
4140 '
4150 '
4500 ' --- INITIALIZE FUNCTIONS FOR TRANSFORMATIONS
4510      SIN.THETA = SIN(THETA)
4520      COS.THETA = COS(THETA)
4530      SIN.PHI   = SIN(PHI)
4540      COS.PHI   = COS(PHI)
4550      RETURN
4560 '
4570 '
```

(The rest of this program is identical to the one in Fig. 8-4.)

One More Example

The program shown in Fig. 8-8 is similar to the one in Fig. 8-7, but instead of changing the viewer's location automatically, this program waits for you to press a key on the keyboard. You can press any one of six keys near the right-hand edge of the keyboard: the four arrow keys and the zero and dot keys. Whenever you press one of these keys, the program modifies the one of the viewer's *spherical* coordinates and redraws the picture.

Fig. 8-8   Program That Allows User to Change Display Interactively

```
1000 ' --- THIS PROGRAM ALLOWS THE USER TO VIEW A PYRAMID
1010 '      ALL DIRECTIONS
1020 '
1030 '
2000 ' --- INITIALIZE
2010      LET THETA = 0
2020      LET PHI = 90 * 3.14159/180
2030      LET RHO = 4
2040      LET DISTANCE = 150
2050 '
2060      GOSUB 21000
2070      KEY OFF
2080      SCREEN 1,0
```

continued on p. 271

continued from p. 270

```
2090 ' --- LOOP TO DRAW THE PICTURE
                     WHENEVER THE USER PRESSES A KEY
2100 '
2110          CLS
2120          RESTORE
2130          GOSUB 4500
2140          GOSUB 3000
2150          COMMAND$ = INKEY$
2160      IF  COMMAND$ = ""   GOTO 2150
2170      IF  COMMAND$ = "8"   THEN GOSUB 2340
2180      IF  COMMAND$ = "4"   THEN GOSUB 2380
2190      IF  COMMAND$ = "6"   THEN GOSUB 2420
2200      IF  COMMAND$ = "2"   THEN GOSUB 2460
2210      IF  COMMAND$ = "0"   THEN GOSUB 2260
2220      IF  COMMAND$ = "."   THEN GOSUB 2310
2240     GOTO 2110
2250 '
2260 ' --- 0 KEY: GET CLOSER
2270          LET RHO = RHO / 1.25
2280      IF  RHO < 3  THEN LET RHO = RHO * 1.25
2290          RETURN
2300 '
2310 ' --- . KEY: GET FARTHER AWAY
2320          LET RHO = RHO * 1.25
2330          RETURN
2340 ' --- UP ARROW KEY: MOVE UP
2350          LET PHI = PHI - 22.5*3.14159/180
2360          RETURN
2370 '
2380 ' --- LEFT ARROW KEY: MOVE TO THE LEFT
2390          LET THETA = THETA - 22.5*3.14159/180
2400          RETURN
2410 '
2420 ' --- RIGHT ARROW KEY: MOVE TO THE RIGHT
2430          LET THETA = THETA + 22.5*3.14159/180
2440          RETURN
2450 '
2460 ' --- DOWN ARROW KEY: MOVE DOWN
2470          LET PHI = PHI + 22.5*3.14159/180
2480          RETURN
2490 '
```

(The rest of this program is identical to the one in Fig. 8-7.)

Note that this program does not use the arrow/number keys as event traps in the way that the game of Erase used them in Section 5.1. It uses them as numbers, and it expects the keyboard to report that number keys were pressed and not arrows. In order to have this happen, you may have to press the num lock key once. If the keyboard is sending arrows and not numbers, the program will never move the viewer around the object; instead, it repeats the same view of the pyramid whenever a key is pressed.

Discussion of the Mathematics

Readers unfamiliar with the mathematics of vector spaces should now go forth and program in three dimensions using the material presented so far.

The simplest way to derive the formulas discussed in this section is to consider a new coordinate system in which the origin is at the viewer's eye, whose z axis points straight back at the origin of the coordinate system in which the object is described, whose x axis points to the viewer's right, and whose y axis points through the top of the viewer's head (which is presumed to be tilted so that the eye points directly at the origin). The formulas for the three temporary variables X.VIEW, Y.VIEW, and Z.VIEW are the linear transformation that converts from the original coordinate system to the new coordinate system, and the variables X.VIEW, Y.VIEW, and Z.VIEW are the coordinates of the point X.SUB, Y.SUB, Z.SUB in the new coordinate system.

The derivation of the formulas is a straightforward, if somewhat complicated, exercise in linear algebra. The transformation is most easily completed in four steps. These steps are a translation to the viewer's location, a rotation through the angle theta, a rotation through the angle phi, and a mirroring (because the new coordinate system is a left-handed one). The formulas above fall out when you multiply the matrices that represent these four transformations.

Once the coordinates of the point to be displayed have been converted to the new coordinate system, it is easy to project them, since the window onto which the points are to be projected is parallel to the xy plane in the new coordinate system. The simple formulas for finding X.SCREEN and Y.SCREEN from X.VIEW, Y.VIEW, and Z.VIEW are the formulas for this special-case projection.

8.2 CLIPPING

In most of our programs, we have assumed that the data we wished to display would fit on the graphics screen, and we have ignored any problems that might have arisen if it didn't. This has caused little trouble, partly because you can often plan ahead and avoid the problem and partly because the examples in this text were carefully chosen to avoid it. In Section 8.1, on three-dimensional graphics, however, we saw that the pictures displayed by the programs became distorted if they didn't fit on the screen. *Clipping* is the process of figuring out what parts of the picture are on the screen and what parts aren't, and of drawing correctly the parts that are on the screen.

Single points present no problem. Whenever the computer executes a PSET statement, it decides either that the pixel is on the screen, in which case the PSET statement changes its color, or that it isn't, in which case the PSET statement does nothing. In other words, the PSET statement does clipping for you. If it didn't—and many graphics systems don't—this simple IF-THEN statement would be sufficient to decide whether or not a point is on the screen:

100 IF 0 < = X.POINT   AND   X.POINT < = 319   AND
       0 < = Y.POINT   AND   Y.POINT < = 199
           THEN PSET (X.POINT, Y.POINT)

This is less convenient, but pretty easy.

Clipping a line is much more difficult, since a line may be entirely on, partly on and partly off, or entirely off the screen. Furthermore, the LINE statement in IBM Personal Computer BASIC offers you no help; all of the work of clipping must be done in BASIC. Whenever it draws a line, a program must decide whether all, part, or none of the line is on the screen (a decision made more complicated by the fact that a line can be partly on the screen, even when its endpoints are both off the screen). See Fig. 8-9. If the program finds that a line is entirely on the screen, it can use a LINE statement to draw it. If it finds that a line is entirely off the screen, it can just skip it and go on to other computing. If it finds that a line is partly on and partly off the screen, then it must calculate where the line crosses the edges of the screen and then use a LINE statement to draw the part of the line that is on the screen.

The LINE statement does not clip lines accurately without help. If you send a line whose endpoints are off the screen to the LINE statement, it is true that the computer draws a line. However, what it draws is *not* the part of the line that is on the screen. Consider Fig. 8-10. The LINE statement does not bother to calculate the location of point Z, the intersection of the line from point X to point Y and the edge of the screen. Instead, it simply moves from point X horizontally to the nearest edge of the screen and draws a line from there to point Y. The resulting line is not a piece of the line from point X to point Y, but is instead part of a much steeper line that does not pass through point X at all.

Fig. 8-9   Clipping Lines

In this figure, line AB is entirely on the screen and hence can be drawn correctly with a LINE statement. Line CD is entirely off the screen. Point E is on the screen, and point F is off the screen. To draw the line properly, the program must calculate the coordinates of point G, where line EF crosses the edge of the screen. Line HI is an example of a line that is partly on the screen even though both its endpoints are off the screen.

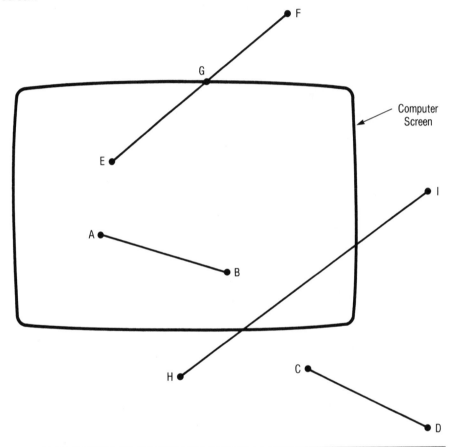

Fig. 8-10   Clipping by Using the LINE Statement

The LINE statement in IBM Personal Computer BASIC does not clip properly because it does not calculate where lines intersect the edges of the screen. Instead, it simply moves off-screen endpoints to the nearest location on the screen.

Line XY is partly on the screen:

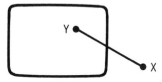

To clip properly, the computer should calculate the coordinates of point Z and then draw a line from X to Z:

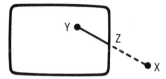

Instead, the computer just "moves" point X horizontally until it is on the screen and then draws a line from Y to this new point:

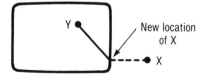

A Sample Program

The program in Fig. 8-11 draws a series of diamond shapes of increasing sizes on the screen. The arrays X.DIAMOND and Y.DIAMOND contain the x and y coordinates of the four corners of the diamond currently being drawn. For programming convenience, the fifth elements of the arrays contain a duplicate set of coordinates for the first corner of the diamond. Statements 1022 to 1080 assign values to the elements of these arrays. The FOR-NEXT loop from statement 1090 to statement 1140 draws the four lines of a diamond by copying the coordinates of their endpoints into array elements X(1), Y(1), X(2) and Y(2) and calling the subroutine at statement 3000. (The lines could be drawn more simply by inserting a LINE statement inside the FOR-NEXT loop, but this program has been written for easy inclusion of a subroutine that clips lines as well as draws them.) Figure 8-12 shows the coordinates of the corners of the diamonds that are drawn by this program. Figure 8-13 shows the display drawn by this program.

As Fig. 8-13 shows, the program draws the smaller diamonds correctly, but when the diamonds get big enough to run off the edge of the screen, the program distorts them. The display you will get if everything is clipped properly is shown in Fig. 8-14.

Fig. 8-11   Program to Draw Concentric Diamonds

This program draws a series of diamond shapes that is too large to fit on the screen.

```
1000  ' --- PROGRAM TO DRAW A SERIES OF DIAMONDS
1010  '
1020  '
1021         DIM X.DIAMOND(5),Y.DIAMOND(5)
1022         LET X.DIAMOND(2) = 160
1023         LET X.DIAMOND(4) = 160
1024         LET Y.DIAMOND(1) = 100
1025         LET Y.DIAMOND(3) = 100
1026         LET Y.DIAMOND(5) = 100
1030  '
1031         CLS
1032         SCREEN 1,0
1040         FOR SCALE = 5 TO 100 STEP 5
1050            LET X.DIAMOND(1) = 160 + 5 * SCALE
1060            LET X.DIAMOND(3) = 160 - 5 * SCALE
1061            LET X.DIAMOND(5) = X.DIAMOND(1)
1070            LET Y.DIAMOND(2) = 100 + 4 * SCALE
1080            LET Y.DIAMOND(4) = 100 - 4 * SCALE
1090            FOR SIDE = 1 TO 4
1100               LET X(1) = X.DIAMOND(SIDE)
1110               LET Y(1) = Y.DIAMOND(SIDE)
1120               LET X(2) = X.DIAMOND(SIDE + 1)
1130               LET Y(2) = Y.DIAMOND(SIDE + 1)
1140               GOSUB 3000
1150            NEXT SIDE
1160         NEXT SCALE
1170  '
1180         END
1190  '
1200  '
3000  ' --- SUBROUTINE TO DRAW A LINE
3010         LINE (X(1),Y(1)) - (X(2),Y(2))
3020         RETURN
```

Fig. 8-12   The Diamonds Drawn by the Program in Fig. 8-11

This figure shows the coordinates of the corners of the first five diamonds drawn by the program in Fig. 8-11.

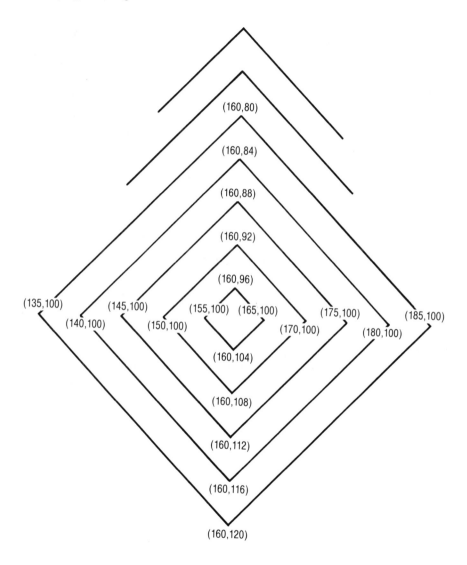

Fig. 8-13   The Screen Display from the Program in Fig. 8-11

This figure shows the screen display drawn by the program in Fig. 8-11.

Fig. 8-14   The Accurate Screen Display of the Concentric Diamonds

This figure shows the display you should get when you draw the diamonds. It is the result of the program in Fig. 8-15.

Fig. 8-15 Program to Draw and Clip Concentric Diamonds

```
1000 ' --- PROGRAM TO CLIP CONCENTRIC DIAMONDS
1010 '
1011        LET SCRN.MIN.X = 0
1012        LET SCRN.MIN.Y = 0
1013        LET SCRN.MAX.X = 319
1014        LET SCRN.MAX.Y = 199
1020 '
1021        DIM X.DIAMOND(5),Y.DIAMOND(5)
1022        LET X.DIAMOND(2) = 160
1023        LET X.DIAMOND(4) = 160
1024        LET Y.DIAMOND(1) = 100
1025        LET Y.DIAMOND(3) = 100
1026        LET Y.DIAMOND(5) = 100
1030 ' --- XX
1031        CLS
1032        SCREEN 1,0
1040        FOR SCALE = 5 TO 100 STEP 5
1050            X.DIAMOND(1) = 160 + 5 * SCALE
1060            X.DIAMOND(3) = 160 - 5 * SCALE
1061            LET X.DIAMOND(5) = X.DIAMOND(1)
1070            Y.DIAMOND(2) = 100 + 4 * SCALE
1080            Y.DIAMOND(4) = 100 - 4 * SCALE
1090            FOR SIDE = 1 TO 4
1100                X(1) = X.DIAMOND(SIDE)
1110                Y(1) = Y.DIAMOND(SIDE)
1120                X(2) = X.DIAMOND(SIDE + 1)
1130                Y(2) = Y.DIAMOND(SIDE + 1)
1140                GOSUB 6000
1150            NEXT SIDE
1160        NEXT SCALE
1170 '
1180        END
1190 '
1200 '
6000 ' --- SUBROUTINE TO CLIP A LINE AND DRAW IT
6010 ' --- LOOP TO CLIP REPEATEDLY
6020            OFFSCREEN(1) = 0
6030            OFFSCREEN(2) = 0
6040            IF  X(1) > SCRN.MAX.X   THEN
                    LET OFFSCREEN(1) = OFFSCREEN(1) + 1
6050            IF  Y(1) > SCRN.MAX.Y   THEN
                    LET OFFSCREEN(1) = OFFSCREEN(1) + 2
6060            IF  X(1) < SCRN.MIN.X   THEN
                    LET OFFSCREEN(1) = OFFSCREEN(1) + 4
6070            IF  Y(1) < SCRN.MIN.Y   THEN
                    LET OFFSCREEN(1) = OFFSCREEN(1) + 8
6080            IF  X(2) > SCRN.MAX.X   THEN
                    LET OFFSCREEN(2) = OFFSCREEN(2) + 1
6090            IF  Y(2) > SCRN.MAX.Y   THEN
                    LET OFFSCREEN(2) = OFFSCREEN(2) + 2
6100            IF  X(2) < SCRN.MIN.X   THEN
                    LET OFFSCREEN(2) = OFFSCREEN(2) + 4
6110            IF  Y(2) < SCRN.MIN.Y   THEN
                    LET OFFSCREEN(2) = OFFSCREEN(2) + 8
```

continued on p. 280

continued from p. 279

```
6120 '
6130 ' ---       CHECK IF LINE IS COMPLETELY OFF SCREEN
6140            IF  (OFFSCREEN(1) AND OFFSCREEN(2)) <> 0
                    GOTO 6900
6150 '
6160 ' ---       CHECK IF LINE IS ON THE SCREEN
6170            IF  OFFSCREEN(1) = 0 AND OFFSCREEN(2) = 0
                    GOTO 6800
6180 '
6190 '
6200 ' ---      IF  OFFSCREEN(1) <> 0   GOTO 6300
6210 '            FIRST POINT IS ON SCREEN; SECOND POINT IS OFF
6220 '            SWAP POINTS
6230             SWAP X(1),X(2)
6240             SWAP Y(1),Y(2)
6250             SWAP OFFSCREEN(1),OFFSCREEN(2)
6290 '
6300            IF  OFFSCREEN(1) < 8   GOTO 6400
6310 '            --- Y COORDINATE IS TOO SMALL
6320             LET X(1) = X(1) + (X(2) - X(1)) *
                    (SCRN.MIN.Y - Y(1)) / (Y(2) - Y(1))
6330             LET Y(1) = SCRN.MIN.Y
6340             GOTO 6700
6350 '
6400            IF  OFFSCREEN(1) < 4   GOTO 6500
6410 '            --- X COORDINATE IS TOO SMALL
6420             LET Y(1) = Y(1) + (Y(2) - Y(1)) *
                    (SCRN.MIN.X - X(1)) / (X(2) - X(1))
6430             LET X(1) = SCRN.MIN.X
6440             GOTO 6700
6450 '
6500            IF  OFFSCREEN(1) < 2 \ GOTO 6600
6510 '            --- Y COORDINATE IS TOO LARGE
6520             LET X(1) = X(1) + (X(2) - X(1)) *
                    (SCRN.MAX.Y - Y(1)) / (Y(2) - Y(1))
6530             LET Y(1) = SCRN.MAX.Y
6540             GOTO 6700
6550 '
6600            IF  OFFSCREEN(1) < 1   GOTO 6700
6610 '            --- X COORDINATE IS TOO LARGE
6620             LET Y(1) = Y(1) + (Y(2) - Y(1)) *
                    (SCRN.MAX.X - X(1)) / (X(2) - X(1))
6630             LET X(1) = SCRN.MAX.X
6640             GOTO 6700
6650 '
6700 '           --- WE NOW HAVE A NEW POINT; REPEAT THE PROCESS
6710        GOTO 6000
6720 '
6730 '
6800 ' --- THE LINE IS ON THE SCREEN; DRAW IT
6810        LINE (X(1),Y(1)) - (X(2),Y(2))
6830 '
6840 '
6900 ' --- THE LINE IS OFF THE SCREEN
6910        RETURN
```

The Cohen-Sutherland Clipping Algorithm

The display shown in Fig. 8-14 is drawn by the program shown in Fig. 8-15, a program similar to the one in Fig. 8-11. The subroutine at statement 3000, which blindly drew a line, whether or not its endpoints were on the screen, has been replaced by the subroutine at statement 6000, which finds where a line intersects the edges of the screen and draws just the part of it that lies on the screen. The four variables SCRN.MAX.X, SCRN.MAX.Y, SCRN.MIN.X, and SCRN.MIN.Y represent the minimum and maximum x and y coordinates that can be displayed on the screen. They are set at the beginning of the program and are never changed subsequently. Their values are used by the subroutine at statement 6000.

The algorithm used in the subroutine at statement 6000 combines the process of deciding if any part of a line is on the screen with the process of finding where it intersects the screen edges. It is not the simplest algorithm, but it is reasonably efficient. "Efficient," in the case of clipping algorithms, means not calculating more line intersections than necessary.

Observe first that a clipping algorithm needn't do anything if both of a line's endpoints are on the screen; it can just use a LINE statement to draw the line. Therefore, a clipping algorithm should test at some point to see if both endpoints are on the screen. Observe next that if both endpoints of a line are above the screen, then the entire line is also above the screen, and the algorithm can stop without drawing anything. Similarly, if both endpoints are below or to the right or to the left of the screen, then the entire line segment is similarly off the screen, and the algorithm can stop. At some point, the algorithm should therefore test to see if both endpoints are off the screen in the same direction. Only if none of these simple conditions holds must the algorithm actually do some calculating.

If no simple condition holds, the algorithm we shall discuss reacts by finding a portion of the line that is clearly off the screen, chopping it off, and then considering the remainder of the line. It first tests the remainder to see if both endpoints are now on the screen; if not, it checks whether both are now above, below, to the left, or to the right of the screen. If the remaining line segment is still not one of the simple cases, then the algorithm finds another part of the line that is obviously off the screen, chops that off, and repeats the process. Therefore, the algorithm is:

IF BOTH ENDPOINTS ARE ON THE SCREEN, DRAW THE LINE.
IF BOTH ENDPOINTS ARE ABOVE OR BOTH BELOW OR BOTH TO
   THE LEFT OR BOTH TO THE RIGHT, QUIT.
OTHERWISE, CHOP OFF SOME PORTION OF THE LINE SEGMENT
   AND REPEAT THIS WHOLE PROCESS WITH THE NEW, SHORTER
   SEGMENT.

Figure 8-16 shows how the algorithm picks the shorter line segment.

Statements 6020 to 6110 determine whether the endpoints of the line are on the screen, or above it, below it, to the right of it, or to the left of it and use these facts to assign values to OFFSCREEN(1) and OFFSCREEN(2). How values in these array elements correspond to endpoint locations is discussed below. Statement 6140 tests to see if both endpoints are off the screen in the same direction. If they are, then the program jumps to statement 6900 and returns without drawing anything. Statement 6170 tests to see if both endpoints are on the screen. If they are, the program jumps to statement 6800, where it draws a line between the two endpoints.

If neither of the two simple conditions holds, the program cuts off a portion of the line segment. If the first endpoint of the line is on the screen and only the second endpoint is off, then statements 6200 to 6250 swap the two endpoints so that when the program gets to statement 6300, the first endpoint is always *off* the screen. Statements 6300 to 6640 find a portion of the line that is off the screen in one of the four directions, calculate the intersection of the line with the corresponding edge of the screen, and make this intersection the new first endpoint of the line. Then the process is repeated.

Fig. 8-16   The Clipping Process

This figure shows examples of the clipping process.

Here, line AB has both endpoints on the screen and therefore is drawn. Line CD has both endpoints above the screen and is therefore not drawn. Line EF falls into neither of these simple categories, and more computation must be done.

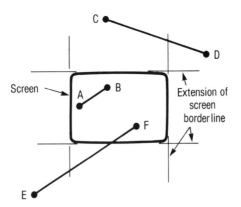

continued on p. 283

continued from p. 282

The algorithm first cuts off the part of the line EF that lies to the left of the screen by calculating where it crosses the vertical line that goes through the left-hand edge of the screen:

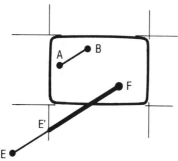

The line E'F is still not a simple case, so the algorithm calculates where segment E'F crosses the horizontal line along the bottom of the screen:

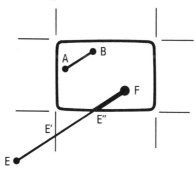

Both E'' and F are on the screen, so the segment from E'' to F is drawn.

Consider line segment GH:

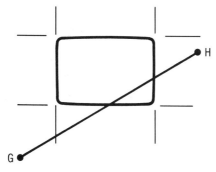

continued on p. 284

continued from p. 283

The part to the left of the screen is cut off:

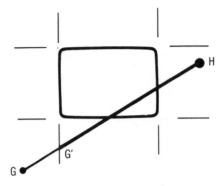

The part below the screen is cut off:

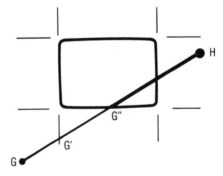

The part to the right is cut off:

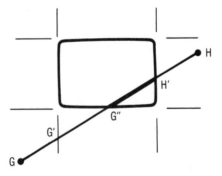

Both endpoints are now on the screen, and the line is drawn.

continued on p. 285

continued from p. 284

Consider line IJ:

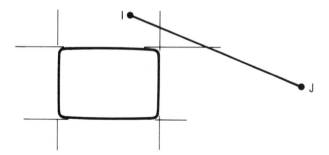

The part of the line above the screen is cut off:

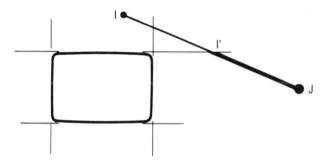

Now both endpoints are to the right of the screen and the line is therefore entirely off the screen.

The OFFSCREEN Array

The OFFSCREEN array is used to figure out if both endpoints are on the screen or if they are both above, below, to the left, or to the right. To understand how this works, we must discuss how the IBM Personal Computer stores integers and how the AND operator provided in BASIC works.

The IBM Personal Computer uses the binary number system to store integers. A complete discussion of the binary number system is beyond the scope of this book, but to understand the program here, you need only understand that the binary number system uses just 1's and 0's to represent numbers and that the decimal numbers shown in the table here translate into the binary equivalents shown:

Decimal Number	Binary Equivalent
0	0000
1	0001
2	0010
3	0011
4	0100
6	0110
8	1000
9	1001
12	1100

The program uses the OFFSCREEN array by using each of the four digits in the binary equivalents to keep track of whether the endpoint is off the screen in one of the directions:

Binary Digit		Direction Point Is Off Screen
leftmost	1	to the right
	2	below
	3	to the left
rightmost	4	above

Suppose that OFFSCREEN(1) is 6. When the number 6 is turned into its binary equivalent, it becomes 0110; since the second and third binary digits are 1's, the first endpoint is below and to the left of the screen. Similarly, if OFFSCREEN(2) is 0, then the second endpoint is on the screen. How decimal numbers correspond to where endpoints are in relation to the screen is shown in this table:

Decimal Number	Binary Equivalent	Relation to Screen
0	0000	On the Screen
1	0001	Right
2	0010	Below
3	0011	Right and Below
4	0100	Left
6	0110	Left and Below
8	1000	Above
9	1001	Right and Above
12	1100	Left and Above

Check to see that the statements from 6020 to 6110 do give the elements of the OFFSCREEN array the appropriate values.

In order to determine if both endpoints are on the screen, the program need only check to see if both of the elements of the OFFSCREEN array are 0, as is done in statement 6170.

Checking to see if both endpoints are off the screen in the same direction is the same as checking to see if the binary equivalents of the two elements of the OFFSCREEN array have a 1 in the same digit. The AND operator in statement 6140 produces a binary number each of whose digits is calculated from the corresponding digits in the original OFFSCREEN elements. A digit in the new number is 1 only if the corresponding digits in both OFFSCREEN elements are 1. Otherwise, it is a 0. Therefore, a 1 in the result of the AND operator means that both elements of the OFFSCREEN array have a 1 in the same digit, and therefore that both endpoints are off the screen in the same direction. Testing to see if the result of the AND function is 0 is equivalent to testing to see if all of the digits are 0.

Calculating New Endpoints

The statements from 6300 to 6640 cut off a portion of the line by calculating where it intersects one of the edges of the screen. To see how this works, consider Fig. 8-17. The line to be drawn runs from point A to point B, but point A is off the left-hand side of the screen. We must calculate the coordinates of point A'.

The program will find out that point A is off the left-hand side of the screen, because X(1) is less than SCRN.X.MIN, the x coordinate of the left-hand edge of the screen. The x coordinate of A' is SCRN.X.MIN, since every point on the left-hand edge of the screen has this x coordinate. With a little geometry, we can calculate the y coordinate rather simply. Consider the horizontal line extending to the right from point A and the vertical line down to it from point B shown in Fig. 8-17. The distances from point A to points M and N are the differences among their x coordinates, and the distance from point B to point N is the difference between their y coordinates, as shown in Fig. 8-17. We will find the distance from A' to M, after which we can add that distance to the y coordinate of A to get the y coordinate of A'.

The triangle whose corners are the points A, B, and N is *similar* to the triangle whose corners are the points A, A', and M. Roughly, this means that the two triangles are the same shape, but different sizes. From geometry, we know that the following ratio therefore holds among the lengths of the sides of the triangles:

$$\frac{A'M}{AM} = \frac{BN}{AN}$$

Multiplying both sides of this equation by AM yields:

$$A'M = \frac{BN * AM}{AN}$$

Filling in the lengths of these lines with their coordinate formula equivalents yields:

$$A'M = \frac{(Y(2) - Y(1)) * (SCRN.MIN.X - X(1))}{(X(2) - X(1))}$$

This formula is used at statement 6420, and the result is added to Y(1), the y coordinate of point A, to give the y coordinate of point A'.

Fig. 8-17   Using Similar Triangles to Find Intersection Points

This figure shows the similar triangles used to find the intersection points between lines and screen edges.

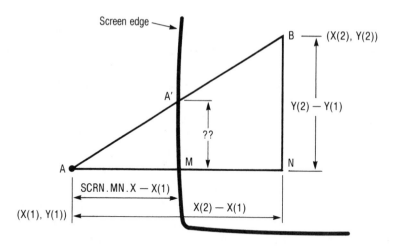

Windows

In graphics, a *window* is the portion of the screen that is used for display purposes. The program in Fig. 8-15 uses the whole screen as its window. However, by changing the values assigned to SCRN.MAX.X, SCRN.MAX.Y, SCRN.MIN.X, and SCRN.MIN.Y, you can have the program use only a portion of the screen. For example, if you change statements 1011 to 1014 to:

```
1011        LET SCRN.MIN.X = 50
1012        LET SCRN.MIN.Y = 50
1013        LET SCRN.MAX.X = 319
1014        LET SCRN.MAX.Y = 150
```

the program would then only use the part of the screen whose corners are:

(50,50)   (319,50)

(50,150)   (319,150)

Areas on the screen outside of this rectangle will remain blank, since all lines drawn in them are clipped off at the new window boundary.

Three Dimensions and Clipping

You can upgrade the three-dimensional program of Section 8.1 to clip lines at the screen boundary by taking three steps. First, add statements 1011 to 1014 to the program:

```
1011        LET SCRN.MIN.X = 0
1012        LET SCRN.MIN.Y = 0
1013        LET SCRN.MAX.X = 319
1014        LET SCRN.MAX.Y = 199
```

Then add the clipping subroutine to the program at statement 6000. Finally, replace statement 3070 with this sequence of statements:

```
3070        IF  FCN = 0  GOTO 3080
3071            X(1) = X.OLD
3072            Y(1) = Y.OLD
3073            X(2) = X.SCREEN
3074            Y(2) = Y.SCREEN
3075            GOSUB 6000
```

This change allows the program to view the object from much closer, since lines that run off the edge of the screen no longer distort the image. However, the three-dimensional program still does not handle situations in which lines in the object being viewed lie behind the viewer's eye location.

Index